To Gary and Sue
as the Third Millennium begins.
Best wishes for an exciting
new 21st Century

*[signature]*
midnight, Dec 31, 2000

# e-Sphere

# e-Sphere

## The Rise of the World-Wide Mind

Joseph N. Pelton
Foreword by Sir Arthur C. Clarke

### Q

QUORUM BOOKS
Westport, Connecticut · London

**Library of Congress Cataloging-in-Publication Data**

Pelton, Joseph N.
    e-Sphere : the rise of the world-wide mind / Joseph N. Pelton ; foreword by Arthur C. Clarke.
      p.   cm.
    Includes bibliographical references and index.
    ISBN 1–56720–390–6 (alk. paper)
    1. Communication, International.  2. Communication—Technological innovations.  3.
Telecommunication systems.  I. Title.
    P96.I5 P33     2000
    302.2—dc21          00–025251

British Library Cataloguing in Publication Data is available.

Library of Congress Catalog Card Number: 00–025251
ISBN: 1–56720–390–6

First published in 2000

Quorum Books, 88 Post Road West, Westport, CT 06881
An imprint of Greenwood Publishing Group, Inc.
www.quorumbooks.com

Printed in the United States of America

The paper used in this book complies with the
Permanent Paper Standard issued by the National
Information Standards Organization (Z39.48–1984).

10  9  8  7  6  5  4  3  2  1

# Contents

Appendixes

# Foreword

*Sir Arthur C. Clarke*

Long before the global network of fixed telephones is fully established, there will be a parallel development that will eventually bypass it completely—though probably not until well into the twenty-first century. It is starting now, with cellular networks, portable radiophones, and paging devices, and will lead ultimately to our old science-fiction friend the wristwatch telephone.

Before we reach that, there will be an intermediate stage. During the coming decade, more and more businessmen, well-heeled tourists, and virtually all newspersons will be carrying units that will permit direct two-way communication with their homes or offices, via the most convenient satellite. These will provide voice, telex, and video facilities (still photos and, for those who need it, live TV coverage). As these units become cheaper, smaller, and more universal, they will make travelers totally independent of national communications systems.

The implications of this are profound—and not only to media news-gatherers who will no longer be at the mercy of censors or inefficient (sometimes non-existent) postal or telecommunications services. It means the end of closed societies and will lead ultimately—to repeat a phrase I heard Arnold Toynbee use years ago— to the unification of the world.

You may think this is a naïve prediction, because many countries wouldn't let such subversive machines across their borders. But they would have no choice; the alternative would be economic suicide, because very soon they would get no tourists and no businessmen offering foreign currency. They'd get only spies, who would have no trouble at all concealing the powerful new tools of their ancient trade.

What I am saying, in fact, is that the debate about the free flow of information which has been going on for so many years will soon be settled—by engineers, not politicians. (Just as physicists, and not generals, have now determined the nature of war.)

Consider what this means. No government will be able to conceal, at least for very long, evidence of crimes or atrocities—even from its own people.

The very existence of a myriad of new information channels, operating in real time and across all frontiers, will be a powerful influence for civilized behavior. If you are arranging a massacre, it will be useless to shoot the cameraman who has so inconveniently appeared on the scene. His pictures will already be safe in the studio five thousand kilometers away; and his final image may hang you.

I wish I could claim that improved communications would lead to peace and general prosperity, but the matter is not as simple as that. Excellent communications—even a common language—have not brought peace to Northern Ireland, to give but one of many possible examples. Nevertheless, good communications of every type, and at all levels, are essential if we are ever to establish peace on this planet. As the mathematicians would say—they are necessary, but not sufficient.

In the closing decade of the nineteenth century an electrical engineer, W. E. Ayrton, was lecturing at London's Imperial Institute about the most modern of communications devices, the submarine telegraph cable. He ended with what must, to all his listeners, have seemed the wildest of fantasy.

There is no doubt that the day will come, maybe when you and I are forgotten, when copper wires, gutta-percha coverings and iron sheathings will be relegated to the Museum of Antiquities. Then, when a person wants to telegraph to a friend, he knows not where, he will call in an electro-magnetic voice, which will be heard loud by him who has the electro-magnetic ear, but will be silent to everyone else. He will call "Where are you?" and the reply will come "I am at the bottom of the coal-mine" or "Crossing the Andes" or "In the middle of the Pacific"; or perhaps no reply will come at all, and he may then conclude that his friend is dead.

This truly astonishing prophecy was made in 1897, long before anyone could imagine how it might be fulfilled. A century later, it is on the verge of achievement, because the wristwatch telephone will soon be coming into general use. And if you still believe that such a device is unlikely, ask yourself this question: Who could have imagined the personal watch, back in the Middle Ages—when the only clocks were clanking, room-sized mechanisms, the pride and joy of a few cathedrals.

For that matter, many of you carry on your wrists miracles of electronics that would have been beyond belief even twenty years ago. The symbols that flicker across those digital displays now often give only the date and time. Soon they will do far more than that. They will give you direct access to most of the human race, through the Internet and the other invisible networks girdling our planet.

The long-heralded global village is almost upon us, but it will last for only a flickering moment in the history of humankind. Before we even realize that it has come, it will be superseded—by what I have called the "global family." This is what Dr. Joseph Pelton, director of the new Clarke Institute of Telecommunications and Information (CITI) has chosen to call the World-Wide Mind. In the 1960s Marshall McLuhan helped us understand the importance of the emerging new electronic media and offered us the concept of the "Global Village" but the rate of change only increases. As we start a new millennium, Joe Pelton suggests that the new paradigm is the newly emerging World-Wide Mind and the start of a true "planetary consciousness," which he calls the "e-Sphere."

## NOTE

This foreword is published by permission of Sir Arthur C. Clarke's agents, Scovil Chichak Galen Literary Agency, Inc.

# Preface

The world of cyberspace is pervasive, persistent, and sometimes a little petulant. The artifacts of this fast-changing world are everywhere. There is the Japanese "smart" toilet seat that takes your blood pressure and vital medical statistics and—reluctant or not—you have to sit still for it. It probably will save many lives, but it also seems to some an invasion of the sanctum sanctorum. You go to a supermarket and find smart carts equipped with business television video displays and scanners that allow you to check yourself out. These scanner/computing devices allow you not only to do your own shopping but scan in your groceries and pay with your handy credit card without a person in sight.

Check-out clerks, equipped with only ears to hear the beep, beep, beep of the laser scanners, are clearly an endangered species. You are now your own telephone operator and bank teller and soon you will be your own filling station attendant and grocery check-out clerk. If you think information technology is eliminating jobs and your own might be next, you could be right. There are indeed millions of jobs that cyberspace technologies can automate, transfer, or eliminate, from salesperson to real estate assessor to accountant.

*E-Sphere* is an attempt to explain, analyze, and even "dialogue" with the reader, if that word can be made into a verb. This is not intended to be an academic book, although a full bibliography can help the interested researcher delve more deeply. The topics covered are diverse, difficult, and I hope maybe on a few occasions even delightful. They include the following:

- The emerging World-Wide Mind and the meaning of "planetary consciousness."
- What cyberspace is and what it might become as it evolves toward the e-Sphere.
- Telecommuting and the changing nature of work.
- The 168-hour work week and the nonstop world.
- The implications of the new $4 trillion-a-year mega-market that combines information, communications, entertainment, and smart energy.
- Jobs at risk and occupations of the future.
- Strategies in cybermanagement.
- Globalism and the decline of national sovereignty in the age of instant communications.
- Race, gender, and bias in the world of cyberbusiness.
- Education for the age of the World-Wide Mind.
- Telewar, info-espionage, and electronic crime.
- Cyberentertainment and virtual reality.
- And, for intellectual dessert, even an exploration of what the next billion years might bring.

This book is organized for the busy reader. Most of the chapters can be read in the order of interest and not necessarily in arithmetic succession. The purpose of this book is to explain that the world of cyberspace is much more than the Internet and that it will change your lives in a host of ways—some of them good, as in Telepower, and some of them bad, as in Teleshock. The emerging World-Wide Mind actually represents a global web of infotelematics, satellites, fiber optics, stratospheric platforms, and wireless radio systems that affect every aspect of our lives. Electronic information systems are redefining education, medicine, and health care, jobs, transportation, recreation, and entertainment. The software and hardware of cyberspace is restructuring the scope, the content, and the size of our world. Your friend, colleague, coresearcher, and competitor for a job may live thousands of miles away.

Cyberspace defines our social, economic, scientific, and cultural environment. It will shape the very nature of our lives and reshape how humanity views itself in a twenty-first century world. No one will escape its impact in the twenty-first century. Furthermore, we will not escape this new century unless we devise ways to use our technology to survive as a species as opposed to optimizing economic growth and productivity.

Pierre Teilhard de Chardin, in his book *The Phenomenon of Man* (1950), discussed the fact that ever since the Renaissance there has been a growing global consciousness and intellectual knowledge that follows what he called the "law of complexification" and what he called the "noosphere." Subsequently, Buckminster Fuller talked about the historical evolution of global civilization and a process he named "ephemeralization." These thinkers and others have noted the fact that integration and development of knowledge is increasing exponentially. This is leading us toward a new world beyond the Global Village known as the "e-Sphere." This process is moving human civilization toward the e-Sphere society that combines complexity, increased speed, and miniaturization.

The purpose of *e-Sphere* is to explain key electronic technologies and their applications in a fast-changing world. It is hoped that it can explain the context of living within the World-Wide Mind and anticipate new trends that range from speed dating to wearable molecular computers, from implanted memory-based skills to new family structures and political processes.

The other more important objective is to explore how humans can maintain our biosphere and our information systems to have the chance to survive as a species. There are already many books that have addressed the emerging new cyberspace networks, but these tend to have a narrow and often quite specific disciplinary focus. This book seeks to be interdisciplinary in scope. It seeks to examine with some candor, and perhaps some occasional wit, how the latest of the electronic technologies and services can and will redefine every aspect of our lives. Those who are Francophiles, for instance, will probably be disappointed by my views that France and several other countries will experience serious problems by using poor telestrategies for survival in the twenty-first century.

Students of communications and information systems as well as denizens of our evolving cyberspace-linked world are invited to explore how all aspects of living, recreation, culture, economics, and business will be changed by this powerful new and ever-expanding technology. The cyberspace duo of "Telepower" and "Teleshock" reflect the yin and yang of networking in an evolving world. These positive and negative forces seem inextricably linked in the century ahead.

The global base of information is now expanding some 200,000 times faster than our global population. We are like turtles trying to catch infosystems that are moving at the speed of spaceships. This is not merely an abstract literary analogy. Our rate of human population growth when compared to the rate of information growth is literally that of an agile tortoise who finds that the hare is escaping in a space shuttle. Our educational and industrial processes are still trying to catch "information spaceships" with turtle-like techniques.

It does not work. It will not work. Speeding up the same old treadmills to improve our educational systems is an exercise in futility.

The answer is not more and more specialization and ever more narrowly focused scholars holding Ph.D.s in obscure topics of study. The fields of study of today's Ph.D.s are verging toward invisibility as they become so deep that they have no breadth. The only hope for humanity is to recover the power of renaissance thinking. The Internet itself is a powerful paradigm of what an emerging World-Wide Mind should and should not be as well.

We must make interdisciplinary connections across an electronically connected world. We must create new types of networked teams of "thinkers" rather than continuing to overdose on info-niche specialists. We must make a "cybernetic shift" away from Cartesian logic and linear thinking and into a new Renaissance where we can exploit multidisciplinary and interdisciplinary creativity. Interdisciplinary teams and other basic reforms in education and industry will become virtually essential to our survival in the evolving world of cyberspace.

The way to deal with the breadth and depth of our emerging global Internet-based brain is to evolve new forms of education and intellectual sharing. It also will likely entail reinventing our economic and social systems as well.

*E-Sphere* celebrates the reinvention of "renaissance people" who can operate in an international, intercultural, and interdisciplinary world. To survive does not mean processing more and more information, but achieving more and more wisdom and connecting more knowledge within an ever more interconnected and interdependent world. The distinction between information and wisdom will never be more important than in the decades that represent our immediate future.

# Acknowledgments

This book represents my latest evolution of thought. It reflects a personal course charted through four books: *Global Talk* (1984), *Future Talk* (1989), *Future View* (1992), and now *e-Sphere* (2000). The last decade has been a time of transition. I have changed from the commercial and operational world of Intelsat to the academic world of the University of Colorado, the international and intercultural environment of the International Space University, and now the George Washington University near the hub of U.S. space and information policy.

The new Arthur C. Clarke Institute for Information and Telecommunications, which I head as executive director and founder, is an actual attempt to create in microcosm a constructive part of the World-Wide Mind. This attempt to create a virtual research institute that draws on the brains and talents of scientists, engineers, and social scientists around the world is highly ambitious yet realizable in light of today's prodigious information technologies.

Throughout the time *e-Sphere* was written in Boulder, Colorado, Strasbourg, France, and Washington, D.C., the one constant has been the affection, dedication, and professional support of my wife and editor, Eloise Janssen Pelton. I dedicate this book to her and a host of friends (especially Lillian Kennedy), plus a number of students, colleagues, adversaries, and soulmates who have enriched my life and challenged my intellect. This book would not have been possible without them, but especially it would have not have been conceived and implemented without Eloise.

# CHAPTER 1

# The Emerging World-Wide Mind

Progress is impossible without change. Those who cannot change
their minds cannot change anything.

George Bernard Shaw

Our world is changing. It is changing in ways that most of us cannot easily see. Over a recent six-month period, the number of
Internet domains in Swaziland increased from 1 to 49 or 4,800 percent. In Sri Lanka the increase was from 6 to 234 or 3,800 percent,
and in Pakistan the jump was from 17 to 386 or almost 2,200 percent. Currently more new information is being created and revised
on Web sites (plus all the connected Intranets) in less than a week
than was available on the entire World Wide Web during its forma-
tive years. For the last five years Internet user growth in South America
has been a staggering cumulative average growth of 125 percent, compared to 119 percent in Asia, 87 percent in Africa, and 80 percent in
the United States and Canada. In the world of cyberspace, statistics that are more than a year old are not very helpful.

Our world is thus changing very fast indeed, and is well on the
way to becoming the e-Sphere. In China, the awakening giant of
the East, some 10 million new telephone lines are now being added
each year. Li Peng, the premier of China, when I met with him
during an international space conference, confessed to know a good
deal more about telecommunications and rocket launchers than he
does about rice. Few free-world leaders in Europe or North America

would likely have his immediate command of trends in electronics or telecommunications.

In India, Indonesia, and China, literally millions of students are linked via satellite tele-education systems that stretch to the most remote village. It is a world of great contrasts. The earth stations used to receive high-tech tele-education courses via satellite in rural Chinese villages are rather incredibly hand carried to their final locations by dozens of villagers simply because there are no roads for heavy trucks. These same Chinese satellite telelearning programs are also being received and taped in Sri Lanka. These tapes are then sent by an air courier service to the United States, where the programs are then once again uplinked from a remote site in west Iowa on Schola's satellite channel to teach American students Chinese!

## IF OUR WORLDVIEW IS TWO DECADES OUT OF DATE, WE MAY BE IN TROUBLE

Today the major export products of countries like Thailand are not rice and timber, but rather computer and telecommunications equipment. Most people, despite the presence of CNN International, see the world as an outdated stereotype. The typical American or European businessman often "sees" the world as it was a decade or even two decades ago. They are not aware of how the cybernetic world of today has transformed other countries as well as other businesses and professions. The Marshall McLuhan paradigm of the "Global Village" is ineluctably (and scarily at times) giving way to the World-Wide Mind and the ever-growing yet ever-shrinking e-Sphere.

The ever-more-swift arrival of the world of tomorrow is quickly becoming today's reality. Kurt Anderson's recent novel, the *Turn of the Century*, blurs reality and tomorrow in a most disturbing way. This novel rather eerily shows that the people in high-tech industries in New York, Silicon Valley, and Seattle, Washington, actually live in tomorrowland—and that it is not really that appealing. Just coping with the blizzard of acronyms is by itself simply mind-numbing.

Many people think of the Republic of Korea as a place that makes dolls, rather than as a nation that has rapidly and successfully developed such high-tech products as 2-billion-byte random access memory chips (or, for acronym lovers, 2 Gig DRAMs). Many were surprised when an earthquake in Taiwan created a major slowdown in the ready supply of computer chips. Others think the world's tallest building is the Sears Tower in Chicago rather than the mammoth Petronis Towers in Kuala Lumpur, Malaysia, or the stunning Hin Hao tower in Shanghai, China. (Chicago is, however, even now plotting to have the world's largest Oedipal symbol.)

Others might be surprised to learn that India is designing, building, and launching with their own rockets state-of-the-art multiton satellites, or to find that Beijing and Shanghai now have thousands of luxury hotels complete with discos and many scores of McDonalds, Wendys, KFC, and TGIF fast-food restaurants. One is hard pressed to argue that this is progress—although one can contend that this may be at least economic momentum if not cultural nirvana. But whatever it is, it certainly pervades the major "advanced cities" of the world. The economic crisis in Asia is only a temporary setback and not the reversal of the historic rise of Asia. A quick check of the Tokyo stock market and recent trade export figures for the Asia-Pacific region shows that the Asian tigers and dragons are coming back strong.

Anyone who is doing business in this fast-moving world of cyberspace and chooses to remain years behind the times could be in for big problems. Rule number one in the age of the World-Wide Mind that exists in the e-Sphere is: "Stay up to date."

### CYBERSPACE AS A FUNDAMENTAL CHANGE ENGINE

The exploding pattern of global change pervades our planet. It is coming to citizens and businesspeople from every direction. It is coming to us via cell phones, fiber-optic cables, high performance and personal computers, satellites, and the all-pervasive Internet. All these complex electronic and communications networks and the advanced software and processing power that support their operation is what is meant by the word "cyberspace."

But what is meant by phrases such as the "World-Wide Mind," the "planetary consciousness," or moving beyond the "Global Village"? As we begin a new millennium we are actually experiencing a new paradigm. The speed of our global economy, the pace of global business, the scope of human knowledge, and the rate at which we change jobs and learn new skills are not merely increasing. No, these changes are now increasing in mathematical terms as if they were fourth-order exponentials. We live in a state of "jerk" or "chaos." In other words, we live in a time where there is an increasing rate of acceleration (what physicists define as jerk) and where nonlinear math and fractals reign supreme over traditional knowledge that is increasingly retreating under intellectual attack (except maybe in Kansas).

Human history has moved from a linear and continuous development to a nonlinear and discontinuous progression that suggests that the world in which we live will no longer be the same. We have jumped to warp speed and the social, economic, and cultural problems that inevitably result are both challenging and frightening to contemplate. The gaps in human history that once spanned a millennium may now occur in a generation or less. Middle-aged people will say, "What is the background on this new development?" Young people of the cyberspace age will respond, "There is no background. This development just sprang out of nowhere. It is a product of cyberspace thinking. It is just what the World-Wide Mind thought into reality."

Transitions in jobs will outstrip in numbers, scope, and speed the so-called agricultural or industrial revolutions. We can use software systems to "think interactively" with a team that spans the planet, or design "solar sail" vehicles that travel to other star systems. New types of artificial intelligence (AI) systems can, in twenty years or less, replace the majority of "people powered jobs." In our new age of planetary consciousness, technology will blanket us with instantaneous communications that drive our economies and threaten our jobs. So far we seem able to automate almost all jobs except that of consumer and citizen voter.

Cyberspace technologies will endow us with wealth and assault our social, cultural, and religious values. In short, information systems will assume a role that is at once omnipresent, omniknowing, and seemingly omnipotent. Their power, reach, and immediacy will create an overarching presence that transcends the Global Village paradigm that Marshall McLuhan defined for us some thirty years ago. McLuhan looked to the power of satellite broadcast television, which could let everyone on Earth receive the same message. Now the Internet and modern telecommunications and computer networks can let us think interactively. Now we are not a village that sees the same image, we are a World-Wide Mind that can think and interact together. This is the great strength of Telepower, but it is also the great challenge of coping with Teleshock.

Cyberspace in the age of the World-Wide Mind threatens to invade our privacy and overload our brains with too much information. It will allow us to link together into integrated thinking networks. The great potential that this can create I call "Telepower." The enormous social disruptions and problems it also creates—the dark side of Telepower—I call "Teleshock." Teleshock will ultimately create "a virtual sense of intellectual claustrophobia" inside our very own consciousness. Telepower will eventually reveal to us

Our links and relationship to what humankind has called God.

Our intellectual limits in understanding the universe.

Our need to confront the chaotic force of entropy and the meaning of "extrophy," the other side of entropy.

Our ultimate destiny as a species.

In short, *e-Sphere: The Rise of the World-Wide Mind* has a double agenda. It tries to explore and interpret contemporary trends in information technology and its application to society. It also tries to explore the limits and challenges of life in a cybernetic society that achieves a truly instantaneous planetary scale. For the pragmatists and down-to-earth readers, please stay on awhile longer. This is really not a concern reserved to dreamers and science fiction writers. These are actually explosive issues that will be directly facing us in only a few decades. Our children will be on the firing line. These fundamental issues are on a collision course with our modern information society. Answers must be found within a timescale that is "immediate" when viewed on a cosmic scale.

## TEN SIGNPOSTS TO GUIDE US TO
## THE IMMEDIATE FUTURE

Over the next decade, ten key concepts will serve as fundamental change engines in the evolving world of cyberbusiness. These ten signposts can help guide us into the first stages of the age of the World-Wide Mind. These forces of change in the world of cyberbusiness can make or break industrialists and infotechnology entrepreneurs alike. Certainly, the information age can generate some almost obscene profits. Paul Allen and Bill Gates, the founders of Microsoft, are between the two of them now worth about $150 billion, a healthy chunk of the total value of the entire NASDAQ exchange companies. If these two cybermoguls were countries rather than people, they would rank in GNP not only well above Tuvalu, St. Kitts, Belize, Rwanda, and dozens of other ministates, but outrival Honduras, the Bahamas, Paraguay, and Afghanistan.

Wealth in the age of cyberspace is more often than not defined by the control, acquisition, and sale of information. This is not new. The challenge is much greater than that. How does one strategically guide that process, at the right time, in the right way, with access to the right capital resources, and thus stay ahead of the competition? This is the ultimate management challenge. Mastering that challenge will, however, not necessarily make us happy. Kurt Anderson explains to us in *Turn of the Century*, his novel turned modern parable, that living in a high-tech world is not going to be all roses. His point seems to be that cyberspace can easily serve to make us more neurotic, more frenzied, and less human. In fact, Anderson, in his contemporary version of an ersatz "1984" nee "Year 2000" novel seems to suggest that the pace of life and a barrage of constant communications in a cybernetic world actually seems to conspire against stable marriage, fidelity, job security, honesty, or even good old-fashioned sanity.

If there were such a thing as a sure-fire formula for managing life and achieving prosperity in the age of the World-Wide Mind, you can be relatively sure you would not find it here in this or any other book. The Bill Gateses of the world may tell us a little about "life at the speed of thought," but his new book gives away few secrets.

There is no one smart enough to create such a strategy that would then be dumb enough to print instructions for everyone to follow. Get-rich schemes and especially cyber-hucksters who try to sell the magic formula are quite simply frauds and confidence people. If you do not believe me, please feel free to spend a few bucks on books, seminars, and videotapes to find out for yourself. Some of these people may be Ph.D.s or professors or computer scientists, but beware of those whose formulas for cyber-riches are based on set, foolproof steps to riches. Today's day traders are simply the latest victims in the "infogreed game."

Here we only seek to record and examine a number of patterns that are evolving. Here we explore possible implications and opportunities that could follow. Here we seek to explore effective strategies to address these key cybernetic shifts. Here we suggest that there is no way to guarantee success, but argue that ignoring these issues and strategies can certainly accelerate failure.

The cyber-manager in the new millennium should create strategies that address the enormous potential locked within ten key megatrends of the cyberspace age as follows.

1. *Teleworkers and Electronic Immigrants.* There are some 10 million telecommuters in the United States and another 15 million in the other developed countries. This will explode to some 60 to 80 million teleworkers worldwide by 2010. These teleworkers are not as visible because they typically work in Europe and North America only two days out of the week in this mode. There is also a new type of teleworker in locations like Korea, Jamaica, Ireland, Barbados, and India. Their jobs in inventory control, word processing, and software development, however, are in Japan and the United States and other developed economies. These electronic immigrants are becoming more and more ubiquitous and today number over a million. In a decade there will be over 10 million teleworkers living in one country and working in one or more others.

2. *The 168-Hour Work Week.* The powerful economic and global impact of the coming 168-hour work week—or, if you prefer, the

1,440-minute day—will be everywhere. It will revolutionize work schedules, global business, and the patterns of stock markets, retailing, merchandising, and more. Nonstop relentlessness will become a major force in the market, and European enterprises will suffer more than others.

3. *Info-Espionage and Telecrime.* The sinister spread of these Teleshock technologies will increasingly hurt the corporate bottom line. Banks, insurance companies, and law enforcement will be reinvented in the wake of changes. This is no longer small time. In Colombia, nearly half of the country is under the control of so-called drug lords who have the latest tools of electronic communications to control their business. In tax-free havens such as the Cayman Islands and Gibraltar there are global electronic activities to exploit the sale of orbital locations for satellites, manipulate shifts in currency values, and so on. In other countries electronic pirating of music, books, and inventions is currently routine. The recent shift in U.S. policy in September 1999 to make highly secure encryption broadly available on a global basis seems to be a calculated risk. Will business, science, drug trafficking, techno-terrorism, or all be the beneficiaries?

4. *The Coming ICEE Age.* The impact of digital electronic convergence and "smart energy" will bring about the marriage or at least cohabitation of information, communications, entertainment, and, most recently, energy (the ICEE-age industries). This high-tech mega-industry will command more than 15 percent of the global economy. The dominance of this "super-alliance" of high-tech industry will create imbalance and even trauma in the global economy.

5. *Jobs at Risk and New Jobs to Come.* There are new jobs in industry and manufacturing, but they are all in the service sector—not on the assembly line. They are not always the most desirable jobs either. Smart software and artificial intelligence will increasingly claim service jobs, too. Beyond the losses that e-commerce will engender for retail clerks, there are going to be "hits" on so-called higher-level professions. Pharmacists and accountants beware. The value-added sectors and infotechnology entrepreneurs will be the "golden geese" of the cybernetic age when it comes to creating new jobs, but artificial intelligence and expert systems may take away a host of service jobs in the process.

6. *Cybermanagement.* Most middle managers were trained for a different world. Most schools, universities, and professional training centers are incompetent to re-train managers for the twenty-first century. Around the world the problems of coping with "disintermediation" (elimination of the middle manager) are severe. It goes from bad in Asia and the United States to wretched in Europe.

7. *Forces of Global Competitiveness.* Industrial policy doesn't work, and France proves it. Korea and Taiwan, however, through hard work and intelligence are succeeding in spite of government control of technological and economic growth. In twenty years the top tier of the national economies of the world will have shifted—dramatically. Net changes that may be anticipated are these: China will be the number-one national economy. The Asia-Pacific will generally win. Europe will generally lose. And the United States and the Americas will face East, not West.

8. *Sex, Race, and Gender in the World of Cyberbusiness.* "On the Internet no one knows you are a dog," the cartoon informs us. But in the world of technological unemployment, uncensored Internet communications, and electronic immigrants the truth is that job discrimination, sexism, and racial intolerance will be all too much with us. Cyberage businesses need to be aware of the dangers that lurk here.

9. *Training Tomorrow's Workforce: The Cyberspace Challenge.* There are more people to be educated and trained on planet Earth in the next thirty-five years than have been educated up to this point in history. We are now 6 billion humans that may swell to 8.5 billion by 2035. The tools of tele-education, teletraining, and cyberspace learning will be key. This is a challenge for developed and developing countries alike. If cyberbusinesses are to succeed in the coming decade, basic problems in education, instruction, learning, and training will need to be fixed.

10. *Info-Entertainment and Virtual Life.* The dangers of a global society hooked on total escapism and virtual lives carried out in cyberspace are not illusory. Health clinics in California are treating severe cases of Internet addiction, and in the world of true "virtual sex" the problem will only escalate. U.S. office workers today cost industry an estimated $50 billion a year just by playing electronic games and surfing the Net. The problem of "cyberdistracted" employees is yet another challenge of the information age. The potentials of virtual reality (VR)–based info-entertainment are, however, not to be scorned, as Sony, Sega, Blockbuster Video, and Disney all jump into the fray.

## THE GLOBAL BRAIN: A NEW RENAISSANCE—OR NOT

As noted earlier, our world is now changing at what seems to be approaching warp speed. This transformation, largely driven by a cybernetic shift in business, education, culture, and employment, is different. It is a change in speed, in scope, and in direction that is more fundamental than any other transition in human history. Let's repeat that for emphasis. This shift in terms of impact on jobs, need for massive retraining of people, affect on income, and much, much more is decidedly larger than the agricultural revolution and the industrial revolution—combined.

A total of about 9 million farm workers shifted jobs over some fifty years during the first part of the twentieth century. Over the last thirty-five years some 15 million workers left assembly-line industrial jobs. The cyberspace revolution of the twenty-first century will see many more people shifting their jobs—many of them several times. Just the number of people shifting from traditional office jobs to telecommuting over the next fifteen years will double the number of workers going from industrial to service jobs. The same type of cybernetic shift will occur in the rest of the developed world as well. The cybernetic shift is thus a legitimate cause for hope and optimism, but it is also a cause for worry and concern.

The thesis of *e-Sphere: The Rise of the World-Wide Mind* is not that the world is undergoing change, but something more basic. We are increasingly seeing fundamental shifts in our ways of living, commuting, and socializing. Alvin Toffler has referred to a "Third Wave" of change, but this is a tidal wave—a tsunami—that alters almost everything from child care to rates of divorce, from job insecurity to general angst. A number of these changes are potentially dangerous or at least disorienting just by their very rapidity. Yet they also give rise to exciting new business opportunities and can stimulate entrepreneurial talent in new and dynamic ways. There is an "intensity of change" unlike previous patterns of the past. On top of it all the rise of human population and advent of new technologies and automated production systems also give new challenges to creating a sustainable biosphere in which we can all survive. Cyberspace technologies and current economic systems are throughput and growth oriented and have not yet made the transition to longer-term survival-oriented goals. In business this "intensity" within the overall cybernetic shift can often mean that new start-up innovators will win and old established firms that fail to see how cyberspace has just redefined their markets will lose.

The industrial age served to separate producer and consumer. In the age of cyberspace, the challenge will be to narrow rather than widen this divide between producing products and mass-market consumption. This may also mean the shrinking of commercial organizations to achieve this goal. The scale of cyberspace enterprises and the speed of their internal communications will be key to their success.

Thus, in some (but certainly not all) markets small will indeed become beautiful again. It has even been suggested that some of the recent megamergers are much like dinosaurs mating. The future of merged dinosaurs, at least in cyberindustries, is not promising—except possibly in a Steven Spielberg blockbuster.

## JERK

As noted earlier, physicists have defined the formal term, "jerk." First, there is velocity, which is simply a measure of speed. Next, there is acceleration (or rate of velocity increase). Last of all, there is a lesser-known concept. This is jerk (or rate of increase in acceleration). Jerk is what happens when you stomp on the gas pedal in a car and your head snaps back with a jerk—instantaneous acceleration. Cyberspace technologies are creating a tremendous jerk within our society.

The cybernetic shift is thus really more of a cyberspace jerk. The rapidity of change is what makes it different from anything we have seen before. This cyberjerk is on the order of ten times faster, bigger, deeper, and more profound than any revolution in human history. Business, in particular, must get ready for the cyberjerk—and fast, very, very fast.

Both society and business are currently experiencing this acceleration as a third or fourth order differential. It is a powerful force indeed. Jerk is almost always uncomfortable, whether in a hot rod or in the cross currents of a cybernetic society.

## THE LAST TWENTY SECONDS IN THE SUPERMONTH OF HUMAN EXISTENCE

If one wishes a visual picture of this process, one needs only to look at a picture of 5 million years of human history condensed into a single cosmic supermonth wherein every second represents two years of time. Figure 1.1 shows that for twenty-nine days and twenty-two hours (all but the last two hours) we were locked in the age of hunting/gathering nomads. Remarkably, the last two hours represent the entire age of human settlements and agriculture. The last four minutes represent the time since the Renaissance, and the last two minutes represent the industrial age. The time represented by the last twenty seconds is the time of lasers, satellites, electronic computers, color television, biotechnology, robotics, spandex, cyberspace, electronic games, and "Baywatch." It seems incredible that these high-tech elements are considered the totality of my Gen-X son's view of the universe.

We are changing, perhaps for better or perhaps for worse, but always at supersonic speeds. Business cycles, product-development

**Figure 1.1**
**The Cosmic Super Month: A Thirty-Day Super Month Illustrates the**
**Startling "Speed-Up Effect" of High Technology in Our Society**

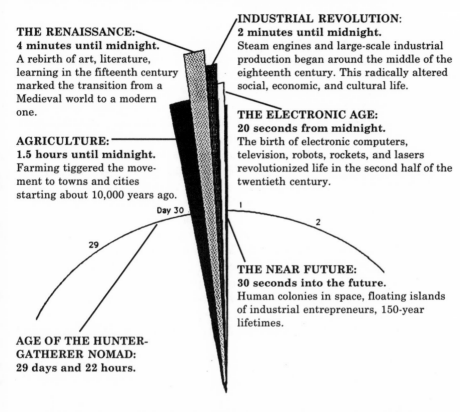

**THE RENAISSANCE:**
**4 minutes until midnight.**
A rebirth of art, literature, learning in the fifteenth century marked the transition from a Medieval world to a modern one.

**AGRICULTURE:**
**1.5 hours until midnight.**
Farming tiggered the movement to towns and cities starting about 10,000 years ago.

Day 30

29

AGE OF THE HUNTER-
GATHERER NOMAD:
29 days and 22 hours.

**INDUSTRIAL REVOLUTION:**
**2 minutes until midnight.**
Steam engines and large-scale industrial production began around the middle of the eighteenth century. This radically altered social, economic, and cultural life.

**THE ELECTRONIC AGE:**
**20 seconds from midnight.**
The birth of electronic computers, television, robots, rockets, and lasers revolutionized life in the second half of the twentieth century.

1
2

**THE NEAR FUTURE:**
**30 seconds into the future.**
Human colonies in space, floating islands of industrial entrepreneurs, 150-year lifetimes.

schedules, marketing concepts, and much, much more will be redefined within the cybernetic shift. Borrowing explanations from the past may prove irrelevant to this remarkable time of change. The future cannot easily be viewed through a rear-view mirror.

It is hard to look at the representation of the super month and argue that future compression is not at work in our cybernetic world. We have gone beyond the age of simple acceleration of knowledge with information now doubling every five years. We are ill-equipped to travel at this pace without making a cybernetic shift in our thinking, our education, and our modes of management and business operations.

Many businesspeople are about to find themselves in a cybernetic pickle. The number-one problem is not obtaining well-trained employees or effective marketing or product development. No, the number-one problem is management, particularly senior and middle management. Many senior and middle managers know very little about optics, electronic technology, satellites, or the Internet. A recent NASA survey of leading aerospace firms confirmed that providing technology training to management was perhaps their lowest priority.

Managers are often inclined to move ahead forcefully into this cybernetic world, with new products, services, and expanded marketing areas. Yet at the same time they are often frightened to death to admit to knowing little of this intimidating new technology. This can be a very dangerous combination of grit and incompetence that is often reserved only for the ranks of administrators at elite universities.

Two decades ago the Exxon Corporation charged into the new world of Telepower and put their oil executives in charge. The results at Exxon only a few years later were almost predictable. The bottom line was a fleet of bulldozers that dramatically demolished the Exxon computer- and fax-producing plants. The tax write-offs (or was it wrong-offs?) were worth more than the residual value of the Exxon computer-manufacturing facilities.

A few years later General Motors under Board Chairman Smith went on a technology spree and acquired both Hughes Aircraft and Electronics and Ross Perot's Electronic Data Systems (EDS). They also found that buying high technology can also buy a lot of red ink. The problem for GM was similar to that of Exxon. In short, there was a lack of key management leadership and planning.

In the 1980s the Comsat Corporation tried to enter the world of direct-to-home space broadcasting. Their entire senior management's knowledge of television programming was nil. They convincingly demonstrated that technically knowledgeable management does not guarantee success in other fields like entertainment or broadcasting. Comsat knew little about programming and even less about commercial marketing. The write-offs for Comsat going into fields in which they had limited top management experience mounted to over a billion dollars in the decade that followed. "Try, try, try again!" should have its limits, even for executives with golden parachutes.

Jim Gavin, chairman of Motorola, decided to take a plunge into satellite manufacturing and space phone operations in the late 1980s. The $5-billion satellite project was finally deployed in 1997, Motorola filed for bankruptcy in August 1999, and officially abandoned the satellites, planning to have them deorbited in 2000. The moral is clear. Don't do what you don't know.

In the world of cyberspace, ill-prepared management is easy to find. Even high-tech managers can still fail brilliantly. Comsat showed this time after time during the 1980s and 1990s. Now, even Motorola has fallen victim to technological overconfidence.

The danger of dramatic management failure in the new and dynamic cyberspace environment is thus very real. The world of cyberspace contains many more perils than ever before. Market boundaries are falling down everywhere. The divisions between communications, computers, cable television, consumer electronics, and content (sometimes called the 5 Cs) are rapidly dissolving in an all-digital world. Further, the advent of "smart energy" is adding a crucial new dimension to this merger of industries. This borderless digital market of the cybernetic shift is like the collapse of an electronic Berlin wall. This wall is seemingly falling like a ton of bricks on ill-prepared senior and middle management.

If we are indeed being "jerked" in the future, what can we do about it? The answer is plenty.

## PREPARE FOR THE WORLD OF CYBERBUSINESS AND TAP INTO THE WORLD-WIDE MIND

We can begin to reject linear thinking and traditional patterns of learning. Problem solving and new-product development in business will increasingly rely on teams of people with diverse and interdisciplinary backgrounds rather than on highly specialized laboratory researchers and engineers. Although specialists and engineers are still very much needed in high-tech industry, the interaction of different disciplines is the key to creative new solutions. The concept is not to abandon disciplines, but rather to diversify into interdisciplinary teams that can act very much like a "multiperson brain" or an integrated consciousness via cyberspace.

In the mid-twentieth century Marshall McLuhan gave us the new paradigm of the Global Village. Now it seems that the World-Wide Mind may serve as the new and important paradigm for both twenty-first century business and perhaps society as well. To make a successful transition to a cybernetic world we must literally learn new ways of thinking. There must be a new approach. It must be a paradigm that creates a plausible new intellectual and cultural vision of the future. This new cyberspace paradigm means a new renaissance in our thinking. It means a new way to approach working, teaching, conducting research, and engaging in business in our increasingly global society. Engineers have not and will not solve our pollution problems. Educators will not solve our educational crises. Politicians will not solve our political problems. Even doctors and life scientists will not solve our health care and medical problems. No, the key to the future is to recognize what our telecommunications, computer, and network-based systems are telling us about the future: We need to "think together." Management and scientific/engineering systems will increasingly form a collective consciousness as we work as electronic virtual teams.

The world of cyberspace is telling us that linked teams of people with a variety of educational backgrounds and cultural and geographic heritages can provide better and more profound answers than highly targeted and deeply focused research teams with a narrow or even a single disciplinary base.

## INTERDISCIPLINARY TEAMS ARE "SMARTER"

An interdisciplinary design team of some forty-seven graduate students from twenty-two countries at the International Space University summer session in Barcelona, Spain, designed a new global satellite tele-education system. What was unique about the system design is that it was a new orbital configuration and it was also some ten times more cost efficient than any satellite system then in planning. It was their plan to sell their unique design to a major satellite system operator for a very small percentage of the system to be used for tele-education purposes that made the proposal truly innovative. Its business and management innovations were more important than their technological designs.

Bell Labs figured out over a decade ago that designing user-friendly telecommunications and information networks and products required more than electrical engineers. When they started hiring psychologists, human-factors engineers, and even sociologists, their products became better. McDonalds, the pervasive hamburger chain, is now using remote sensing analysts and satellite data to decide where to buy land for the future. Fast-food restaurants in general have learned they must combine skills that range from chef and nutritionist, to network design engineer, to architect, to psychologist to make their businesses run smarter and better.

If interdisciplinary skills and multidisciplinary teams work well in designing new systems and products, then the same goes double for effective management. One of the largest projects in human history, the international space station, provides a key case in point.

## THE HAZARDS OF MANAGING
## LARGE-SCALE PROJECTS

Recently, astronaut Jim Newman, who flew on the first assembly mission for the international space station, showed other colleagues from the International Space University and me through the full-scale mock-up of this orbiting human habitat. This facility, located in the heart of the Johnson Space Flight Center in Houston, is truly Texas sized. It is an awesome creation that fires the imagination about what humanity might achieve in the twenty-first century.

On closer inspection, however, the flaws in the space station design start to emerge. This mega-billion-dollar "human living environment" is not very "human." Instead, it is stark and sterile. The computer control system for the station is based on low-bandwidth and slow-speed 386 processors. The first question is this: How can a scientific marvel like the space station be so low tech?

The answer seems to be exceptional caution in qualifying systems for manned spaceflight, plus very complicated and internationally complex management systems. The desire to project a "no frills" image to respond to the demands of Congressional budgetary watchdogs has likewise served to lock the space station into technologies that are years out of date. The essence of the overall space station design derives from the singular focus on engineering optimization and caution.

A team of interdisciplinary graduate students could not design and build such a huge project. Here coordinated efforts of specialists are essential. But it seems a good bet that such a creative and interdisciplinary team could actually conceptually design something that is more fun, human, and adaptable than the current design, and perhaps even at lower cost.

The problem with disciplinary-led planning is not just restricted to large-scale government projects. The same can be equally true in private enterprise. The Ford Motor Company recently spent over a half million dollars just to decide where to place the rear-view mirror on the redesigned Ford Taurus for driver convenience and aerodynamic flow. Then, after it was all done, top management reversed the entire study effort back to square one.

Huge projects, whether conducted by private enterprises or governments, seem to have major built-in dangers. These dangers can often be overcome by the use of well-integrated interdisciplinary design and management teams.

## CYBER ZEN

To cope with the age of cyberspace we must also effect a basic shift from hierarchical to horizontal systems. It is a shift from precise linear and structured mathematics to nonlinear and "fuzzy logic" concepts. In nontechnical terms, it implies becoming more Zen-like.

The switches we currently use in telecommunications systems are based on linear math and hierarchical architecture. Our digital processors have only recently been equipped with fuzzy logic systems that approximate how the human brain works. We define most of our problems in terms of a discipline such as chemical engineering, medicine, health care, education. We assign a team of experts with exactly the same background and training to solve a problem. It usually works, but often not very well. It often lacks creativity and innovation.

This "digital" or "either/or" approach to thinking, along with highly focused expertise, will within the next few decades give way to what has been called the subtle logic of Buddha as opposed to the digital reasoning of Aristotle. French intellectuals, pedantic literalists, and others, however, will not give up their reliance on Cartesian or Aristotelian logic without a fight.

Linear and rigid patterns of thinking may still be employed in some areas of the world even at the end of the twenty-first century. This reliance on rigid logic systems will likely remain, however, only in areas where order and precision are given the highest value, even over creativity and progress. But in scientific, engineering, medical, and management circles and most information societies, linear thinking will have been totally rejected as painfully wrong or at least horribly limiting.

In many ways this cybernetic shift in our thinking and learning patterns will turn us toward the ideas of the East. We will become more Zen-like. It means that Aristotelian concepts of right and wrong and digital concepts of zeroes and ones will have been rejected as crude analytic tools. Most of all, disciplinary thought will give way to the much greater power of interdisciplinary teams. Fuzzy logic and nonlinear math will no longer be nurtured just within the cloisters of the Santa Fe Institute, but instead will become widely recognized as providing a "pathway to wisdom." Management can be the greatest beneficiary of all.

What little we know about the brain is that knowledge and information is distributed throughout the cortex and that memory is something like small wells of information and data. These wells are linked together by associative patterns. The more these patterns of interaction are used, the pathways become stronger and more powerful. If, on the other hand, the associative patterns are not used they wither away.

The brain is seemingly like a network of interdisciplinary teams that are linked together as new thought processes and new information is gained. Time after time, traditional approaches are working counter to what cybernetic processes suggest are the best ways forward. In education, the capabilities of the Internet are being adapted to traditional schooling techniques. Instead, traditional forms of education should be adapting to cybernetic opportunities.

In business, and particularly in services industries, highly hierarchical management and communications systems are likely to produce overstaffing, high costs, slow response, and generally poor results. The brain and services industries apparently need different types of communications networks to achieve good results.

The hierarchical switched network, whether it is applied in telecommunications or business management, is hopelessly inefficient. New satellite systems like Hughes's Spaceway, Astrolink, Skybridge, and especially Bill Gates's and Craig McCaw's Teledesic system intend to directly connect all the PCs around the world. The vision is to create a flexible and dynamic communications system that reflects the true dynamic characteristics of a cybernetic world.

Traditional telecommunications monopolies based on fixed fiber-optic networks are trying to sustain expensive ground switching systems. They may, in another decade, find themselves ill-equipped to operate in a highly mobile and dynamic information society. There is great flexibility in an infinitely interconnectible network that a satellite network can provide (see Figure 1.2).

What we know about the cybernetic shift is today largely defined by economic, industrial, and technical trends. The social consequences are still largely unknown. We know, for instance, that telephone and computer density in a country is a remarkably accurate predictor of economic prosperity (see Figure 1.3). We also know that communication services, at least in terms of volume, are shifting away from telephone calls and toward video, multimedia, and data services (see Figures 1.4 and 1.5). We know that person-to-person communications is shrinking in relative volume, while person-to-machine and machine-to-machine communications are on the rise (see Figure 1.6).

These technology trends have led to the merging of the information, communications, and entertainment industries. Further, deregulation and competition are accelerating the forces that moves us toward powerful, digitally mandated industrial collisions that have been called the "big bang" (see Figure 1.7).

The social consequences of these and other cybernetic shifts are still far from understood. It is impossible to argue, however, that these basic transformations that arise from the world of cyberspace are not inducing important social, moral, and cultural changes. The Telepower opportunities and the Teleshock dangers charted here

**Figure 1.2**
**The Cybernetic Network: Routing Flexibility of Mesh Architecture in Telecommunications**

**Heavy lines indicate high-throughput links**

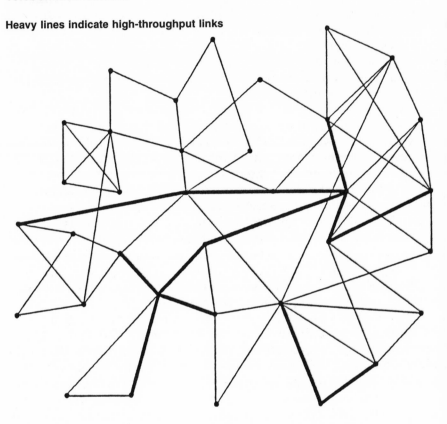

are only the tip of an iceberg. What is important is to recognize that this overall pattern of change is happening. It is happening relentlessly, systematically, and globally. It is thus important to note that in the twenty-first century we are likely to see the following key and basic shifts occurring:

| The Fading Paradigm | The New World of the World-Wide Mind |
| --- | --- |
| Traditional Disciplines | Interdisciplinary plus Disciplines |
| Management Hierarchy in Charge | Teams in Charge |
| Piecemeal Thinking | Synoptic and Synergetic Thinking |
| Hierarchical and Large Systems | Distributed or Mesh Networks That Are Agile and Nimble |

**Figure 1.3**
**Telephones versus GNP per Capita: Still a Key Global Correlation**

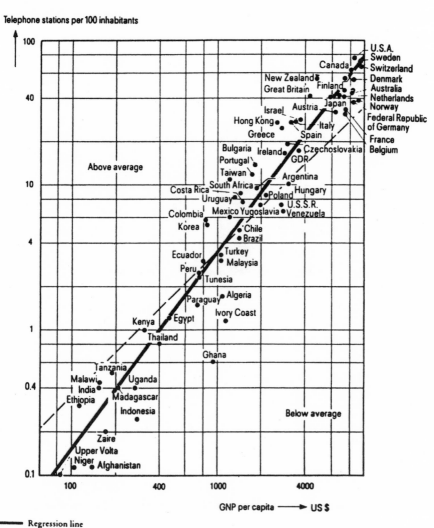

Telephone stations per 100 inhabitants

GNP per capita ———➤ US $

━━━ Regression line
－－－ Regression line, if relationship were proportional

| | |
|---|---|
| Traditional Warfare | Just-in-Time Military Systems |
| National/Local Systems | Planetary Systems |
| Linear Math Predominant | Nonlinear Math Predominant |
| Traditional Education | Participatory and Lifelong System |
| Traditional Industrial Patterns of Supply and Distribution | Emerging World-Wide Mind |

**Figure 1.4**
**Video and Data Will Dominate IT Growth in the Twenty-First Century**

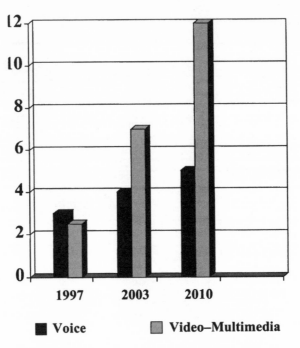

Although the broad scope of change is characterized in abstract terms in this list, the precise patterns of change throughout our economic and business systems are even more important to consider. In the chapters that follow, the road map to cyberbusiness and cybermanagement is charted along the pathway of coming change. The force of the ten megatrends of cyberspace will dramatically redefine business, management practice, and cyberprofits. Further, it will do it in new and often daring ways. Those who hesitate or doubt that a cybertsunami of change is going to sweep through twenty-first-century business practices—and especially those who fail to prepare for its arrival—will undoubtedly regret it.

And now it is time to explore our ten signposts to the future of cyberbusiness. In each case the key is finding the proper cybernetic shift. Watch out for these signposts to the future. Cyberbusiness is coming to your electronic neighborhood soon.

**Figure 1.5**
**Communications, Cable TV, Computing, Consumer Electronics, Content**

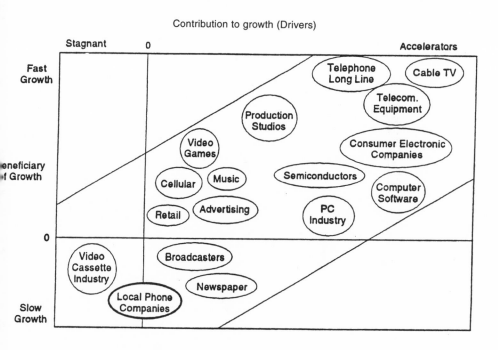

**Figure1.6**
**Person and Machine Communications**

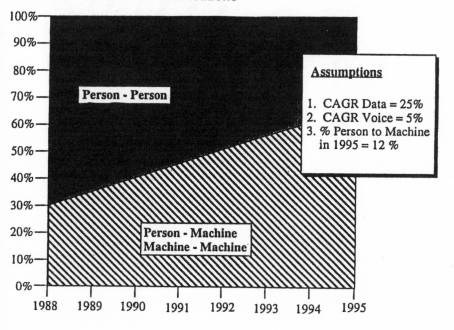

**Figure 1.7**
**Digital Integration of Markets and the Big Bang**

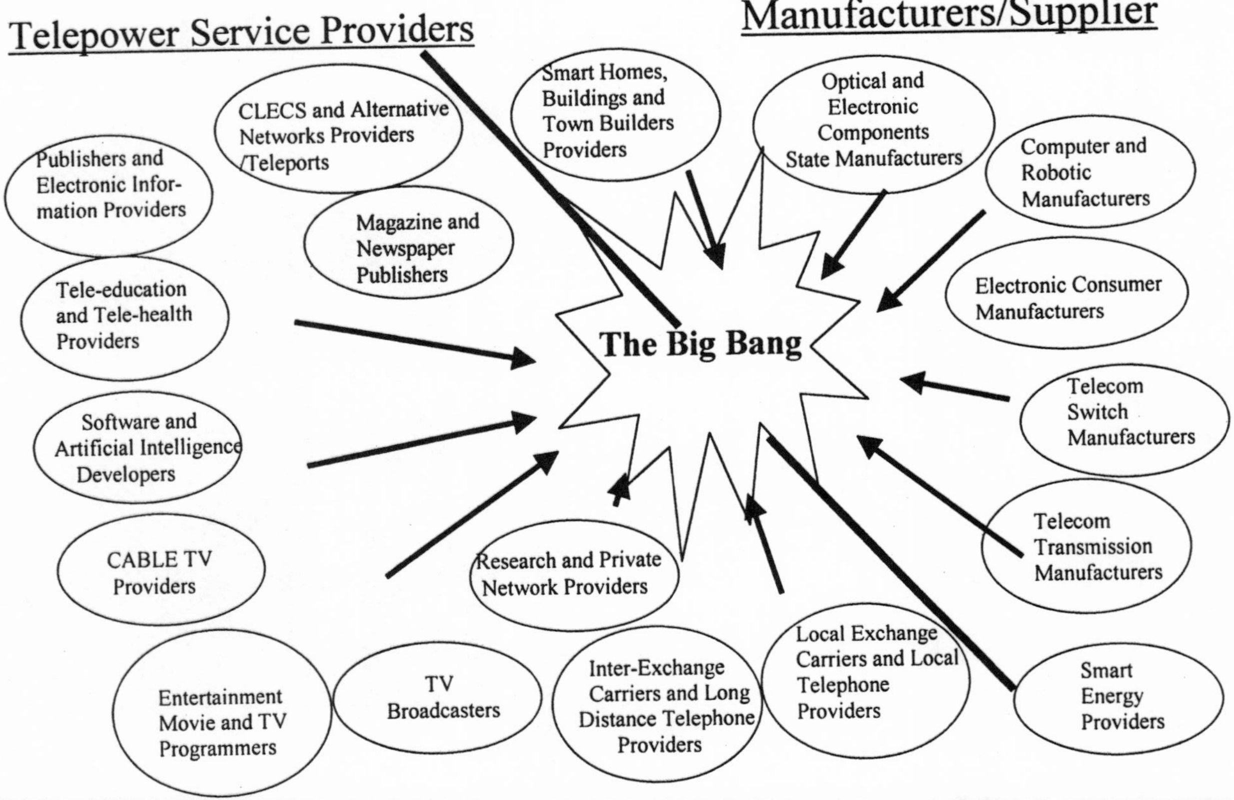

## Manufacturers/Supplier

## Telepower Service Providers

The Big Bang

Computer and Robotic Manufacturers

Electronic Consumer Manufacturers

Telecom Switch Manufacturers

Telecom Transmission Manufacturers

Smart Energy Providers

Optical and Electronic Components State Manufacturers

Local Exchange Carriers and Local Telephone Providers

Smart Homes, Buildings and Town Builders Providers

Inter-Exchange Carriers and Long Distance Telephone Providers

Research and Private Network Providers

CLECS and Alternative Networks Providers/Teleports

Magazine and Newspaper Publishers

TV Broadcasters

Publishers and Electronic Information Providers

Tele-education and Tele-health Providers

Software and Artificial Intelligence Developers

CABLE TV Providers

Entertainment Movie and TV Programmers

## THE CYBERSPACE CHANGE AGENTS

- Telecommuting and electronic immigration
- The 168-hour work week
- Info-espionage and tele-crime
- The coming ICEE age
- Jobs at risk and new jobs to come
- Cybermanagement
- Global competitiveness
- Race, gender, and bias in the world of cyberbusiness
- Training tomorrow's workforce—the cyberspace challenge
- Info-entertainment and virtual life

# CHAPTER 2

# What Is Cyberspace?

Exactly what is cyberspace anyway? Some think, even violently contend, that cyberspace is the "Super I-Way." These cyberjunkies contend that the Internet, a vast maze of computer networks with hundreds of million of users, is the be all and end all of cyberspace. Clearly, the Internet is the biggest and most powerful electronic messaging network in the world. But as noted in a recent study of the Chicago-based international engineering consortium the Internet still moves only a tiny percentage (i.e., on the order of 2 percent but moving up fast) of the world's total information. Further, it is still possible that the first-generation Internet will ultimately turn out to be a failed experiment that teeters out of control under the weight of too much "junk" information. Do not fear, however. Internet 2 (an upgraded, higher speed, and larger database-compatible version of the Internet) is coming to your local university or government research center, if not to your home office PC, and soon.

In this case, "junk information" is defined as databases that are either out of date, too hard or too slow to access, too irrelevant, or simply wrong. There is also concern about too much "spam." This is the unwanted advertising or other messages that come to you unsolicited. There is even a Web site actually devoted to viewing a rotting piece of spam in case someone didn't understand that uninvited e-mail is a pretty rotten thing.

Even if the Internet should fail due to information overload, bad information, and spamming—and it probably won't—there undoubtedly will be a son or daughter or grandaughter of the Internet that will lead us toward an improved global data network.

The next generation of the Internet will be more managed and centrally controlled to allow network growth to be planned, and for spurious information to be weeded out or updated. It will also likely achieve much higher levels of storage capability, along with improved speed and accuracy.

The Internet is thus central to cyberspace, but it is nevertheless just a part of the whole. What is key to understand is that all forms of optical and electronic communications and all forms of electronic processing and software represent a part of this complex new electronic environment. Let's review the basics of cyberspace:

- Cyberspace is not necessarily related to a particular transmission or switching technology. (Although the essence of the Internet is the Transmission Control Protocol/Internet Protocol (TCP/IP), and IP-based communications systems may ultimately take over the public switched telecommunications networks [PSTN].)

- Cyberspace is a hybrid combination of copper wire, coax and fiber optic cable, satellites, radio frequency (RF), and infrared wireless communications, and stratospheric platforms, not to mention Local Area Networks (LANs), Metropolitan Area Networks (MANs), Wide Area Networks (WANs), and much, much more.

- Cyberspace is networked capabilities achieved through user terminal equipment, which can be personal computers, mainframe computers, remote processors linked by telephone or cable-TV-based modems, personal data assistants (PDAs), new "smart" television sets, DVD, and, soon, wearable antennas.

- Cyberspace is now centered on the industrialized countries, the Internet, and corporate electronic networks called LANs and WANs, but in the twenty-first century it will increasingly blanket our world and in time link billions of people together. As noted on the Internet society's Web site, the cumulative annual growth rate of the Internet in South America is 125 percent, in Asia 110 percent, and in Africa 80 percent. It is about 90 percent per annum in the most advanced countries.

- Cyberspace is ultimately a state of mind that represents the evolution from mass-media, broadcast-oriented networks to a true many-to-many electronic system with enormous flexibility. This highest level of expression for cyberspace in the twenty-first century may ultimately be called the World-Wide Mind.

- Cyberspace is not Nirvana, nor access to ultimate wisdom. It is rather an expanded, responsive, and complex information system. It can be used for many different purposes that range from intellectual pursuits to low-brow entertainment, from humanitarian ideals to the darker side of society.

• Cyberspace is the beginning of a new paradigm called the World-Wide Mind, where we leap forward from the age of global television that satellites brought us in the 1960s. Now, at the start of the new millennium, we have entered a new time where we can see the same worldwide image, and think together via a vast global network of ganglia to create the future faster, and faster, and faster than ever before.

Rather than being an ultimate capability, the Internet is, in fact, a morass of unregulated and uncontrolled data systems and networks that is actually in danger of spinning out of control.

## THE GLOBAL ELECTRONIC MACHINE
## AND CYBERSPACE

Telecommunications, information systems, and services, plus entertainment, will represent an economic enterprise equivalent to about $4 trillion as of the start of the new millennium—or so World Bank studies tell us. This means that one dollar in twelve will be devoted to this activity on a global basis. A massive electronic network will be in place to support this insatiable sharing of digital bits back and forth across the world. As a result of standards, international communications, and global business, this network will evolve toward what has been called the Global Information Infrastructure (GII) or more simply, the Global Electronic Highway or even the Global Electronic Machine. In one guise or another it will ultimately reach everywhere on our planet.

This vast array of communications satellites, fiber optic and coaxial cables, twisted and open copper wire, electronic and mechanical switches, microwave and cellular radio towers, wireless LANs, computer terminals, earth stations, and hand-held transceivers are collectively being merged to create the world's largest and most expensive machine. This machine never stops running. This machine never stops expanding.

Encompassed in this vast network are national civil and military communications systems, corporate enterprise networks, and yes, even the Internet is a part of this whole interconnected network. Altogether, this vast electronic machine represents a capital investment of perhaps $15 to $20 trillion. Despite its huge size and geographic dispersion it is a kind of integrated and interlinked machine, but one that is highly decentralized. Nevertheless, it grows smarter and more interconnected and more capable every day. This means that it can impact our lives more profoundly, offer us new opportunities, and also cause us more misery and grief. It is the sword of Damocles, the two faces of Janus, Pandora's box, and ultimately a new portal to information and the universe. Its watch-words should be "Handle with Care!"

The information that passes through the commercial and private parts of dedicated data networks is highly structured and controlled, but the Internet itself is somewhat like an unstructured and almost random data dump. For better or worse, the Global Electronic Machine with its bells and whistles, warts and scars, is the first step in creating not the Global Village, but rather the World-Wide Mind. In another century or so we may get there, but first we will have to repair or reengineer quite a few synapses and neurons before we get it right.

## THE INTERNET TODAY AND TOMORROW

The Internet is today close to 200 countries or political territories linked through interconnected data networks that will soon number 200,000. The biggest of these networks are NSFNET, Bitnet, IP Internet, UUCP, and Fidonet, but some are a "network" of one or two people who have obtained their own domain. A complete list of all these networks is not very helpful, because their names, nature, and existence change daily.

The dramatic increase in the size and interconnectivity of the Internet must nevertheless be placed in perspective. Of the nearly 200 million users of the Internet that will balloon to over 1 billion by 2005, it should be noted that it is still heavily dominated by males and by higher-income and highly educated people. This is shifting, but it will still be a quite elite group even decades from now. Further, in terms of geographic focus it is still highly populated with American users (about 50 percent worldwide). NSFNET, which is named after the U.S. National Science Foundation, is still essentially the backbone of the system. Some 60 percent of all Internet traffic actually flows through Washington, D.C. Almost every major route in the world of Internet systems flows to and from the United States. If one wanted to visually see why and how the United States is now the only superpower, you would only need to look in the *Telegeography Report 2000* and see how "U.S.-centric" the Internet really is.

There are more than 6 billion people on the planet today and it will be a very, very long time before the Internet could be considered a public utility that is generally available to the entire public even in the United States. Telephone, television, radio, and newspapers reach a higher percentage of the population than the 35 to 50 percent of U.S. citizens that have consistent to partial access to the Internet. The Internet in the United States will probably reach the same penetration levels as telephone today around 2005. It is not clear if it will ever reach the levels represented by the availability of radio and television, which now reach over 5 billion people on our planet.

Nevertheless the Internet (and all of the interconnected corporate Intranets) represents by far the largest global data network. Here, hundreds of millions of people can exchange e-mail messages. The primary means of connection today is through public commercial telephone networks linked via home computers equipped with modems. One can access public laws, government archives, video coverage of space missions, underwater explorations, or literally millions of topics. Home-page presentations on the World Wide Web are one of most effective ways that information about almost any topic can be shared across the Internet—from astrophysics to zoological pornography. Not overly surprising, a recent report from the U.S. Congressional Research Service tells us that the most visited home pages are the ones that offer X-rated video images. A key word search for "sex" leads to literally thousands of sites. Internet users, as noted previously, are still mainly male, and a great deal of e-commerce is X-rated.

The Internet will, of course, change and grow a great deal in just the next decade. Change could be even more dramatic than in the last ten years. In the 1960s Marshall McLuhan gave us the image of the Global Village, but in the twenty-first century the cyberspace environment made possible through the Internet and other forms of electronic communications will begin to define the World-Wide Mind. Perhaps tens of thousands of terabytes will be stored on Internet 2, outstripping the size of the Library of Congress or the British Museum a thousand times. But today, our great libraries actually still contain much more information than the Internet. The date when the Internet will contain more data than the top twenty libraries is rapidly approaching, but today the World Wide Web is about 1 billion pages and 1 trillion bytes of information— less than the Library of Congress alone.

One might ask, if there is so much information out there on the Internet, how to possibly find it. The answer, despite what the cyberjunkies tell you, is that it is really fairly difficult to find. There are, however, some emerging tools that are being designed to help. Some of the key weapons with which to attack the Net are directories. One of these is known as Yahoo, perhaps the best known "yellow pages" of the Internet. There are also other valuable tools out there, known by such names as Argus, Alta Vista, Infoseek, Open

Market's Commercial Sites Index, Infominc, and the Whole Internet Catalog. Some of the big Internet service providers like AOL provide their own "browsers" (or information seekers) as well.

Perhaps the most common way to enter the Web is through a browser like Netscape Navigator or Microsoft Explorer, the doors to the world of multimedia-based hypertext. Through Net directories you can begin to browse cyberspace by linking up to a host of directories that are either general (such as those already mentioned), or highly specialized. Through Net search you can also undertake more serious and selective research by using search engines to find a particular topic such as "structure of galaxies" or "Dell Comics Super Heroes." (Who is to say exactly what serious research is in the world of the Internet). Once launched, with the help of a friend who at least pretends to be a cyberspace guru you should be able to find almost anything. This could be current magazines (from *Playboy* to *Business Week*), a video of the latest space astronomical image just in from the Hubble telescope, Julia Child's or Martha Stewart's latest recipes.

Despite its size and electronic reach, the Internet, even in the early twenty-first century, will still only be a part of the vast electronic machine that is our twenty-first-century global information infrastructure. Commercial and mobile telephones, cable television, and satellite networks will still remain a part of the mix. In fact, the Internet will still be highly dependent upon this information infrastructure for linking to users. Even so, we can look to a rather astonishing future for cyberspace networks.

## EIGHT WAYS THE INTERNET OF TOMORROW WILL BE DIFFERENT

Few people knowledgeable about the Arpanet (Advanced Research Projects Agency Network) in the 1960s would have predicted something that looks and acts like the global computer system of 200,000 networks and hundreds of millions of users that constitutes the Internet today. Clearly, forecasts have their flaws and it may be highly embarrassing to review these predictions a decade from now. Predictions about the future are just that. These forecasts have at least some good evidence and trend lines behind them, but only time will tell if they have any real merit.

### Getting More Organized: Combating the Infojunk Problem

Today a number of experts claim that the Internet is at great risk. They fear that the Net is in danger of crumbling under too much unedited, wrong, irrelevant, out-of-date, or simply "junk" information. British Telecom's much-vaunted videotext system of the 1980s, known as PRESTEL, failed simply because too many people loaded junk information onto the system. As a result, paying customers could not find the information they wanted. Some believe that commercial services through high-speed portals will evolve to provide high-quality information nodes on various subjects within the Internet. Others believe that perhaps educators, publishers, financial analysts, and other commercial organizations will provide needed structure, editing, and control. There is a near consensus in most developed countries that the government should not be the one to organize and control information on the Internet. The dangers of "controlled information" and totalitarian abuse would simply be too strong.

The *Penthouse* and *Playboy* Web sites are consistently among the most active in the world. This rise in nudity and pornography on the Net may, however, give rise to new controls that will limit and focus the content on the Internet and serve to limit creativity or experimentation. Parents can subscribe to services that can shut off access to most of these sites, and the so-called V-chip technology or other subscription services can also be employed to keep teenagers and children from pornographic access.

One thing seems clear. If the twenty-first century Internet is to succeed, it must get better organized. Most important, it must find a way to rid itself of a growing mountain of infojunk. Censorship may or may not become a part of this process, and if it does that will very likely be a strong negative rather than a positive. Some sense of self-policing of Web sites and global standards against infojunk is badly needed. If we are lucky this will come in the form of a noncensored and nonauthoritarian answer.

### The Mobility Factor: The Internet Goes Mobile

The biggest surprise in the field of telecommunications in the last decade is the huge success of mobile telephone services. As noted in my recent study for the IEC on the wireless industry, it is still the most rapidly growing segment of the overall market. Internet users on the move want to have instant connectivity anytime and anywhere. Using everything from wireless LANs, infrared modems, and a maze of satellite systems, inveterate Internet users will get "info-fix." They will get their connections at airports, on planes and trains, and in the jungles of Brazil. This means that the Internet will increasingly be connected not just by wires, but by radio waves and even infrared short-distance links. The success of such products as the Palm Pilot and Sprint PCS enhanced cell phones underscore this trend.

Already, satellite systems such as Orbcomm, INMARSAT, American Mobile, Telesat Mobile, Globalstar, and Satellife provide global Internet interconnectivity to mobile or semimobile terminals. Within the next five years the number of mobile satellite systems allowing Internet links will mushroom tremendously. Some of these will be in low and medium Earth orbit, and others will be in the conventional geosynchronous orbit. Look Ma, no hands, no wires, but lots of phone bills! These systems will be accessible and user friendly, but rather expensive. As usage grows the costs will come down. One of the reasons that Internet access is so pervasive in the United States is that the cost of hooking up and using the system is much less than in Japan or Europe. The fact that one pays a flat fee to use the Internet in the United States and Japanese and European users must pay by the minute makes a great difference. Even cell phone connectivity is down to two cents a minute in the United States.

### Beyond the Personal Data Assistant: Is the Personal Computer on the Endangered Species List?

The tool that made the Internet possible is the personal computer. Perhaps over 95 percent of all users access the Internet this way. Today we see the move from PC to laptop to palm top, while others are using even simpler systems like Web TV. We are now seeing seen the advent of "smart" mobile telephones offered by companies like Nextel, Sprint, Vodaphone, and others around the world. This trend will be followed by the so-called personal data assistant, with artificially intelligent "agents."

These new hand-held units will have to be a good deal better than the old Newton 2, which evoked a yawn from the user market. This is because these first PDAs were too hard to use, and no one wants to punch in text with a tiny pencil. The Internet-compatible PDAs will use voice input via software like "Dragon" to allow you to talk to your handset and see your input in text.

Within the decade, a PDA with artificial intelligence, fast processors, voice input and output, wireless modem, and a chip for mobile voice and data and even space navigation (i.e., GPS) will likely be available in one compact package. Such a product could become the number-one consumer product in the world and certainly become the predominant means of accessing the Internet. Some of these PDAs will be multipurpose and others will have specialized functions, but most will be equipped for Internet access through a wireless or plug-in modem. Some will represent the concept of the so-called Internet Lite, with limited processing power but able to draw upon all of the software power stored within the Net. The PDAs of the future do not need to be powerful, but just have powerful access. The use of the systems will vary greatly by age. Young people of the twenty-first century that are raised with this technology will almost inhale these systems as an essential part of their lives. They will be almost as essential to life as one's arms, legs, lungs, or brain.

### Voice and Real-Time Interactive Services

The Internet was designed for asynchronous data messaging. Today "asynchronous" e-mail has been supplanted as the key application and increasingly we will have real-time multimedia exchanges. Gopher and now the omnipresent World Wide Web first introduced video images on the Net. These multimedia images in HTML, XTML, and the newer languages that are replacing it are now becoming the primary product in terms of throughput of bits on the Net.

Increasingly, users want to use the Internet for real-time interactive services. Those who plug into Earthcam want to see the images they see of London, New York, or Hong Kong instantly updated, rather than wait thirty minutes or even ten seconds for the next screen. There are a number of customer kits that can be purchased today to use the Internet for free long distance telephone services. The quality and reliability of these services are rapidly improving. After all, the Internet was never designed for this purpose.

As the Internet is upgraded, however, especially NSFNET, one can foresee voice, interactive computer games, and even radio and television shows operating seamlessly through the network. At this time a number of new companies are building new ultra-high-capacity fiber networks that are designed as private business networks. These dedicated business networks use Internet Protocol (IP) as their basic switching protocol and can offer voice and multimedia services at rates that are four times cheaper than the supercarriers like AT&T, British Telcom, NTT, or France Telecom. This change will alter the world of telecommunications and information all over the world. These technologies and new business practices will advance the coming of the World-Wide Mind, the global business, and the global university.

The key question here is to what extent providers of telephone and commercial telecommunications services will seek to impose legislation or regulations to block such efficient and global network usage. At this point most of the big telephone companies have hedged their bets by becoming Internet service providers (ISPs), but unless they adjust their business plans to become cyberspace and IP-centric they could lose 40 percent of their business in the next five years as indicated by recent studies of the International Engineering Consortium.

### Horizontal versus Hierarchical Webs:
### Bill Gates versus the Telephone Giants

Today we have conventional telephone systems, mobile radio phone companies, cable television networks, electric power systems, Alternative Network Providers (ANPs) or Competitive Local Exchange Carriers (CLECs), and a variety of satellite system operators. All of these erstwhile providers of the information highway have acquired customers and in doing so have tended to aggregate customers and consolidate traffic through switches or concentrators so that heavy trunks of telephone service can be carried over large and efficient links. This architecture is the basis of international standards as agreed to by the International Telecommunications Union (ITU), the U.N. specialized agency in Geneva that seeks to standardize global telecommunications and networking.

The advent of the PC and the Internet architecture suggests that the old rules do not apply. The new paradigm of what might be is expressed boldly in the Bill Gates and Craig McCaw 1994 proposal for an 840-satellite system known as Teledesic that today has been rescaled to 288 satellites (and may be dramatically changed further still).

This low Earth orbit satellite system can link anyone to anyplace and bypass the conventional telephone system. The Hughes Spaceway Satellite system, the Lockheed Martin and Liberty Media Astrolink system, and Alcatel's Skybridge networks carried the Teledesic approach of broadband satellite services directly to the desktop forward to become a trend. These satellites, to be launched between 2003 and 2005, can bypass conventional on-the-ground telecommunications networks and in many cases offer direct wireless mobile Internet connections as well as telephone, data, multimedia, and videoconferencing services.

### Virtual Reality as an Internet Driver

Just as video-based services such as the World Wide Web have overtaken data messaging on the Internet, it seems likely that new applications such as scientific visualization, interactive multimedia video, and especially virtual-reality applications will predominate another decade in the future. Innovative new products such as the Sensart virtual-reality stock market will be highly popular but will require the transmission of huge amounts of data back and forth over the network.

### Megascience

Increasingly, the tremendous potential of the Internet for truly global megascience projects will be understood. Systematic linking of databases, interconnecting the world's observatories, and collaborative research with interlinked high-end machines will generate a huge amount of new communication on the Internet. Research projects such as NASA's Earth Observation Satellite System alone will generate many tens of thousands of terabytes of data. This is the equivalent of 10,000 Libraries of Congress!

### Globalism: Industry and Trade versus Science

Today there are over 190 countries and territories around the world linked to the Internet, but this means that some forty countries or territories have not yet linked into the Internet. This will change rapidly, and virtually every political entity on earth will be interlinked within the next decade.

There will be different patterns of international communications, however, as total global interconnectivity is achieved. Industry- and trade-driven communications will still be predominantly on telephone fiber, satellite, and commercial radiotelephone links. This is because of considerations related to privacy, confidentiality, quality of service, system availability, and customized requirements. It in large part relates to commercial self-sufficiency and not wanting to be dependent upon a large amorphous system without a single network control being responsible. Traffic can and will migrate off the Public Switched Telephone Network (PSTN) and on to private Internet Protocol (IP)–based fiber networks operated by entities like Level-3, Qwest, Frontier, and Williams.

In contrast, a great deal of academic and scientific collaboration will be carried out on the Internet—or at least Internet 2. Ties and relationships that transcend local or even national politics will take place and give rise to new forms of international collaboration, new international teams developing patents, and new stresses and strains to concepts of national sovereignty. Some governments may indeed see the Internet as a direct threat. Electronic immigrants who use the Internet to work via electronic means in other countries may well see the Internet as a form of virtual immigration.

## THE DARKER SIDE OF CYBERSPACE

At times our advanced information systems seem to be creating a more and more hostile, user-unfriendly, and overhyped information society. This Teleshock phenomenon may not be your imagination. Technophobia and technoneurosis may have some very real and legitimate basis. Futurists John Naisbitt, Alvin Toffler, and others who have attempted to chart the likely future courses of cyberspace have missed some of the most important trends. Toffler's reference to the so-called Third Wave would really be much more on target if he referred to the Great Flood.

Major challenges have been underestimated and coming economic opportunities undervalued. Attempts to see these issues within the framework of U.S. political views of "liberal Democrats" or "conservative Republicans" is not only foolish but most likely irrelevant. The issues of Telepower, Teleshock, cyperspace, and survival techniques in the information age are largely orthogonal to conventional theories of government or political strategies. Information and service industries that are being driven by cyberspace technologies are reshaping every aspect of society: our jobs, our culture, our transportation and energy systems, our environment, our education, our health care, our leisure time, and, yes, even our sex lives. New strategies and approaches are needed for America, for the Western Hemisphere, for the developed countries of the world (i.e., the Organization for Economic Cooperation and Development [OECD]), and for the developing countries as well.

## TOWARD A BETTER UNDERSTANDING OF CYBERSPACE TECHNOLOGIES

Cyberspace may have seemed to have sprung out of nowhere, but it does have a rich and interesting history. More important, its future will likely have a dramatic effect on the future of the human race.

### The Prehistory of Cyberspace

The definition of humanity and civilization is closely linked to communications and language. For millions of years communications was confined to verbal and body language. This meant that knowledge was limited to the memories of individuals and the traditional oral-based learning processes within a community.

About 40,000 years ago in the Neolithic age, drawing and written languages emerged. Suddenly knowledge could be stored, transmitted, and exchanged in a systematic way. Humans had created institutional memory. More important, they had created for the first time an intellectual tool. Instead of the practical use of fire or the invention of the wheel or sledge, they had embarked upon a new path—the path of "intellectual prosthetics." Humanity had gone beyond the individual's own capabilities to create a thinking tool. This was the path to the future world of cyberspace. In this sense, cyberspace is the modern embodiment of collective memory and collective thought and collective human experience. It is the ultimate in late twentieth-century intellectual prosthetics that began only 40,000 years ago in stone-age caves. One says "only" because humanity has been around for some 3 to 5 million years and thus 40,000 years is by comparison only a short time.

The progression from written language to today's electronic networks has not come in a series of neat, predictable steps, but in a series of sudden jerks. The only real pattern has been that these jerks have come closer and closer together. Thus, it was only about 10,000 years ago, after the last ice age, that agriculture and permanent settlements began to arise. This innovation brought stability and prosperity, but in an intellectual and societal sense it allowed specialization of labor and the creation of new types of occupations, such as educators, librarians, engineers, craftsmen, and inventors. Suddenly there were people who could specialize in thinking and innovating.

In the nineteenth century came the invention of digital communications. This event was Samuel F. B. Morse's invention of the telegraph. In the late 1830s Morse, a New York portrait painter, religious zealot, and active political figure of his day, also engaged in amateur tinkering. His first invention in his twenties, a firefighting water pump, was a failure, but his subsequent development of the telegraph brought instantaneous communications to the world. Morse, dubbed the American Leonardo, ran for Mayor of New York City, introduced the daguerreotype into America, created the American Academy of Fine Arts in New York, and assisted Samuel Colt in the development of electrically discharged mines for the U.S. Navy. His greatest contribution, however, was the creation of electrically encoded messages that allowed people to have instant contact.

The next key step toward modern cyberspace was the invention of the telephone in 1865 by Alexander Graham Bell. Bell, like Morse, was an amateur inventor and tinkerer rather than a trained scientist or engineer. The telephone allowed not only instantaneous communications, but broadband links as well. At first the telephone was seen as a home entertainment system. Western Union's top management, who were offered the Bell patent for $100,000, did not foresee an important future for the telephone nor envision how it could rival their efficient electronic messaging system. They just said no to one of the greatest industrial opportunities of all time.

There next was a wait of more than three decades until Marconi demonstrated the feasibility of wireless communications using radio waves. In fact, the Marconi experiments with long-distance short-wave or high-frequency telecommunications was a colossal act of serendipity. The ionosphere, which reflected the Marconi-generated radio signals back to Earth, had not even been discovered in the early 1900s. Thus, no one, including Marconi, knew why long-distance short-wave radio communications actually worked.

Following the invention of the telegraph, the telephone, and radio communications, the next few steps toward the world of cyberspace came in rapid succession. These key steps were television, electronic computers, transistors, satellite communications, and fiber-optic cable systems. In a span of only fifteen years from the late 1940s to the early 1960s, all these key technologies grew from concepts to practical realizations. The following list provides a brief history of the key inventors and innovators who developed the essential technologies that have led us forward. These innovative broadband interactive electronic telecommunications and information systems constitute the hardware and software that enable the existence of cyberspace.

| | | |
|---|---|---|
| Telegraph | 1838 | Samuel F. B. Morse |
| Telephone | 1876 | Alexander Graham Bell |
| Radio | 1895 | Gulielermo Marconi |
| Television | 1923 | Baird and Zworykin |
| Computer Programming | 1935 | Charles Babbage |
| Electronic Computer (ENIAC) | 1944 | Howard Aiken and others |
| Transistor | 1948 | Shockey, Bardeen, and Brattain |
| Fiber-Optic Cable | 1955 | Kaparry |
| Satellite Communications | 1958 | U.S. Signal Corp./NASA |
| Arpanet/Internet | 1958 | Advanced Research Projects Agency |

## THE ACCELERATION OF CHANGE AND ITS RELATION TO COMPLEXITY THEORY, NONLINEAR MATH, AND THE EMERGING WORLD-WIDE MIND

The list of key inventions that lead to the age of cyberspace continues. It is, in fact, even increasing in pace. The invention of large-scale integration, very large-scale integration, monolithic devices, micromachines, expert systems, artificial intelligence, soliton (or solitary wave) pulse transmission systems, super conductivity, dense wave division multiplexing, code division multiplexing, active phased array antennas, optical switches, and much, much more detail the technological progress of information systems over the last forty years. The flowering of electronic and optical technologies since the 1960s has indeed allowed the creation of the cybernetics age.

The key to understanding this new age we are now entering is founded in millions of years of human history. This long history cannot be evenly divided, as scholars are often wont to do. The history of humankind can be best understood as follows:

The Age of Hunters and Gatherers. This covers virtually all of human history. From the dawn of the Southern ape man some 5 million years ago up until 10,000 years ago, this described the compass of human activity. Since this mode of existence required virtually everyone to hunt and gather food, there was limited opportunity for innovation or specialization of labor.

The Age of Agriculture. This age began with the discovery of the art of farming and the planting of seeds. This allowed permanent settlements, and the agricultural surplus allowed some to farm and others to develop special skills and to create new ideas and customs. This age began about 8000 B.C. in Mesopotamia, and matured as higher seed yields were obtained.

The Age of Industrialization and Scientific Inquiry. This age, an outgrowth of the enlightenment and the Renaissance that began in the fifteenth century, flowered at the end of the seventeenth century and the beginning of the eighteenth. The pace of innovation again quickened as a new system of societal research, learning, and innovation created new wealth and a profusion of new professions. This is what Teilhard de Chardin called the birth of the "noosphere."

The Age of Global Telecommunications, Artificial Intelligence, and Cybernetic Networks. This age is now just beginning. It involves much greater complexity. The combination of networked hardware, sophisticated software, collective research, and globalized economic activity define an entirely new age for humanity. It has already helped to move modern human society toward the Marshall McLuhan vision of the Global Village, and before it ends it will likely serve to create the World-Wide Mind. We are thus making the transition from the "noosphere" where individual interactions led us forward to the birth of the e-Sphere, where global interconnectivity and "Big Science" can define our future.

The new age of the e-Sphere can and will produce startling new Telepowers, but it will also give rise to pernicious new dosages of Teleshock. The e-Sphere allows higher levels of interactivity, increased global linkages, and increasing choices between more specialization or more interdisciplinary cross-pollination. The unique ability of the Internet to probe to new depths of specialization while also allowing collaboration across an almost infinite number of traditional lines of learning and scholarship may constitute a critical path to the future in terms of how we work and learn in the twenty-first century. There is in this latest stage enormous power to stratify, to segregate, and to bias and distort human, societal, and cultural relationships.

It is not new to think of human development as a series of stages. Futurist Alvin Toffler has, for instance, written of the Three Waves of history. The gentle image of rhythmic waves lapping against the seashore as presented to us by Toffler is not even close to an accurately scaled history of human development when he talks of these historical waves as somehow being parallel or proportionate. If we were to reckon the human stages leading up to the cybernetics age, we would find that the first stage consumed 99.8 percent of the entirety of human existence. The second stage would consume 0.19 percent of the total time, the third stage would represent less than 0.01 percent of the time, and the last stage would almost be off the scale of measurability. The importance of these stages to human intellectual development is, however, inversely proportional to their duration. This is because the information in the human store of knowledge is expanding some 200,000 times to a million times faster than the growth of human population. Today, information doubles every five years. By 2005, the doubling will occur in three years, and so on.

If one were to visualize human history as the building of two buildings—one that measures time and another that measures human knowledge—we would create two dramatically different images. The first building, built to reflect the time domain, would be about 32,000 meters or nearly 20 miles high. Of this building 10,000 stories high, 9,980 stories would be devoted to the first stage (hunting and gathering). Only 20 stories would be devoted to the second stage (agriculture and permanent dwellings), one story or two meters would be devoted to the third stage (the industrial age), and about 1 foot would represent the latest stage (the cybernetic age).

The second building, representing the totality of human knowledge, is also some 32,000 meters, 20 miles tall, or 10,000 stories tall. It represents the ever-increasing growth of global information. This edifice of knowledge represents by its height the cumulative information of world civilization. The height of this building reflected in the four stages of human development would show a dramatically different picture than our preceding graphic. Here, the first stage, which actually represents millions of years, contributes less than one meter to the height of our building. The second stage of farming and agriculture would be about 5 meters high. The third stage of industrial growth and development would be about 200 meters high. The last stage, representing only the last forty years of advanced technical development, represents a staggering addition. This forty-year period represents over 9,500 stories of our building of knowledge—95 percent of the global knowledge base has been added in under a half century. The dramatic difference between the two buildings represented by elapsed time and acquired knowledge is essential to understanding how quickly information is now growing. These two images should instill a sense of awe, and even more important, fear about the modern human condition. These startlingly different views of human history are shown in Figures 2.1 and 2.2.

The old mathematics with which we have for centuries attempted to describe the physical universe has long rested on the concepts known as linear equations. Dramatic shifts are occurring in how effectively and quickly human intelligence interacts within a cybernetic society. These changes, that come in forward jerks rather than smooth progressions, are more than a little daunting. It is indeed different—fundamentally different—from the past. Cybernetic communications seems to represent a new evolutionary pathway to the future. In terms of models or analogies, nonlinear equations and fuzzy logic systems may well be better suited to describe how this process works. For thousands of years, since the age of Socrates and Aristotle, we have placed our faith in linear math and Carthesian logic to find solutions to social and practical problems. Today we find that nonlinear mathemathics and strange concepts called fractals and complex logic systems are letting us solve problems in new ways. These new ways of thinking reject the idea that by thinking in terms of "either" or "or" we can solve any problem. It turns out that weather patterns, stock market behavior, and coastlines are predicted better by the new math that allows us to think in terms of shades of gray rather than black and white.

Humans in a network may tend to communicate more efficiently and link together much like neural networks inside of a brain, rather than based on the math of Boolean algebra and Western logic we have treasured for two millennia. These new nonlinear interactions may ultimately prove to be best modeled in terms of set theory based upon "gray" or overlapping results. The variations in these sets are not easily predictable. They reflect patterns of development of increasingly higher complexity. They nevertheless seem to reflect dynamic and recurring patterns of development. The importance of the new way of thinking (the math inside our brains, so to speak) may serve to accelerate even more the speed of our intellectual evo-

**Figure 2.1**
**Building of Human Historical Development (10,000 Stories or
20 Miles High)**

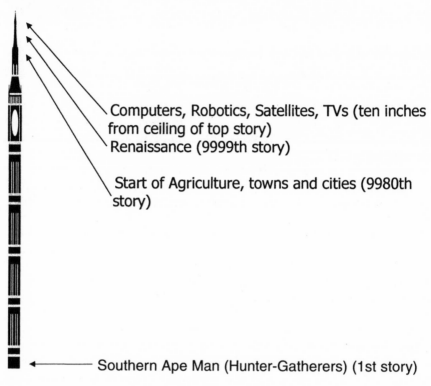

Computers, Robotics, Satellites, TVs (ten inches from ceiling of top story)
Renaissance (9999th story)

Start of Agriculture, towns and cities (9980th story)

Southern Ape Man (Hunter-Gatherers) (1st story)

lution. This may be the key breakthrough that leads us more quickly to the age of the World-Wide Mind.

At such places as the Santa Fe Institute, scientists are using this chaotic or nonlinear math to seek and find these interconnecting patterns that seem common within life forms. These patterns can be seen starting from replicating molecule chains, to cells, to organism, to complex societies. The first phases may be slow or at least primitive in structure, but the last phases are fast and highly interactive.

The challenge of modern society goes well beyond issues such as illegitimate birth, divorce, criminal rehabilitation, welfare reform, juvenile delinquency, job retraining. or even how to seek to overcome poverty and war. It ultimately involves the structure of a twenty-first-century world and the role that people of all types and all countries will play in it.

**Figure 2.2**
**Building of Human Knowledge (10,000 Stories and 20 Miles High)**

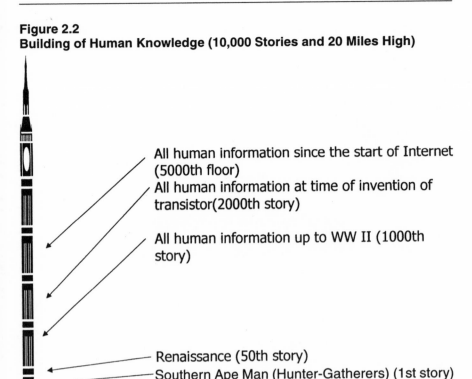

All human information since the start of Internet (5000th floor)

All human information at time of invention of transistor(2000th story)

All human information up to WW II (1000th story)

Renaissance (50th story)
Southern Ape Man (Hunter-Gatherers) (1st story)

Today's political platforms in the United States and abroad, on both the left and on the right, seem almost equally irrelevant and ineffective in coping with the range, the speed, and the magnitude of the coming changes. The building of time and the building of knowledge are shifting apart every day, and more and more so. The solutions of past centuries, including those of the twentieth-century industrial age, are going to be of virtually no help. We need new cybernetic solutions for the coming age of "extreme future compression."

## THE CHALLENGES OF TWENTY-FIRST-CENTURY CYBERSPACE AND THE WORLD-WIDE MIND

A quick synopsis of the issues and challenges presented by living in a cyberspace-dominated world and the potential of the new technologies to respond to the vagaries of high-tech Teleshock are presented in the following list of Cyberspace Dilemmas:

| Cyberspace Challenges | Potential Cyberspace Cures | Potential Cyberspace Pitfalls |
|---|---|---|
| Loss of Jobs | Structured Career Migration Restructured Corporations | Erosion of Identity Lack of Permanence |
| Globalization | Telework/Telecommuting | Global Economic Gaps Overcentralization |
| Crime and Violence | Surveillance/Security Systems, UPC Monitoring, GPS and Satellite Tracking | Privacy Invasion Totalitarian Repression |
| Privacy | Encryption Systems Electronic Screening | Corporate and Public Intrusion into Private Liberties |
| Obsolete Educational Systems | Interactive Multimedia Life-Long Learning Experiential Learning Systems | Mega-Training Decline of Public Education |
| Health and Medical Care | Telehealth and Telemedicine Systems | Depersonalization of Care |
| Energy and Resource Depletion | Information-Based Recycling "Smart" Energy/Resource Systems | Overbuilding Deserting of Key Conservation Concepts |
| Environment and Pollution | Telework "Smart" Economic and Transportation Systems | Overbuilding Deserting of Key Conservation Concepts |
| Man–Machine Interface | Improved Voice and AI Interfaces | 168-Hour Work Week AI-Driven Society Cultural Decline |
| Societal Values | Interactive Education and Entertainment, Life-Long Learning | VR Escapism, Underclasses Two-Tiered Society |
| Information Overload | Electronic "Filtering" AI Databanks, Knobots | Political Apathy Overspecialization |
| Balanced Urban Development and Rural Living | Telework, Service Economy | Urban Blight Suburb Flight |

The opportunities of cyberspace technologies to address key issues of education, health care, transportation, energy, job creation, international trade, and peaceful relations among and between people at the local to the global levels are enormous. They are so important that the future could be said to depend upon the effective application of these technologies in the twenty-first century. The dynamic tension of this critical set of technologies in a very real way seems to hold the entire fate of our species in its hands.

CHAPTER 3

# The World of Telecommuting: Electronic Immigrants and Teleworkers Unite

There's more to life than increasing its speed.

Mahatma Gandhi

## ELECTRONIC IMMIGRANTS AND TELEWORKERS

The concept of telecommuting is actually nearly four decades old. The first known instance involved banks hiring suburban housewives in Chicago, Illinois, as typists. The work was all handled via phone lines, and the housewives did not have to spend money on transportation, lunches, or child care. Their salaries were, however, "adjusted downward" to be about 40-percent less than their downtown counterparts. To the advocates of equal rights for women this was hardly seen as progress.

Today the practice of telecommuting has spread across a wide range of jobs, across the sexes, and includes many parts of the world. The patterns of work have also greatly diversified to encompass many more professional activities. Telecommuting during the 1990s even embraced electronic immigrants all over the world. Rural and remote workers, environmentalists and energy conservationists alike have thus seen telecommuting as a boon. In fact, telecommuting is neither pure panacea nor a problem to dread, but like most technologies born of cyberspace, suspended in-between.

What is clear is that the nature of jobs is experiencing a cybernetic shift. As the entire world moves to an increasingly service-based economy, the nature, form, and structure of jobs will experience a paradigm shift born of the emerging World-Wide Mind. People will pursue multiple careers over their lifetimes or they will spend their lifetimes being trained either to keep the jobs they have or to prepare for new ones.

In the United States some 10 million people have joined the ranks of telework via home-based computers with modems and printers and other electronic aids such as faxes, e-mail, and even broadband lines. (This figure of 10 million U.S. teleworkers comes from a recent Yankee Group study. It should be noted, it is only a subset of the 25 million people who work out of their homes but are not necessarily electronically connected to a main office.) There are also millions of teleworkers in Europe and the Asia-Pacific. In Japan the concept of telework, however, is focused around satellite telework centers rather than home-based electronic offices for social and cultural reasons.

Teleworkers or road warriors in North America and Europe typically work part of the time at home or out of suitcases on the road. They typically also spend a good deal of the time at a central office as well, since professionals feel disconnected and potentially overlooked if their telework actually becomes full time. The exception is again in Japan, where the satellite telework office largely replaces the need to go to a central office at all. Indeed, the primary motivation for telework in Japan today is to eliminate the need to build more office space in the high-cost, high-density urban centers of Tokyo or Osaka.

The most popular option in the United States is working two days a week at home and three days at the office. Here, professional workers seek to avoid being permanently lost in cyberspace or telework limbo for fear of being overlooked for promotion and advancement. Independent sales representatives, real estate agents, and others that are truly home-based workers are thus not included in the concept of a true teleworker.

It is anticipated that these home-based telecommuters and so-called road warriors, who are equipped to operate on a global basis by means of electronic communications, will continue to grow in number and geographically expand to more and more countries. The Yankee Group study and other consultant reports suggest that by 2010 the number of teleworkers worldwide may rise to 60 to 80 million. There are some projections for 2025 that suggest that 40 to even 50 percent of all service workers within the developed countries will be electronic telecommuters. These projections are based on the following factors:

- Current growth rates of 15 to 20 percent per annum in telecommuting jobs.
- The requirements of energy conservation regulations and clean-air laws in the United States, Europe, and Japan that encourage the creation of telecommuting jobs within industry.
- The high cost of real estate in major urban centers, which makes the creation of new centralized office space increasingly expensive and hard to find (particularly key in Tokyo, London, New York, Chicago, and other areas where urban office space is so prime).
- The high productivity factors and general satisfaction levels reported on the part of employees and employers with telecommuting jobs.

This quiet revolution is spreading across the United States and most of the Organization for Economic Cooperation and Development countries of the Western world. It may be quiet, but the scope and speed of change represents a truly fundamental shift.

Telecommuting is not without some problems. It gives rise to a number of troublesome issues. There are concerns about the application of workplace rules. The U.S. Occupational Safety and Health Agency (OSHA) does not have the same power and rights in the home that it does in the traditional workplace. A recent attempt by OSHA to hold large corporations liable for "unsafe" home working conditions ended in a fiasco, with the top OSHA administrator totally retreating from this position. Issues of health standards, child labor laws, and excessive work hours are difficult to enforce with regard to "electronic cottage industry" carried out within the home workplace. Exceptional measures, such as an electronic log-on with an electronic fingerprint being used to prevent child labor, have been seriously proposed by Professor Jack Nilles, University of Southern California (USC) telecommuting guru. The AFL–CIO has also suggested that telecommuting has become yet another means of breaking the force of unions. Clearly there are fewer reasons and incentives for one to join a union in a decentralized electronic work environment that is largely home based.

Certainly a key element of dispute and discussion is the issue of wage compensation. Some argue that wages should be higher or lower depending on such factors as commuting time and expense, use of home space and equipment, more self-management, and greater convenience in terms of child care, shopping, and so forth. Others argue that wages and longer-term employment no longer should apply and that telecommuters should be hired and compensated just like independent contractors. Yet others suggest that compensation should be on a piece-rate fee of so many dollars per unit of service rendered. This viewpoint suggests that so-called handicapped, "challenged," or lower-productivity workers should be able to work and compete for telecommuting jobs but be paid for their individual level of production rate rather than at a standardized salary rate.

One of the major opportunities that telecommuting can almost effortlessly enable is the possibility of part-time or flex-time jobs. The idea that rural and remote communities can be the source of labor for service-based activities in urban centers is really not at all far fetched. A farmer or construction person during off-peak hours or adverse weather conditions could easily work four hours a day entering insurance records or formatting copy for a magazine. This is not only theoretically feasible, but actually happening in rural North Carolina, Arkansas, Colorado, and elsewhere. There are actually daytime rural chicken pluckers in North Carolina who serve as data-entry insurance clerks by evening. Their employers are hundreds of miles away in Connecticut and Nebraska. Availability of time is more important than availability of place.

Rural telecommuting can work many different ways. Farmers can exploit cyberspace to work at virtual urban service jobs or surf the Web to make their farms more profitable or productive. One of the expected breakthroughs in agriculture is in what has been called "precision farming." In this approach to farming, remote sensing satellite data accurate down to two- to three-meters resolution is analyzed almost on a square yard by square yard basis. It is used to determine exactly how much water, fertilizer, seed, and nutrients are needed for each subplot of farmland.

This approach to "smart farming" has been tested at several university research centers in the United States and Europe. These experiments, as reported by University of North Carolina studies, showed that crop yield can be increased 30 percent, while the needed resources (water, fertilizer, seed) can be reduced as well. Within a decade or so, large farms may have their own satellite terminals to inform them how to manage their crops, increase their yields, and bring their crops to the right market at the right time.

In rural Colorado the farmers in the town of Delta are already using the Internet to increase their productivity and to sell their products on a global market. A systematic survey of agricultural prices finds the top value, makes the sales transaction, and sends crates of broccoli packed in dry ice and shipped off by air freight to Tokyo or London or Wellington. Nearby ranches have begun to catch on as well. Instead of putting up prize bulls for the local auction, they surf the Internet to obtain the best possible price. In short, telecommuting now means not only going to work electronically from a home location, but also seeking the best prices for a product or service through the Internet and other electronic networks.

## THE WORLD OF ELECTRONIC IMMIGRANTS

In a book called *Global Talk* that I published in 1981, the concept of "electronic immigrants" was discussed as a possible major trend for the future. The idea was simply that highly trained individuals such as computer programmers who worked in a lower-income country such as India would be hired to work in a much higher-income country such as Japan or the United States. The "innovation" was that the worker would remain in his or her home country and get assignments and deliver the work product via electronic means. In economic terms the worker would immigrate to another country, but would physically remain in his or her home environment. At the time the main reaction beyond skepticism was to view the idea as "visionary speculation," and it was largely ignored.

In 1990, however, the World Future Society (WFS) chose this topic for one of its top ten predictions. This prediction was chosen by the WFS on the basis of an article I had done for their *Futurist* magazine when readdressing this subject in 1989. Johnny Carson highlighted this particularly "loony" prediction on his New Year's Eve show with the remark, "What in the heck is that all about."

In that very same year, however, AT&T realized that developing electronic immigrant commerce was a new way to make money. AT&T became a partner in a satellite teleport project in Jamaica based on the idea of promoting electronic immigrant industries between the United States and the Caribbean. Now it is estimated that there are more than 1 million electronic immigrants worldwide. Politicians in Congress who are interested in the U.S. trade balance have begun asking why no one ever addressed this new problem in international labor exchange.

## THE WORLD OF THE LONE EAGLE

The idea of telecommuting is as simple and as basic as connecting a worker to a job from a remote office or a workplace via electronic means. The advent of electronic immigrants suggests that there are few geographic limits to the distance one might phone in to work, and not many limits on the type of service performed. NASA is even experimenting on highly sensitive devices for telerobotic brain and eye surgery for astronauts in space. It is truly the ultimate in remote telework, but there are probably few volunteers who would want to be the first to go under the NASA teleknife.

If you can bring people to work electronically, you can also connect them to markets in the same way. Thus, a professional teleworker who deals in information, software, or intellectual products can be free—totally free. They can pretty much live wherever they wish to locate. Increasingly, states in the sunbelt as well as picturesque states like Colorado are seeing an influx of so-called lone eagles. These lone eagles are typically specialized computer software developers, designers of expert systems, writers of professional newsletters, or entrepreneurs who are developing new info-products or services.

They can opt for a tele-resort, a spa, or a city of their choice. They and not others decide where they—or they and a few close colleagues—want to live and what they want to do. Is their life's ambition to sail, to ski, to play golf and tennis? They can in today's electronically defined service environment move to their dream location and set up shop just as well as anywhere else. The rest of their needs can be largely met by the Internet, private computer or telecommunications networks, or courier delivery services.

A friend who is a former state department foreign officer and now a telecommunications consultant and entrepreneur has taken the idea of moving your work to where you want a step further. He has explored with Jamaican officials the idea of a state-of-the-art tele-resort where a corporate bigwig cannot only have all the amenities of the beach, golf course, and tennis courts, but has also an "infocottage" equipped with the latest in telecommunications and computer equipment. Instead of asking for options like a king-size bed or a nonsmoking room, the televacationer must focus on choosing a large flat-screen video display, 384 kbs video conference, or T-1 high-speed Internet interface. Furthermore, with Computer Aided Design and Computer Aided Manufacture (CAD/CAM), these exotic resort techocottages might even be robotically manufactured in Colorado and shipped anywhere in the world for assembly at extremely low cost. So far this concept is still a concept, but give it a year or two.

In a Boulder, Colorado, neighborhood where I lived for a number of years it was possible to find a stockbroker with a seat on the New York Stock Exchange and a publisher of a national magazine on inline skating. They and other like-minded telecommuters could go to work around the United States or even overseas via a dedicated Earth station mounted on their roof or via a cable modem or even an advanced, broadband telephone line with ISDN or DSL capability.

These lone eagles have defined where and how they wish to live and then used tailored telecommunications networks to serve their economic and business needs. A lone eagle aerospace consultant to NASA operates out of (appropriately enough) Eagle, Colorado. A few miles to the south lives a specialized manufacturer of precision aircraft parts and satellite entrepreneur named David Wine. Wine, an individualist whose living room is equipped with chandeliers purchased from the movie set of *Gone with the Wind,* is the lone eagle par excellence. He has his own plane, a high-speed swamp boat, and one of the best views in the world. In order to pay for it all, he also has a CAD/CAM-driven computer hob and printer that can cut machined parts to 1/5,000 of an inch tolerance at extremely high speed. The technology is very impressive, but the location of this high-tech facility in Montrose, Colorado, in a 10,000-square-foot mansion (a monstrously large log cabin this individualistic lone eagle constructed using his own saw mill) is perched at 9,000 feet overlooking an unspoiled five-mile stretch of the San Juan Mountain Range.

Dr. Matt Nilson, the founder of the Friendly Skies Corporation (more familiarly known as Tongasat), is an international version of a lone eagle. Tongasat was created as a very "enterprising" enterprise that records satellite frequency assignments for satellite systems with the International Telecommunication Union on behalf of the Island of Tonga. Then the next step is to "lease" the assigned spectrum at attractive prices to satellite-system owners without orbital slots. Matt Nilson, a Scandinavian, and his wife from the Philippines have homes in San Diego, California, and Singapore. He, very much the ultimate international lone eagle, lives where he wants. Currently he has given up the Tongasat enterprise, but his next enterprise could be anywhere in the world and likely could be managed from one of his global nesting places.

In the age of farming, the farmer was bound to his land. In the age of industrialization, both the worker and the factory owner were bound to the plant and their suppliers. The same was true of mines and miners, of forests and foresters, and even of banks and retailers, who needed to be close to their customers. Lone eagles can have complete freedom of time and place. As this trend grows, there must be concerns about a totally "rootless society" where there is no commitment to local needs or political process. The World-Wide Mind can come to mean a society where no one feels connected to his or her local community. This trend can already be seen in falling voting rates, rapid moves from job to job and city to city, and other indices of transience.

Thus, in an electronic service economy that is more heavily based on Amazon.com than the local bookstore, the old rules of proximity have begun to fade away. QVC is a multibillion-dollar electronic enterprise that has grown up almost overnight with cable television. Its revenues are based on selling cable television customers products at a distance. Retail sales catalogs have grown dramatically over the past decade on the basis of highly competitive prices (low-cost overhead and highly efficient operations) and the convenience of shopping at home or office, where and when the consumer wishes. The next decade will raise the stakes and expand the scope of these operations.

Consumers in countries where it is difficult to shop on weekends or evenings will be attracted to teleshopping via the Web. Likewise, those who find their localized national market prices for consumer goods are now 50- to 100-percent higher than global market prices on the Internet will become the inverse of electronic immigrants. They, in short, will become global teleconsumers. The amazing global spread of McDonalds, Pizza Hut, Sony Walkmans, and Honda Accords in the last few decades will have explosive new twenty-first-century counterparts in the age of the World-Wide Mind.

With the rise of global teleservices via the Global Information Infrastructure or Global Electronic Highway (as first projected by Al Gore), almost every part of the services industry worldwide will change. Small consulting firms, inventors, one- and two-person digital production studios, agents, and a host of others can increasingly operate via a cleverly devised Web site on a flexible gobal scale. Millions of little guys can act and "feel" like big guys with big-name logos. In the area of global products, the transition may be even more dramatic. The idea of truly planetary sales and distribution networks that can sell anything to anybody at any time is a potential new mega-industry of the twenty-first century. The key would be access to the world's global satellite broadcast systems and cable television networks in order to promote worldwide sales.

Although this might start with an emphasis on personal apparel, jewelry, household goods, and so forth, such a global electronic sales network could become like a huge and integrated electronic catalog. The range of products could range from fountain pens to Rolls Royce luxury sedans, from a turtleneck sweater to a high-definition television set, or from a bottle of perfume to a Caribbean cruise. These electronic sales networks would operate in dozens if not hundreds of countries. Key elements that will be needed are actually not all that demanding:

- Access to people through television, radio, or telephones.
- Commercial agreements with key suppliers around the world and competitive prices that are below national suppliers.

• Local or regional warehouses and distribution, delivery, and service centers.

• Low-cost global communications and air-freight contracts.

• Better enforcement of constraints of trade regulations in products and services by the World Trade Organization (WTO), the European Union, NAFTA, APEC, and so forth.

• National and regional enforcement of antitrust provisions to ensure true competition.

Countries such as Germany, Sweden, Norway, France, Spain, Japan, and others that have limited shopping hours, high consumer prices, and complicated procedures for shopping may find themselves very vulnerable to the "global electronic merchandise shop." This means that while on one hand we will have electronic immigrants going to work electronically around the globe, on the other we are likely to have global merchandisers selling their products nonstop all over the world to global electronic consumers as well. This will make a large impact on balance of trade and national economies, and even stimulate backlash over open-trade agreements and regional trade alliances. This, however, will likely move production and consumption further apart and make preservation of the biosphere and inclusion of "survival values" in twenty-first-century economic systems even more difficult. Further, the continued moving of jobs further offshore will likely never be politically popular.

Beyond these obvious economic impacts, the labor, cultural, and general society impacts will likely be even greater. In this new environment a growing number of employees will work for overseas corporations, and traditional employees and established trade unions will feel the pressure of this new global competition. The proponents of global electronic marketeering will claim they are bringing reform, efficiency, responsiveness, and lower consumer prices. On the other hand, the "invaded territories" will claim that the Philistines are assaulting their long-established national traditions without regard to local culture, local traditions, and local needs.

There are now some seven global telecommunications "super-carriers" emerging that control some 65 percent of global long-distance revenues. Within another decade a number of transnational "global electronic merchandisers" may emerge that will control a huge new share of retailing and commerce. (This will be a broad shift that covers everything from new car sales to household goods to clothing to even housing, leisure, and travel services. In Japan you can today even buy on the Web, a house built in California.) These new megamerchandisers will be able to reach everywhere with compelling advertising, attractive prices, and rapid delivery. The bottle-necks will come from local support staff, responsive national service, and warehouse and distribution systems.

The critical success factors of the new megamerchandisers will include the following:

- Global availability of television-based marketing at low per-viewer population cost. Rupert Murdoch of the News Corporation has already largely accomplished something very much like this feat.
- Complete transparency of global telecommunications. This means that local, national, and international calls and communications cost much the same and that faxes and e-mails are much less costly than letters.
- Ability to exploit the inflexibility of shopping hours and artificially high cost/price structure by offering rapid (twenty-four-hour-a-day) service and user-friendly and responsive local service, warehousing, and distribution services.
- Rapid and efficient establishment of local distribution and service centers that work to standards of efficiency and accept an any-time, any-place user-oriented philosophy.
- Sufficient political strength and influence to prevent backlash efforts to cut off transborder access and restrict open-trade markets.

In this new cyberspace environment, Tom Cross, the Colorado-based telecommuting expert, in his book on telecommuting, has said: "The advent of tele-work within the global cyberspace economy may prove as fundamental as the plow to the agricultural revolution and as the assembly line was to the indusrtrial revolution." Already telework has become absolutely fundamental to the growth of jobs in America. Within the next twenty years telework, including electronic immigrants, will have a predominant effect on new employment and labor patterns. Today, teleworkers are "harvesting" billions of dollars in revenues, but in another two decades the electronic crop of teleservices could mount into the trillions of dollars.

By that time, of course, such huge numbers in terms of revenues, wages, insurance coverage, and so forth will give rise to controversy and political hassle. There will be disputes over which of the affected countries or local jurisdictions collect income and sales taxes, social security, health and retirement taxes. There could even be transnational disputes over voting entitlement, divorce law, and the military draft.

Here is a recap of some of the problems we have already noted:

Electronic Sweat Shops. It will not take long for telework to move from being a panacea to a problem. As noted earlier, home-based electronic cottage industries can and will involve child labor. If electronic commerce is seen as moving its operation from within a single nation to operations with no international boundaries involved, how does OSHA or any other national regulatory body oversee work conditions that can shift across national borders at will?

The Split-Shift Rural Teleworker. Already rural farm workers who pluck chickens by day are inputting data for insurance companies by night. Again, how does one regulate such a complex environment?

Cyberspectra for Sales. "Raiders of the Lost Orbital Arc" such as Matt Nilson can and do exploit national regulatory processes. They can easily capture information in telecommunications satellite filings before national agencies and then reformat the data to make preemptive filings at international entities like the International Telecommunications Union (ITU) to cut in line in front of those "following the rules."

Global Cybermarketers versus Traditional Retailers. The cybermarketers will claim they are making shopping easier and less costly for global consumers. Local retailers will claim that this is not only an attack on their livelihood, but their very culture. Collection of sales tax alone will create big disputes.

There can be no doubt that telework, electronic immigrants, flexplace employment, access to diverse talent, and lower-cost labor pools will affect almost everything. It will affect international alliances, and the meanings of distance and rural and remote. It will impact service corporations and living and commuting patterns most. It could also have some important side benefits, such as reduced energy consumption and a reduction in pollution, and could also impact urban, suburban, and rural housing development and even the planning of transportation systems. To date the issue of electronic immigrants and teleworkers has been considered as essentially a labor issue, but if this trend continues and grows to affect tens of millions of workers, its broader implications and impact on society and international relations will be increasingly recognized and studied.

## CYBERCHALLENGES AROUND THE EMERGING WORLD-WIDE MIND

It is important to note that patterns of telework are quite different around the globe. The motivations for workers to operate from remote locations can and do shift around the world. In the United States most teleworkers have a computer, modem, fax, and other key equipment in a home office. In Japan there are now a good number of remote teleworkers, but for cultural reasons these do not operate from home tele-offices but from satellite work centers that are connected to the central office. The NEC corporate headquarters building is linked via fiber optics to over fifty satellite work centers clustered around Tokyo in reasonably close proximity to the workers' homes. The point here is that these satellite work centers not only save commuting time, but they are a cost-effective solution to the fact that adding new office space in Tokyo is not economically viable. A study of central Tokyo real estate concluded that if the Imperial Grounds were to be developed to current levels of density and expense this several-square-mile area would be equivalent in value to all the residential real estate in all of Canada.

Telework will evolve rapidly around the world, but it will vary a great deal in terms of where, when, and how it occurs. Densely populated cities with expensive core city real estate values and air-pollution problems will dominate the first wave of growth. The second wave can emerge almost anywhere.

Workers near Shannon, Ireland, are now the back-office workers for several key Wall Street firms. They process the previous day's stock orders and the regulatory paperwork. Then they send it back to New York before the NYSE opens the following day. Here the workers go to work in a very normal way in normal offices, but the source of their work and income is located a quarter of the way around the world. In work that does not require instantaneous feedback the World-Wide Mind can operate quite normally today. Recent studies by Telegeography, Inc., however, have shown that the strategic relation between any two points on the planet is determined by the size of the throughput channel and not distance alone. If one has access to a truly high-data-rate satellite or fiber link, offices in New York City and Singapore can be "virtually closer" to each other than a low-speed channel from the Big Apple to Muskogee, Oklahoma.

With today's technology, almost anyone can be a teleworker and the "home office" can be anywhere on the planet. A farmer in Kenya who uses remote sensing data processed at Goddard Space Research Center in Maryland is thus one remote form of teleworker. Likewise, the sheepherder in New Zealand who uses a local loop wireless connection to an international satellite to find out when to shear her sheep and bring the wool to market is also, in a sense, a teleworker. The astronauts and cosmonauts on board the international space station will define yet a new form of teleworker, as will the interplanetary explorers who begin to terraform Mars before the end of the twenty-first century.

Recent ITU studies indicate that about 4 billion of the Earth's 6 billion people are linked in one form or another to modern infosystems. This means, however, that 2 billion are still excluded from the e-Sphere. Rural Asia, Africa, Latin America, and remote islanders are simply often not linked to the rest of the world. People in these remote locations typically lack telephones, educational systems, potable water, health care, and electricity. Their quality of life and standard of living suffer.

Urban dwellers and the residents of the wealthier nations, on the other hand, are linked to the emerging World-Wide Mind. They are, in a sense, all teleworkers who have access to a great deal of information. This access is often taken for granted. Few people within the vast population of the information rich realize the various ways they are actually interconnected when they read a newspaper or magazine that is printed via a satellite connection or receive in print form a stock quote or real estate listing derived from an electronic database. We are more linked to the World-Wide Mind of the emerging e-Sphere than ever before. As the Internet doubles in size every year, the linkages will be more and more pervasive. Each day about two-thirds of the human population are connecting to the World-Wide Mind and becoming teleworkers, some a lot, others just as little.

But then there are the great mass of the rural and unconnected humans who inhabit our planet jointly, not collectively. This great throng of the "unplugged" is not only outside of the World-Wide Mind, but in some senses also outside of our planetary culture. Some would argue that this is good and others that it is bad. For better or worse, the anthropological experiment that separates our global culture into those that are plugged in and those that are not cannot continue. Before the twenty-first century is through, either of two things will have happened. Either we will have all joined together within a new culture of the World-Wide Mind, or we will have failed to survive as a species. There may be some desired in-betweens, but our infotechnology will, for better or worse, force one result or the other. Technology, especially infotechnology, is a one-way gate. The question is whether entropy or extrophy will win out in the next crucial century—the century of human survival. The answer to the question of chaos versus intelligent evolution is key. It is the creative solution to this teleological issue that may well be the key to our long-term survival.

The problems associated with telecommuting are thus only going to increase. We will see tensions in patterns of work and promotion. It will complicate links to the rest of the world and the relation between developed and developing countries. There will be dilemmas and even agonies in the social problems driven by various forms of telework in the decades ahead, but somehow we will all survive. Those who can adapt to the new and preserve that which is good of the old will not only survive, but perhaps even prosper in a social and cultural sense that transcends material wealth.

## OVERALL TREND REVIEW

### Potential Pitfalls

- Global trends, attitudes, and acceptance of telework will be widely different.
- Discontinuities born of telework and electronic immigration will give rise to international and national social, religious, cultural, and economic tensions.
- New problems associated with electronic sweat shops and child labor issues.
- Handicapped and disadvantaged labor will present special issues and challenges.
- Loss of jobs by obsolete middle management.
- Special transnational political and economic issues to be solved will include those involving income tax, health insurance, retirement, disability, social security, immigration, and equity of pay and promotion.

### Opportunities and Challenges

- Potential for energy saving and pollution reduction.
- Transferable real estate value: high-cost urban office space and shopping malls can be electronically or virtually shifted to low-cost suburban and rural areas.
- Increased global and national access to a wider pool of skilled and lower-cost labor and professional services.
- Lower overhead and more effective cybermanagement in virtual global corporations.
- Relative competitive advantage achieved through leveraged application of telework strengths.
- Improved employee morale (at least on a short-term basis).

# CHAPTER 4

# The 168-Hour Work Week

A global economy is one that can operate as a working unit in real time. Capital is now truly global and instantaneous.
Manuel Castells

## THE NEVER-STOP WORLD

Our world, and especially the world of business, is changing in a blur. Robots that work nonstop are now more efficient and cost effective than human labor in industrial countries. In ten to twelve years this will also hold true in most so-called developing countries as well. The corporate gurus who believe the wave of the future is to move offshore had better rethink in cyberspace terms. They will likely need to recoup their investment within a decade or prepare to explain why their low-cost labor has vanished in the wake of fully automated, software-managed manufacturing plants.

Already in Taipei, Shanghai, and Seoul industrialists are worried. They look at their current crop of Nike- and T-shirt-wearing teenagers and wonder where their low-cost and zealous workers will come from in the twenty-first century. In less than two decades the salaries in China and India (at least in Beijing, Shanghai, Bombay, Calcutta, Madras, and New Delhi) could skyrocket as much as ten times or more. Already the urban heart of Bombay is the most expensive place in the world to build.

The intensity of the 168-hour work week and the superspeed pace of change in a cybernetic world creates a mutual feeding frenzy. It is like two great white sharks escaped from the set of *Jaws* that consume each other with unrelenting fury. Nonstop intensity generates speed and urgency. This speed of change reinforces the need for constant design, engineering, production, and innovation at ever higher rates of speed. There is danger in this. Management that believes the key to success is to work harder and longer rather than smarter and better is doomed to lose in the age of the World-Wide Mind. A key management rule for the highly competitive e-Sphere is that one must work harder, better, and smarter. But of these, working smarter is the key. This is simply because one can also count on the competition to work smarter longer, harder, and better as well.

The issue of a nonstop economy and the 168-hour work week may lead some skeptics to say, "So what?" If some computers and some communications networks work all the time, well, let them. For regular workers isn't this a trivial question? The first issue is that of the human–machine interface. There is a growing gap between what people and machines are willing to do and capable of doing. In industrial terms machines are winning and workers are losing. When one goes from hardware to software, the issue becomes even more focused and more critical, and involves many more jobs. Smart software will replace somewhere between 2 and 3 million jobs a year in the United States for each of the next five years. Far more than industrial and manufacturing jobs are at risk. What is not so clear is how many new jobs new value-added services and "smart software" will generate by 2005.

The point is that not only are things going to change, but that they will change faster and faster and more and more. These changes will occur twenty-four hours a day, seven days a week, fifty-two weeks a year, and all 100 years of the century. (Some very impatient people in the news media, however, have recently insisted in putting only 99 years into the twentieth century and only 999 years into the millennium.) But as the Royal Astronomer of the United Kingdom, Arthur C. Clarke, and others know, the new millennium starts 1 January 2001.

The work week of smart machines, and by implication of cyber-managers, is moving in one direction, while the bulk of typical workers are moving in the other. In short, the 168-hour work week will bring major conflicts in the workplace. How do you spell the 168-hour work week in the twenty-first century if you are a labor union or an employee in mining, agriculture, manufacturing, or a low-skill service job? You spell it three ways, and none of these are attractive to the worker:

• Technological unemployment.

- Cyber-based underemployment.
- Increased dumbing down and skill loss in routine jobs.

In short, the nonstop world is a frightening concept to many people, and labor unions are at the top of the list of those concerned.

As noted in Chapter 1, the speed of change, innovation, and development of a cyberspace world is horrendously fast. The world of the Internet, e-commerce, portals, and the enterprise networks operated by large multinational corporations all increasingly look like the operation of synapses inside the brain. Patterns of behavior become established, experience a learning curve, and ultimately operate at split-second speeds—or should we say nanosecond—efficiency. Soon supercomputers will be operating at speeds much faster than the alpha waves inside the human brain.

Consider these facts: Information is growing at least 200,000 to 1 million times faster than our human population. Our ability to assimilate all new knowledge is about as realistic as a turtle catching a space ship. Most of the world's patents were issued within the last two decades. More and more of our data networks and robotic factories are now on-line and operate three continuous eight-hour shifts twenty-four hours a day, without any stoppage except for occasional maintenance, repair, or upgrade. Most upgrades are now instantaneously achieved through smarter software. These and dozens of similar factoids suggest that the pace of our global economy is now hurtling along at breakneck speed.

People really do not like to work much more than forty hours in a regular work week. Exceptional effort for exceptional times may be all right, but workers do not like a steady diet of overtime. Taiwanese and South Koreans, the reigning world champs at workaholism, are still putting in about fifty-four hours a week. There are not many countries that can still claim to give hard work a good name.

I have had the pleasure of waiting impatiently at the trucker's blockades in France during a wildcat strike where angry workers righteously demanded retirement at age fifty-five and a thirty-five-hour work week. There were riots in Germany (rock throwing, sit-ins, and arson) when new legislation was proposed to allow shops to stay open on Saturday afternoon. It is safe to say that organized-labor support in Europe for a nonstop world with instant service anywhere at any time is nil to nonexistent among rank-and-file workers. They may well be right in their views, but in the long run it does not matter. The 168-hour work week is still coming.

The birthing pains associated with this brave new never-stop world are occurring every day. During the dog days of summer 1999, the European Union was pressing for the creation of a European

Stock Market to rival the NYSE and to equal its schedule of eight holidays a year. This is not easy to do when you find that there are at least fifty major holidays celebrated throughout Europe. Trying to wrest Bastille Day away from the French or Queen's Day from the Netherlands is not a job for which anyone of sane mind would volunteer. Yet global competition is the driver that pushes us relentlessly toward automated telephone systems, airline reservation systems, catalog order services, stock markets, and "never off-line" escort services.

So what are the implications for the future? Some of the prospects are almost dizzying. One possibility might be called "automated freighters." In future years, with the advent of intelligent highways and navigational systems with fuzzy logic on board, automated vehicles could transfer goods from one warehouse or industrial plant to another or directly to retailers. Amazingly, this could occur in the skies as well. There is some thought that Fedex could, with automated avionics and robotically controlled air freighters, fly above commercial air space (i.e., above 65,000 feet). Fuel-efficient and crewless air freighters, such as converted 747s, could provide improved or at least cheaper transoceanic service. This would allow them to fly air cargo at all hours of the day. Such a concept could give new meaning to the phrase, "Look, no hands!" In fact, there might indeed be one person on board to be wakened in the case of some emergency or mechanical malfunction, but only as a backup.

Everywhere one looks, the move toward nonstop activity suggests that workers' penchants for vacations and disdain for long work hours could lead industrialized countries to turn to Option B. Option B, unfortunately, is to replace the worker by inventing a machine and the necessary software to do the job instead. Increasingly we are hearing the phrase "software-defined equipment." This suggests that smart electronic devices with the right software (things we used to call computers but now are merely dubbed "smart processors") are today performing a host of new functions.

Software-defined equipment now includes electronic keyboards, guitars, oscilloscopes, cell phones, personal data assistants, calculators, CAT scanners, robots, television sets, radios, communications switches, washing machines, air conditioners, and more. Amazingly, Japanese designers at the Ministry of International Trade and Industry (MITI) are working on what might be called the ultimate software-defined product: the sexbot. Their first prototype is remarkably like a mock-up of Marilyn Monroe. Apparently its function would be to replace the world's oldest profession.

It is for these reasons and more that the European economies with the lowest hourly work weeks in the world may be in particular danger. There are other special problems for Europe in terms of education, patterns of innovation, and the ascendancy of the Asia-Pacific. Although Ireland appears to be a bright spot on the economic horizon, the prospects for the euro are really not all that positive. The amazing shrinking European work week and the shrinking value of the euro currency certainly compound the problem rather than help. France, with its highly unsuccessful attempt to create new jobs by authorizing retirements at age fifty-five and signing on to a thirty-five-hour work week is seemingly determined to lead the charge to economic chaos. In short, the nonstop economy and the 168-hour work week could prevent the European Union from faring well in the twenty-first century.

At first blush it may seem cranky and culturally insensitive to harp on this point, but the truth is that the 168-hour work week is, in fact, relentlessly assaulting century-old traditions with a powerful economic insistence. French culture has a rich and abiding belief that about six hours a day should be devoted to eating and drinking and that two months a year should be devoted to being "en vacances." This lifestyle does not fit with global corporations constantly on the move and poised to deploy the latest cyberspace information at lightening speed anywhere on the planet. In short, the current patterns of human work weeks (especially in Europe) are increasingly incompatible with a nonstop cybernetic world. In thirty years several European cultures (France prime among them) may well be clinging to their ancient and admirable culture and also to a potentially crumbling Third World economy.

In contrast, our airline reservation systems, our commodity trading networks, our retail-call distribution centers, our insurance and banking networks, and much, much more are webbed together to provide full-time, anytime service. Corporations like DEC have created a global enterprise network so that they can use their global offices to create a twenty-four-hour-a-day workforce. The idea is that they could hand off assignments from Europe to the United States to Japan and so on around the world. Ordinary firms, organized on work cycles of the past and wedded to national business markets, will have trouble competing with cyberbusinesses such as DEC, Deloitte and Touche, and NEC.

In short, our machines are going to work longer hours (168 hours a week) while weak and pleasure-seeking mortals are going to work shorter hours instead. There are more late-night shifts, more weekend stints, and more non-9-to-5 work assignments ahead for some. This is in response to digital integration of markets, the onset of the ICEE age (i.e., the age of information, communications, entertainment and "smart" energy), globalization of the economy on an increasingly planetary scale, and the worldwide cybernetic shift. The smarter and faster our world moves, the harder it will be to stop and rest. The treadmill keeps going faster and faster and working smarter seems only a part of the answer.

The forces of culture are usually thought to be language, art, shared history, religion, and cultural artifacts such as rituals, patterns of behavior, holidays, and mores. We usually do not think of time in terms of culture, but in our modern world it is an extremely powerful differentiator. We can, in fact, divide cultures in the following way:

| | |
|---|---|
| *Primitive Culture* | Respect for ancestors and tribal traditions. |
| | Change is unwelcome. |
| | Time not important to day-to-day life. |
| *Ancient Civilizations* | Respect for ancestors and accumulated knowledge. |
| | Time is still a mystery: Devolution, evolution, or steady state? |
| | Fundamental religious beliefs often define concepts relating to the nature and meaning of time and structure society. |
| | Time on annual cycle is key to agriculture. |
| *Renaissance Civilizations (Agrarian)* | Time is known and measured. |
| | Time is important to daily life and to commerce. It is thus often a source of progress. |
| | Time is still local. |
| *Industrial Civilizations* | Time and place is known and measured accurately. |
| | Time and schedules are central in daily life and commerce. |
| | Time is key to transportation, banking, finance, and communications as well as to society in general. |
| | Time is still predominately national. |
| *Cyberspace Civilizations* | Time is both knowledge and money in terms of competitive commercial edge. |
| | Every successful cyberservice and industry is time dependent. |
| | Broadband communications can overcome both time and distance. |
| | National cultural differences in perceiving time is a major cybermanagement challenge. |
| | Global economy runs on a global clock. |

Today represents a watershed where there are both clashes and a blending of cultures. One can find all five types of cultures just described on the planet and this makes for some fundamental conflicts. These radically different cultural time and efficiency clashes will only get worse. In the nineteenth century the spread of trains created the cultural imperative to have standardized time zones and to force all people, from farmers to merchants, from preachers to teachers, to follow a single clock.

In the age of cyberspace, the global telecommunications network, the Internet, and digital precision sometimes force advanced information systems to levels of precision of better than a millionth of a second. Humans tend to resist this degree of regimentation. In the nineteenth century Henry David Thoreau, the American philosopher, said, "Things are in the saddle and ride mankind." One could update this for today's concerns and wonder if "relentless time schedules are in the saddle and ride humankind."

Certainly, in each of the five time cultures there are dramatically different thoughts about the organization, meaning, and significance of time in daily life and in commerce. The main conflicts of the coming century will be over clashes in values, religious beliefs, ethnicity, money, and resources. The powerful tools of cyberspace will not help. They will bring conflicting cultures and values into closer and closer proximity—at least in an electronic sense of the term.

A global corporation that tries to standardize its rules of operation with a range of employees in Duluth, Cannes, Seoul, and Nairobi will find that the allocation and use of time is more than a simple set of management rules. Likewise, a global agrobusiness trying to implement precision farming on a planetary scale may find that cultural problems and work schedules are a larger challenge to success than technology or information distribution.

The move to the nonstop world involves far more than resetting a watch or changing a weekly work schedule. A person in France expects major breaks in the day for meals and socialization. A person in Yemen expects to pray to Mecca several times a day. A person in Japan may spend four hours a day commuting to and from work. A sophisticated sensitivity to how and why people spend their time and how it might affect a standardized world work schedule is actually a key cybermanagement challenge.

Finally, there is a more fundamental issue to consider. Is economic efficiency coupled with more industrial throughput and material wealth the answer? This issue was first raised in the opening chapter and is again addressed in Chapter 8. Relentless pursuit of efficiency and conventional scientific and engineering models are not going to produce the "correct answers" in the twenty-first century. As we stand on the threshold of the power of planetary consciousness as realized through the World-Wide Mind, we must go beyond new thinking processes. We must define new goals for life in the e-Sphere.

The brain is an effective, integrated entity that calls on each and all of its resources in what might be seen as a democratic arrangement of neural networks. Our emerging nonstop global economy is anything but an efficiently arranged and integrated network. Incresingly we are creating "vertical economies," in which production and consumption are further and further removed. Quality, teamwork, trust, and synergy all seem more likely to be subtracted than added to our increasingly automated, depersonalized, and detached business systems.

We are designing systems that traditional Western logic, based on digital logic and economic efficiency, has told us to create. As we enter the twenty-first century we may be forced to realize that survival, clean energy, and recycling of resources are a key part of the equation. This means that subjective or "inefficient" values such as beauty, esthetics, and diversity of thought are crucial to creating a sympathetic environment in which a true World-Wide Mind can exist.

The speed with which we are relentlessly pursuing a one-dimensional and rigid value system is potentially just as dangerous as religious fundamentalism, racial bigotry, or other extremist cults. The collosal failure of the Biosphere 2 experiment in the Arizona desert should be a clear sign that rigid conceptions of how to create complex economic and biological systems are potentially very dangerous. We need to spend more time figuring out where we want to be in the next eon, rather than increasing productivity a few percentage points next year. The speed we are traveling on the threshold of a new century is not scary in itself. But the lack of goals and the lack of understanding of what we do not know is scary indeed.

In the chapter on cybermanagement one of the modern management concepts analyzed is that known as Time-Based Management (TBM). Some would jump to the conclusion that TBM is above speeding up production. Indeed many would claim that their job is to keep things faster in a new and improved version of Fredrick Winslow Taylor's classic time and motion studies—the unabashed father of something so pretentiously and inaccurately called "Scientific Management." Actually, the TBM approach is headed in the opposite direction. It advocates working smarter rather than faster. It advances the idea that better planning, communications, teamwork, education and training, and systemic thinking will win the day—not turning the same old crank faster and faster. What this system lacks is caution.

Today's science, mathematics, and engineering are still just at the infancy of what humans can and will know in a few more centuries. We must not only do better planning, but also use some reserve in applying our scientific and modern management tools. Is the goal to deliver larger quarterly profits or longer-term survival of the species and wisdom? Can we actually begin to design systems that attack the "arrow of time" or entropy? Is the creation of new intelligence the same as "extropism," and through human intelligence can we reshape our world and ultimately the universe? Albert Einstein said the most difficult intellectual challenge is asking the right question rather than supplying the correct answer.

The message embedded in Time-Based Management is that speeding things up and running production units and information systems on a nonstop basis is not a solution or an end in itself. It seems ironic and even mystifying to note that speed by itself provides few answers. Even though we now have fax, electronic data interchange (EDI), e-mail, and personal computers with a host of software packages it still seems to take the same amount of time to prepare a business plan or conclude a contract or a meeting as it did decades ago. It seems that Parkinson's Law (i.e., work expands to fill time available) has indeed survived the efficiencies that are supposedly imbedded in cyberspace.

Many efforts to measure productivity gains set out to measure a specific task or subroutine, but do not look at the overall time required to complete overall tasks. If there is a key bit of wisdom to be gained here it is this: Speed does not necessarily produce improved or more cost-effective results. Throughput is not an end but an optional means to be employed in a intelligent way. Video-based instruction may actually be less effective than audio-based instruction in some areas. The ability to sort and index information eight different ways may inhibit a marketing campaign as much as it helps it.

Over two decades ago, amid much hype and hullabaloo, a new enterprise known as the "Paperless Office" opened in Washington, D.C., in the middle of the famous (or infamous) Watergate complex. This office was going to be more efficient, more networked, and much, much less paper oriented than a traditional modern workplace. This group was not only going to be a model showplace of the future paperless office, but they were going to provide consulting support to corporations that wished to drink from the holy grail of electronic office efficiency. Where is that group today? Bankrupt. Out of business. A failed enterprise.

Today people have access to enormous electronic files, databases, and electronic graphics on their own computers and file servers. They also send and receive a tremendous volume of e-mails and faxes and spend a great deal of time on the phone and even in videoconferences. This sounds a great deal like an electronic office, but there's a rub. These same offices have tons of filing cabinets filled with documents and bookcases filled with books, reports, monographs, and videocassettes. There also is a large supply of hard-copy market studies, computer printouts, transparencies for overhead projectors, slide projectors, and paper forms, brochures, flyers, pamphlets, business cards, rolodexes, and index sheets to keep track of where everything is located.

Like so often in the past we embraced the new and kept the old. Now we have four or five times more information to deal with than ever before. And maybe, just maybe, we know less than we did before about what our key objectives are and how to achieve our basic goals and objectives. Too many as well as too few tools can prevent you from getting a job done.

Our current problems that derive from information overload are seemingly a function of too many different media and sources of information spewing forth data with no physical or intellectual constraint. Now that we can communicate easily with people around the globe, they can send and receive information twenty-four hours a day. Automatic fax routers can automatically send your messages out at the lowest telephone tarriffs in the middle of the night. God help you if your number should ever end up by accident on such a fax list.

The 168-hour work week is thus in some ways a logical consequence of the building information overload in our system. This mushrooming information is spilling out in volume and geographic coverage, and now expanding into the time domain to demand attention from any sentient being at the end of a fax, telephone, PC, or television or radio receiver at every hour—or every minute—of the day. Some experts project that we will need "cyberfilters" to protect us from information overload and something like a "time zone" filter to protect us from the never-ending 168-hour work week.

**OVERALL TREND REVIEW**

### Potential Pitfalls

- Cultural clashes over intensivity and length of work week.
- Quality control and communications become much more difficult.
- Data updates must become continuous and unforgiving of lapses.
- Staffing, annual leave, vacation, and holidays all become more demanding.

## Opportunities and Challenges

- Consumer desire for ever more convenient and nonstop market access.
- Time-integrated global service and supply corporation has strategic market advantage.
- Greater agility to respond to new global developments on a rapid-response basis.
- New niche markets of special opportunity and special time-urgency emerge.
- New types of North–South and East–West synergy become possible.
- Nonstop stock and commodity markets.
- Second- and third-shift jobs will remain highly compensated and in demand.
- Just-in-time commerce and war fighting will become the norm.

# CHAPTER 5

# The ICEE Age: The Merger of Information, Communications, Entertainment, and Smart Energy

> As soon as we recognize our environment it becomes something
> else.
>
> Marshall McLuhan

## THE "ICEE-CAPADES"

It appears to many cyberspace zealots that we are entering a new ICEE age. The recent spurt of megamerger deals related to ICEE age industries is staggering. We have seen ABC–Capital Cities being taken over by Disney, Ted Turner acquired the MGM film library and then was taken over by Time Warner, which in turn is being acquired by AOL. GM owns companies that make cars, manufacture robots and satellites, design solar cells, and operate direct-to-the-home TV programming in partnership with Microsoft and AT&T. Who knows? Maybe the merger of Exxon and Mobil will allow them to start thinking in terms of smart energy derived directly from the sun, rather than oil pumped from the ground.

Meanwhile, Bill Gates and Microsoft are everywhere in a network of enterprises that involves over 500 companies that range from satellites (Teledesic) to television (MSNBC). Vodaphone is trying via acquisitions to become the world's largest mobile-telephone operator. AT&T is in global partnership with British Telecom in a venture named Concert that might spawn the next megamerger.

Across the Pacific, Mitsubishi, through its various families of businesses, now controls 10 percent of the Japanese GNP and commands operations that include cars, computer chips, satellites, ocean thermal energy conversion, solar cells, and robotics.

Rupert Murdoch, who sees the world as his oyster, has taken over Fox, the Dodgers, and a growing percentage of the free world's television and satellite media. Today, with a growing number of satellite television broadcast and distribution systems around the world, he comes the closest to having a complete worldwide direct-broadcast satellite system.

Then there is the Paramount deal, where one corporation has become a publisher, a movie maker, a key television studio, a video merchandiser, a cable television system, and a dozen other enterprises as well.

We have also seen in the energy and transportation industries that South Korea's number-one *choebel*, Hyundai, has moved to become a major aerospace, electronics, and computer-chip company. Clearly South Korea has been shaken by the financial reversals of the last few years, but count on the industries of Korea coming back strong.

In Japan, Toyota, Honda, and Toshiba have moved into electronics, computer networking, and robotics. In Europe, Thomson has moved from electronics into solar energy, and Alcatel, Aerospatiale, and Matra-Marconi have strengthened and consolidated their research into solar cells and advanced energy systems, including regenerative, unitized fuel cells.

In the United States, General Motors and Raytheon have moved from their traditional roles into new areas such as computer-system networking, spacecraft fabrication, energy transmission, and nanotechnology. Ford, in counterflow mode, now has a single-minded focus on vehicular manufacturing and services, and thus divested itself of Ford Aerospace some years ago. GM, whose experiment with technological integration and high-tech "telecomputer-energetics" has also been plagued with problems, selling the manufacturing arm of Hughes to Boeing. Integration and merger may be the dominant theme throughout the high-tech world, but corporate restructuring, spin-offs, and renewed focus on a single key market will also occur. This is especially so when new CEOs assume command and come to view the vast integrated global digital market as a threat rather than an opportunity.

These and dozens of other industry moves of every conceivable type continue to happen and transactions topping $100 billion now seem to happen with frequency. The methods of merger, stock acquisition, sharing of markets and intellectual property, and so on have themselves continued to multiply. Today we can see not only straightforward mergers and acquisitions, but investment as minority stakeholder, joint venture, joint licensing agreement, corporate diversification systems, technology transfer agreements, and investment in entrepreneurial start-ups with takeover or buyout options. Companies now buy national or established local brands to enter a market restricted by trading units, such as the European Union.

The megadeals, wherein billions of dollars change hands in the vast new global digital marketplace, are certainly the visible part of the process. This new market has been labeled as the Big Bang or the Five Cs. The Five Cs are computers, cable TV, communications, consumer electronics, and content. Whatever you may call it, this is yet another part of the World-Wide Mind paradigm shift that comes from digital technology and the nonlinear power of the Internet.

The drive to become bigger and absorb as much as possible of the vast digital market defined by the Big Bang is today almost all-consuming. Beyond the constantly reported move toward large-scale mergers and acquisitions there is also a much less visible but ultimately perhaps more important process. This is sufficiently subtle that it allows conventional antitrust provisions to be eluded by a gradual absorption process. Examples of these more invisible shifts are those by the French giant, France Telecom, for example. In 1994 they first acquired only a 40-percent interest in Keystone Communications, a company that had a predominant position in international satellite video services. They lease satellite channels on the major global systems and then, in effect, serve as an importer and exporter of video news and entertainment. Then, in 1997, some three years later, France Telecom bought total ownership under a buyout option. Although the name has now changed to Globecast, it is in no way clear to the general public or even to its customers that the company once known as Keystone (and Wold and Bonneville Communications prior to that) has now shifted in several basic ways. Globecast has changed from being a U.S. company to being a totally French-owned company, and this satellite television business is now concentrated in one of the world's so-called supercarriers.

In many cases the strategy of gradually buying into an enterprise allows antitrust and other high-level government reviews to be minimized. While the Keystone/Globecast deal would not likely have triggered such a review, even though its forty-plus satellite television channels represented over 60 percent of this particular global market, other such subtle takeovers by giant corporations have found that gradual acquisitions can minimize government red tape.

In today's world it is hard to know who owns what. In these icy and increasingly murky waters the extent of complex ownership patterns is almost impossible to follow. Most large multinational computer or telecommunications corporations have dozens of subsidiary corporations under their control or in which they have dominant holdings. In theory, the blending of information, communications, and entertainment markets can produce innovative new products and services. Some of these new products and applications will be developed for business customers and then be adapted to the mass consumer market. Likewise, we can also see the development of new entertainment offerings for the general public. These in turn can sometimes be adapted to new business or educational applications. Virtual reality, 3D television, and immersion instruction technologies have the potential to create powerful learning tools and even more powerful, absorbing, and potentially even destructive entertainment media.

There is solid potential here for trivialization, bastardization, and old-fashioned schlock as well. In the world of ICEE-age megamergers there is the very real possibility that products and services could be designed for the "lowest common denominator." There is a disturbing trend toward the dumbing down of almost every electronic product or service. Already, news programming is written for a "typical consumer" with an eighth-grade education. A *Washington Post* review of President Clinton's inaugural speech found that in vocabulary and syntax it was written at the ninth-grade level, one grade above network news. Business systems are designed for "easy learning" and mass-marketing appeal. There is now confusion and overlap between entertainment markets and business applications. The same overlap exists between information systems and computer games.

Today there is even starting to be similar overlap between news journals and home entertainment. Such a merging of entertainment and news is potentially dangerous when taken as a steady diet. Media that challenges people to critical thinking is shrinking. On the other hand, the amount of passive and dumbed-down information is expanding. In the language that George Orwell gave us in *1984*, this is "ungood."

There seems to be serious questions about our future direction when Mickey Mouse is the primary symbol for the largest television network in America. Are there not dangers in insufficient division between news and entertainment? This blurring into the world of infotainment has already been developed to almost an art form in U.S. commercial television network news and is spreading. In Japan and Europe the infusion of entertainment into news shows has increased over the last five years under the influence of cable television and satellite-distributed programming. Tie-ins between news and entertainment shows are now worldwide phenomena.

There is also the parallel danger of oversimplification of the information content so that vocabulary and syntax begin to rival the *Cat in the Hat* phrasing of a Dr. Seuss primer. There is little doubt that education systems will migrate toward electronic formats and mediated systems over the next twenty years. This could accelerate a tendency to "massify" and simplify content, erode vocabulary, and generally debilitate the thinking skills of students. These changes at first may well be gradual and almost imperceptible over many years. In one course literary references might be simplified and in another the math exercises might be streamlined. At the end, however, we may see the unfortunate results. These may be lower test scores, more functional illiteracy, and a "mass electorate" with reduced critical-thinking skills.

And there is the danger that we will blame the wrong organizations and technologies for our problems. The general public and workers are, for instance, concerned about privacy, electronic surveillance, and information overload, but they are not sure who or what to blame. There are other problems of massification of the media and dumbing down of content and the loss of jobs due to market and technology consolidation. Many others, including the author, are finding it hard to cope with the 168-hour work week. Particularly tough are the omnipresent automated information centers that computers, automatic call-distribution centers, and robots now control. Who is, in fact, to blame? Would it be a better world without infotainment and infomercials? If there was less television and less cartoons would we stop the ongoing decline of educational standards? What should American parents make of the American Pediatric Association's recent call for no television for infants under two years of age and limited television for children that are older? Should the FDA have labels printed on television, DVDs, and computers warning consumers that "viewing may be harmful to your health and make you stupid as well?"

The easy way out is just to ignore the issue and focus elsewhere on smaller and more specific problems that we can solve. Yet we ignore these issues at the peril of generations to come. It is easier to detect the "false prophet" solutions that the merchants of World-Wide Mind technologies and products hold out to us. There is the idea, for instance, that personal computers and decentralized networks offers an escape from huge integrated systems. This is largely a myth. Monolithic software is today busily massifying personal computers, computer games, and cable TV channels as well.

Many have bought into the idea that personal computers will allow the flowering of diversity, independent thought, and self-directed learning systems. When Macintosh was introduced at the Olympic Games in 1984, the commercial showed a female athlete tossing a hammer to smash the monolithic and totalitarian control of an Orwellian society run by centralized computers. It was a powerful image that took a mighty poke at the "controlling" influence of IBM, but it was only creating an illusion. The nearly pervasive control of software by Microsoft is today almost as complete. Its power is far greater than the once dominant "Big Blue" hardware systems.

The fact is that the predominant trend of our time is the move to network computers together. This is being accomplished not only through the Internet but through literally millions of interactive systems represented by LANs, MANs, WANs, and now even enterprise networks or Global Area Networks (GANs). The most common term for private networks today is simple: "Intranets." Five to ten times more information flows through Intranets, LANs, WANs, and Extranets than through the Internet itself.

The advent of distributed processing networks and essentially global operating systems and quasi-universal software systems just keeps accelerating. This is dramatically portrayed by various versions of Windows. The gigantic success of this software on a global scale suggests that personal computers really are not "personal" but in many ways integrated and massified products cleverly disguised. In some ways today's personal computers and their software are no more decentralized or personalized than individually owned but highly standardized fast-food franchises. And the future suggests that our individual personal computers will be even more webbed together.

One only needs to look to the proposed twenty-first-century global broadband satellite system known as Teledesic to get a preview of our networked PC future. This so-called mega-LEO (Low Earth Orbit) satellite system would deploy a huge number of satellites to create a huge telecommunications capacity equivalent to the total capacity of a Bell operating company like Bell Atlantic or SBC. Each of these high-tech satellite systems as first designed would have the equivalent of a CRAY supercomputer crammed into a shoebox. This remarkably innovative design is based on so-called "star wars" research into smart tiny satellites, known as "brilliant pebbles." The financial failure of the Motorola Iridium system is creating serious market and capitalization problems for all the new systems, and thus Teledesic as originally designed may never be deployed.

The key to the Teledesic satellite system, however, is not its innovative design, but its backers. This system was filed with the FCC in 1994 by Microsoft's Bill Gates, venture capitalist guru Ed

Tuck, and Craig McCaw, who sold his McCaw Communications empire to AT&T for billions of dollars.

Gates and McCaw are not only among the wealthiest men in the world, they are visionaries who see the potential of personal computers, personal data assistants, and wireless communications to create a mobile, flexible, high-throughput network built upon the individual rather than a huge, integrated infrastructure of the Bell operating companies. The vision is that of liberation and freedom, but in truth the new wireless-based World-Wide Mind will ultimately be unifying and limiting as well. In short, if we look to an integrated network of the future as envisioned by Bill Gates it might look like this: It would combine a personal computer equipped with Windows, a new type of Microsoft software designed to provide low-cost computer telephone service that can run on your PC, and Teledesic satellite services that can connect to your desktop. These terminals will be able to support up to two megabits per second and are quite small in size and cost (i.e., 65 cm and under $1,000). The Bill Gates, Craig McCaw, and Ed Tuck vision is thus to reinvent networking, global access, and even the global telecommunications infrastructure.

So far, the concept of a global electronic revolution that lets Bill Gates and friends bypass virtually everyone has been better theory than practice. There have been real-world problems. These difficulties include the rather thorny partnership agreement between Motorola and Teledesic, the market failures of the new personal-communications satellite systems like Iridium and ICO, and the delay in finalizing the design of this broadband system. This has not only created problems for Teledesic, but also tended to adversely affect the plans of the other players in the field, such as Hughes (Spaceway), Loral (Cyberstar), Lockheed Martin (Astrolink), and Alcatel (Skybridge).

In parallel with the idea of broadband, multimedia satellite systems in the sky there have also been megachanges in global networking through deployment of almost unlimited fiber-optic networks (i.e., Oxygen, Global Crossings, Flag, Club, TAT-14, TPC-2, etc.). There literally will be the ability to send over ten terabits of information a second across the Pacific or Atlantic oceans at will as the twenty-first century begins. This is equivalent to sending the Library of Congress across our ocean of choice every second, or 3,600 times an hour. This prodigious capability is the information and communications infrastructure that makes the World-Wide Mind possible today. Further, these speeds could well reach 100 terabits per second across the oceans by 2010.

Yet despite these enormous gains in global and national linkages, the problem of adding knowledge and wisdom still eludes us within our new global and integrated digital markets. This much we know: There will likely be further massification of thought. Performance on standardized educational test results will continue going south. The gap between producers and consumers will continue to widen. Economic systems will continue to ignore the need for "survival values" to be included in consumer markets.

There will also be broad conformity, not only in terms of popular culture, but also in business operations and in educational systems. The biggest motivation to have Windows on your personal computer is the ability to network with anyone, anywhere, anytime. One of the implications of integration and mergers within the ICEE age is indeed massification. So-called personal computers, despite their name, will really not help to counter this trend.

The key market factors creating the current turmoil of mergers and strategic alliances seem chaotic and unpredictable. These shifts, however, follow some clear patterns that include the following:

- Globalization.
- Total digital integration of all information, entertainment, and communications products and services that allows easy market crossovers.
- High profit potential (especially for value-added digital services).
- Merging of hardware, software, and firmware interests and markets.
- Capital-intensive infrastructure needs.
- High debt/equity ratio (especially in cable TV and new Internet companies) being balanced by traditional telecom companies with "deep pockets."
- Stagnating markets for the old guard (especially video rentals, TV networks, book publishers, and local telephone carriers), forcing these corporations to find new Telepower partners.
- Global market opportunities for a new guard, allowing access to new global capital.
- Importance of brand-name identification and using "acquired brands" to transcend trade-bloc barriers.
- Rising importance of secondary value-added markets (e.g., electronic catalog sales, security, etc.).
- Unique characteristics of energy companies to complicate these Telepower formulas (e.g., energy companies with deep pockets and key rights of way).
- Increasingly permissive regulatory environment in the United States and other parts of the world will continue as long as they mirror new electronic prosperity (i.e., open "standards," open competition, and lenient antitrust laws).

When taken collectively, these factors literally invite rapid crossover, mergers, joint partnerships, and aggressive competition. Cable television is poised to provide telephone and data services. Communications carriers are beginning to provide video services to the home. Energy companies are taking over local communications networks and using their existing rights of way and deep-pocket capital to launch themselves into the high value-added telecommunications market. Transportation and automobile manufacturers are using their rights of way, their information and robotics expertise, and their capital-raising abilities to enter broader service markets. Consumer electronics companies are saying they can sell products that eliminate much of the need for cable television systems, the set-top black box, or specialized communications networks. All in all, it should be one heck of a fray.

At stake in all this redefinition of markets and expanded opportunities is the ability to reach directly to the end user, thus bypassing national governments and local merchants. As noted in Chapter 2, the combined global telecommunications, information, and entertainment market is projected to reach at least $4 trillion by 2001. With the addition of smart energy, smart transportation, plus the smart car industries, the total becomes very large indeed—over $5 trillion. Even today—a trillion here and a trillion there—it is still considered real money.

This new activity that crosses so many market boundaries of the past has no proper name. In *Global Talk* we experimented (unsuccessfully) with the long and awkward phrase "telecomputer-energetics." Not surprisingly, it did not work. At least it still has not found its way into Webster's Dictionary or the Oxford English Dictionary.

What do we mean when we apply the word "smart" to energy, transportation, buildings, or whatever? The idea is simply to take advanced information technologies and apply them with significant and positive effect. In most cases we make things better. When we use these technologies with regard to cars, trucks, trains, and highways we hope to make them safer, less polluting, and able to handle more traffic. In the case of energy, cities, and buildings we seek to clean up the environment, save electric and fossil-fuel energy, and make life more comfortable. It does not always work, but we need to keep trying. Following are some brief examples of new "smart" systems.

### Intelligent Highways

We can make a highway system "intelligent" by installing sensors, video cameras, computer controls, and electronic control devices. This process can double or triple the flow of cars and trucks. These same techniques can also make highways safer and increase the speed and energy efficiency of the overall network.

These improvements can be achieved by better routing, closer spacing, and improved timing in the traffic flow. During adverse weather conditions smart highway performance can increase even further, particularly in terms of safety. Experiments conducted in both urban environments and on roadways often subject to adverse weather conditions have shown impressive gains in all areas: safety, traffic flow, fuel efficiency, net cost per vehicle (in terms of both capital and operating costs), and overall throughput performance against traffic density.

Simply adding ice sensors, motion detectors, radar systems, and electronic-messaging systems to the stretch of I-70 where the Eisenhower Tunnel penetrates the Rockies at nearly 12,000 feet has already paid off handsomely in terms of reduced traffic jams and decreased accidents. In future decades far more sophisticated techniques will be applied. It is quite simply a cheaper, better, and faster transportation system.

There are also alternative transportation systems, such as magnetically levitated transport systems for urban and long-distance transportation, that are designed to move larger numbers of people. A plan to create such a MagLev system between Los Angeles and Las Vegas would likely increase total traffic volume, reduce energy (especially gasoline) consumption, and reduce traffic fatalities. In these areas, the United States is actually behind Europe and Japan where higher energy costs and greater population density have forced research and implementation ahead.

### Smart Energy

The rate at which petroleum is being depleted as a fuel source is alarming. In fifty to seventy-five years, given current trends, oil will become so scarce (as the global population reaches near 10 billion) that it will become too expensive to be used to power cars or trucks or to heat buildings. An alternative source of power that is cheap and environmentally clean, such as fuel cells, solar cells, ocean thermal energy conversion, or advanced batteries, is crucial. The answer is clearly to harness recyclable fuel, which ultimately comes from the sun in one way or another. One extreme clean-energy strategy, in fact, would be to burn up all the available oil and gasoline quickly so that the economics of developing new smart energy becomes profitable and feasible soon. Or at least one might claim this is what our farsighted leaders are attempting to accomplish.

The options are many. They include advanced solar cells, regenerative and unitized fuel cells, wind turbines, Ocean Thermal Energy Conversion (OTEC), geothermal energy, and solar energy platforms in space. One does not have to follow the extreme strategy of burning up all our fossil fuels in the hope that smart energy can save our future. The other option is to convince the communications and information-technology companies that they can make profits from applying their software and networks to the world of transportation, energy, and construction.

Already, research for computer chips in gallium arsenide and other high-valence solid-state materials can be applied to improved solar cells. The best processors developed for general commercial applications can be used to save 30 percent of annual heating and cooling bills for office buildings and apartments. The use of smart highways and smart air-traffic routing can save billions of gallons of gasoline and jet fuels.

### Smart Buildings

The remarkable differences in buildings and their performance is not widely known or appreciated. If one compares the energy-efficient INTELSAT headquarters building with the Rayburn Office Building of the U.S. Congress, both located in Washington, D.C., one finds dramatic differences. The average energy consumption per cubic foot per year is 50,000 BTUs for the INTELSAT building and over 200,000 BTUs for the congressional office building. The application of passive energy conservation as well as active energy-generation technologies to modern building can produce energy savings and overall cost savings, help lessen environmental pollution, and even enhance employee comfort. Life cycle cost analysis can show that a few million dollars of investment in a building can pay back tens of millions of dollars in operating costs.

## SMART ENERGY IS THE CRITICAL NEW ELEMENT IN THE ICEE AGE

Many people accept the idea of the digital integration of information, communications, and entertainment (ICE). Several big-name consulting firms even have a division that specialize in the ICE industries. The recognition of that energy mix included in this new mix is winning acceptance among industry analysts. Smart energy to most is still just a slogan. But this too will change.

What assets do these power companies have on their side to launch an offensive into the war of the smart digital markets? In the past they were poorly armed. Exxon lost hundreds of millions of dollars when it tried to be market nimble in the 1960s and 1970s and enter the fray. Today much is different.

Power companies have utility rights of way, transmission facilities in cable conduits and on utility poles, billing systems, and brand-name identities with consumers. They also have deep pockets and the desire to expand into higher-profit-margin markets. Furthermore, several railroads, such as Southern Pacific and Santa Fe, plus electric power corporations in Georgia, Alberta, Canada, and elsewhere, have been edging into telecommunications and networking markets for several years.

The highest-capacity communications in the province of Alberta today is not the local telephone company, but a U.S. power corporation that has been thinking ahead. Indeed, a number of gigantic power corporations are poised to jump right into the middle of the telecomputer-energetics market. This flexibility and access to capital are not perceived as good news for the telecommunications companies.

The tides of change will ebb and flow, but in twenty years the clear pattern of a digitally linked ICEE age will have emerged. Even oil-based energy companies see the need to change and move over the next twenty years to new forms of energy (or at least say they do). The end result is that once-clear divisions of markets that one could define by AT&T (telecommunications), IBM (information), Disney (entertainment), and Con Ed (energy) are simpy no longer there. Everybody is everywhere that digital technology can go and just a little bit further. It is like the sexual revolution has come to the high-tech village and experimenting is a very compelling thing to do. They just can't seem to stop from doing it. (Today is what might be called the "heavy-petting" stage of the ICEE-based sexual revolution.)

Energy is starting some decades behind in digital assets, but especially deep pockets count for a lot. They give the power companies the chance to learn from past mistakes (i.e., avoiding the mistakes of Exxon and Southern Pacific Railway) and give them the chance to buy into technical credibility in the coming ICEE age. Having access to a few billion dollars never hurt in launching a new business venture. Here the power companies and Bill Gates (who has been on a buying spree himself) have something in common.

A current business where virtually every thing about the ICEE age comes together is automobile manufacturing. Thus, Mitsubishi, Toyota, and GM are already well along this road, with investments and technical capabilities in computers, computer chips, satellites, robotics, and advanced energy systems. If one just takes GM as a minicase study, the results may be surprising. GM, together with its subsidiaries Hughes, DirecTV, EDS, and several robotics and artificial-intelligence companies, for instance, already has quite a diversified base in telecomputer-energetics. These capabilities allow GM to have the following:

- robots to build automobiles.
- computers and processors to implant through the engine and the cabin interior.
- cellular communications for road emergencies (i.e., GM's Onstar).
- two satellite companies to provide entertainment-service distribution (Hughes, DirecTV, and PanAmSat).
- a research capability to provide advanced fuel cells, batteries, solar cells, and high-tech gallium arsenide computer chips and phased-array antenna systems.

GM, in fact, has a full ICEE-age competency. Further, Mitsubishi, Daewoo, Hyundai, and Toyota are also pretty strong technology players across the board. Almost every major automobile manufacturer will bring a smart energy car or at least a hybrid (gas and electric) car based on batteries, fuel cells, or solar cells to market by the early 2000s. Honda is already there.

## OVERALL TREND REVIEW

### Potential Pitfalls

- Obstructive campaigns by traditional oil and energy interests.
- Collision versus creative convergence.
- Antitrust considerations.
- Mentality that equates bigger and faster with better and smarter.
- Slow spinoff and market development of new products and services by ICEE-age giants.
- Lack of global diversity and responsiveness in meeting local needs.

### Opportunities and Challenges

- Technological spinoffs, especially in solid-state semiconductors, fuel cells, and artificial intelligence.
- Leverage marketing, sales, and distribution across digital convergent markets.
- Improved customer interface and synergies (for ICEE service providers).
- Globally integrated protection of patents, copyrights, and intellectual property.
- Deep pockets and labs to develop new technology and software.

CHAPTER 6

# Jobs at Risk and Occupations of the Future

The basic things expected by the people of their political and economic systems are simple. They are:

- Equality of opportunity
- Jobs for those who can work
- Security for those who need it
- The preservation of civil liberties for all.

Franklin D. Roosevelt

## VANISHING JOBS

Are you considering becoming a property appraiser, a pharmacist, an accountant, or maybe a geologist? These are good, solid, and well-paying professions with job security, right?

In the unvarnished language of Teleshock, "No way, Jose." These and dozens of other jobs are very much at risk to the rising tide of Telepower and e-commerce. Cyberspace technologies are being applied today not just to assembly lines. They are being aggressively deployed in both professional and highly trained service-level jobs. Even writers may be at risk. There is computer software today that can generate a plausible storyline for a movie. This same software can also weave together credible dialog by drawing on a bank of recorded conversations coded for such use. Such software could give new meaning to the term "hackers."

You might say that the jobs mentioned are very different. They require very different types of education and training. Why are all these and other professional jobs at risk? What is the formula? And even more to the point, how can I find a "safe" job? Are there jobs or professions that will not be zapped away by Telepower within the next decade or so?

What is indeed common to these diverse professions (even writers of potboiler movies) is that there are a rather limited or well-defined set problems or issues to address. In a growing number of service jobs the "work" is being reduced to a series of algorithms. By accessing databases, entering information, and applying the algorithms or formulas, a professional judgment or report can be rendered.

An expert appraiser, for instance, must address issues such as location, size of house and lot, property assessments, date and type of construction, and so forth. It turns out that expert systems designed to develop "program appraisals" come within 95 percent of what trained expert appraisers conclude after two days of work. Banks thus tend to like the computer-generated program appraisals because they are much cheaper and much, much faster.

A recent study at the University of Colorado at Boulder of the appraisal industry in the United States projects that up to 80 percent of existing jobs in appraisal of property will be eliminated over the next ten to fifteen years. This same study suggests that many other jobs in the real estate industry will also be adversely impacted by the application of new high-powered information databases and the use of expert systems. There are even artificial intelligence systems that can provide a range of professional services, such as developing marketing strategies and projecting optimum prices for a house or property. Of real estate related jobs, however, the appraisal industry will be hit the hardest and the soonest.

## IS THERE A CYBERPHARMACIST IN YOUR FUTURE?

Pharmacist may sound like an unlikely profession to be targeted for Teleshock. Here, too, large-scale use of information systems can and will have a big impact. In this field the trend is toward large-scale integration. Very large drug supply houses can hire a single "master pharmacist" to oversee large crews of "packagers" who put together literally millions of orders. The longer-term plan of many large drug store chains is to consolidate operations at only a few national drug packaging and distribution centers. From these huge centers there would then be an "automated" system for consumers to get their products.

UPC codes for individual prescription drugs could, for instance, be issued by doctors and then taken to a drug dispensing laser scanner system that would give you the right medical supplies or drugs. It would at the same time also charge you the UPC encoded price for your prescription. The theory is that the system would be more foolproof and would cost much less to operate than a neighborhood pharmacy. Clearly the system would be a lot less personalized, but then again, so was banking, once, and dining out or getting information from a telephone operator. The difference here is your life could be in the balance if all your prescriptions are not cross-referenced and checked.

## CUT TO THE QUICKEN: THE UNCERTAIN FUTURE OF ACCOUNTANTS

The accountant was once among the most secure professions, but here too the risks of Teleshock are high. One needs only to visit a local computer or business supply store to pick up a low-cost software package like Quicken to understand the dilemma of the accountant. Prepackaged accounting systems such as Last One, available in the United Kingdom, or Quicken can convert a secretary or file clerk into the office accountant in a few hours time. Clearly, highly specialized accountants with quite specialized tax- and tariff-related information will stay in demand for some time, but the routine accounting exercises that track revenues and expenditures are easily obtained in "no-brainer" software packages. Other specialized accounting systems with voice-directed or ordered modifications for customized accounts are also starting to become available.

In professions that involve a process that can be covered by a systematic set of rules, technological obsolescence may not be far behind. The concept is really quite simple. Any job that is subject to routine or recurring instructions can in time be replaced by expert systems or automation. Accounting is clearly a case in point.

## CAD–CAM VERSUS THE CYBER-ENGINEER

Some may think that at least scientists and engineers are exempt from this type of automation. Surely an aerospace or mechanical engineer is not subject to replacement by expert systems. This is, however, not necessarily true. The modern geologist and geophysicist have found that automation and technological obsolescence can strike almost anywhere. In the past they were the ones who structured and catalogued information about the Earth's upper crust and strata, classified remote sensing data from satellite radar systems, and organized other similar data to assist in finding natural resources.

This information no longer has to be sorted and organized by human processors, but instead can be organized by expert information systems. These systems have shown excellent results in identifying high-probability sites for petroleum reservoirs, mineral deposits, and other natural resources. While the demand for geologists remains, the number of available positions within oil and mining companies is definitely phasing downward.

When a company begins to design a new bridge or conceive of a new airplane, they now likely turn to Computer Aided Design and Computer Aided Manufacturing (CAD–CAM) software to do much of the work. The key result is that the number of registered mechanical and aerospace engineers required is now decidedly less. If automation works to reduce costs on an assembly line, then it can be even more powerful when applied to highly salaried professionals.

More and more expert systems will be developed to perform an increasing range of jobs over time. There will be systems that can design an effective advertising layout or that can design car body shapes or dashboard configurations. There will be other systems that can do architectural layouts or improved engine propulsion or help coach a high-jumper or a sprinter. The increasing capabilities of fuzzy logic systems that are now applied to simple tasks like air conditioning controls, smart washers and dryers, and self-focusing cameras will be reapplied to a wide arrange of service jobs as well. Ultimately, the most economically important application of fuzzy logic intelligence may be to replace middle-management jobs.

Lots of jobs like crop harvesting, warehouse storage, and so forth cannot be effectively modeled by linear math and conventional math systems but are well handled by fuzzy logic systems. There is increasing evidence that fuzzy logic systems based on nonlinear math concepts work very much in parallel to the human brain and thus allow for the increased automation of advanced service jobs.

## SUPERSERVICE JOBS: THE FOURTH SECTOR
## OF THE ECONOMY

The loss of agricultural and mining jobs in the late nineteenth and early twentieth centuries was followed by the rise of manufacturing jobs—that is, until they began to recede in the late 1950s. Today service jobs are still surging in number as the so-called primary sector (farming and mining) and the so-called secondary sector (industry and manufacturing) both continue to shrink. Today, to have a service-sector job tells us very little. You might be making seven figures or more or minimum wage. Service employees range from stockmarket traders to neurosurgeons to McDonald's fast-food workers. Service professionals include almost everybody from astrophysicists to sanitation engineers (who used to be crudely called garbage collectors).

So how do we pick the high-value and "safe" service jobs? The answer is far from clear. Nevertheless, for starters, those service jobs with the highest information, communications, specialized skills, and judgment components will command the top salaries as well.

In the future, the application of artificial intelligence and expert systems to service jobs will increase the rate of technological unemployment. There are very few positions absolutely guaranteed through the middle of the twenty-first century given the rapid advance of artificial systems in every aspect of industrial and governmental services. The era of multiple professional careers and life-long job retraining has arrived. If you are an accountant, a property assessor, a teacher, or a pharmacist, you among others may be in for big trouble unless you upgrade your cybernetic skills starting now.

Over the nineteenth and twentieth centuries the profile of jobs in the United States changed dramatically. The shift from mining and agriculture to industrial jobs was in turn followed by the shift to service employment. Today there are subcategories within the service industry (such as sports, entertainment, recreation, and hotel and restaurant) that are much larger employment sectors than industrial manufacturing. What is particularly interesting is the pattern of change in employment in the United States over the last 200 years (see Figure 6.1). It actually mirrors the pattern of employment around the world based on level of economic development. Countries with per capita income of less than $500 per year resemble the employment patterns of the United States 150 to 200 years ago.

In a review of the total global economy, a dramatic shift in the pattern and nature of jobs can clearly be seen as economic development increases with rising GDP per capita. The pattern of employment in a country is closely linked to development. The current level of economic prosperity of a particular country as measured in GDP per capita serves as a highly accurate predictor of employment patterns, and vice versa. Thus, countries with low income levels are still predominately agrarian and mining economies. The so-called primary sector of the economy (namely, farming, mining, and logging) represent the vast majority of jobs. Industrializing countries at middle income levels show a much higher percentage of industrial jobs. Finally, the wealthiest countries of North America,

**Figure 6.1**
**Distribution of U.S. Jobs by Major Categories (1775–2000)**

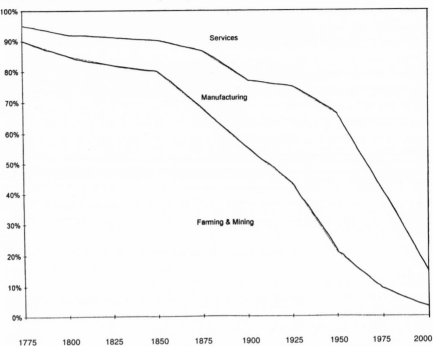

Japan, and Europe (i.e., the OECD countries) have the great bulk of employment in the service economy. As income levels rise and economic growth occurs in developing countries, they more and more reflect a job structure that is dependent first on industrial and then on service jobs. In coming decades these countries will reflect a job structure that resembles the United States, Japan, or Europe today. By 2050 the majority of jobs will be in the service sector in most of today's developing countries. They too will have become a part of the e-Sphere.

Information, robotics, and communications technologies have engendered tremendous changes in the job market. A lot of people have learned in the past decade to spell "technological unemployment." In the last decade nearly 20 million manufacturing jobs have been lost in the world's most economically prosperous countries.

In addition to the industrial workers, many service workers have had to adjust to change as well. Grocery store check-out clerks have learned about technological underemployment. Many such clerks resent being seen as people with ears but no brains in the age of laser-scanner check-out systems. The advent of "intellectual pros-thetics" that range from spell-check to Quicken electronic account-ing systems have substituted computer power for human skills. If computers keep getting smarter, does it mean service workers are doomed to become "dumber"?

But the news is not all bad. These same technologies are increas-ingly being used to help people find new and sometimes more chal-lenging jobs as well. Over 100 Web sites are now devoted to matching up people looking for jobs with new positions. Many of these sites are specialized. There are sites for the aged, those over fifty, young people just entering the job market, and very specific groups such as those with specific physical handicaps.

Many corporate Web sites are being developed to aid both poten-tial employees and employers. Web pages and companies like Monster.com that are devoted to finding new employees are, in fact, expanding rapidly and now handle many tens of thousands of jobs per month.

If we anticipate now that service-sector jobs will begin to decline in quality and quantity in the twenty-first century, what next? Suggestions have included the rise of the entertainment, recreation, and sports sectors on one hand and the rise of the intelligence sec-tor or super-service jobs on the other. This will be at least part of the answer. Clearly we already see within the service sector the large number of tiers of jobs that vary enormously in salary level, job interest, and economic impact. The spectrum ranges from low-tier and low-value service jobs (e.g., fast-food workers, teachers' aides, and nurses' aides) up to the high-tier and high-value service jobs on the other end (e.g., stockbrokers, systems analysts, patent attorneys, investment bankers, and electronic engineers).

Table 6.1 shows the pattern of the most prevalent jobs in the U.S. economy over the last century. Added to this official listing from the U.S. Census Bureau is a hypothetical projection of what the predominant jobs in 2005 might look like.

The changes that will come in service jobs will involve more than trying to overcome technological obsolescence. The nature, struc-ture, and geographic location of jobs will also be changing. The changing structure of service jobs will thus include the following:

- Electronic telecommuting to work (by over 50 million people by 2010).
- Lone eagle service industries in rural and remote areas.
- Global corporations linked together to maintain twenty-four-hour-a-day, 168-hour-a-week operations.
- Global television and entertainment networks with live news, sports, and movie feeds to over 100 countries at a time.

**Table 6.1**
**The Most Predominant Jobs Over the Last 100 Years in the United States**

| 1900 | 1960 | 1990 | 2005 (Estimate) |
|---|---|---|---|
| Farmers | Retail Sales/Managers | Retail Sales | Teachers/Teacher Aides |
| Farm Laborers | Teachers | Health Aides/Nurses | Health Aides/Nurses |
| General Laborers | Secretaries | Teachers/Teacher Aides | Retail Sales |
| Servants | Truck/Tractor Drivers | Truck Drivers | Programmers/ System Analysts |
| Merchants | Secretaries | Farmers/Farm Managers | Engineers/ Technicians |
| Clerks | Private Houshold Workers | Janitors/Cleaners | Waitresses/ Restaurant Workers |
| Salespeople | Farm Laborers | Bookkeepers | Auto Mechanics/ Repair |
| Carpenters | Manual Laborers | Engineers | Truck Drivers |
| Railroad Workers | Bookkeepers | Cooks | Aides/Bookkeepers |
| Miners | Carpenters | Auto Mechanics/Repair | Telemarketers |

*Sources*: 1900, 1960, and 1990 U.S. Census Bureau statistics and projections from the *Futurist* magazine.

- Global booking agencies and travel bureaus on-line anytime, anywhere.
- And much, much more.

Almost all the old rules of services industries will be broken or altered in the process. The following is a review of the rules, both past and future:

| **Old Rule** | **New Rule** |
|---|---|
| Physical proximity is key | Electronic proximity is key |
| Prime real estate is essential to succeed | Electronic prowess is the critical factor |
| Service availability— eight to ten hours a day | Service availability— twenty-four hours a day |
| Location determines labor pool | Labor pool can be globally defined |
| Service is highly localized | Service is geographically flexible and can be globally leveraged |
| High level of interactivity is key | High level of interactivity is key |

Three of the biggest changes for service-related jobs, as already discusssed in Chapter 2, may well be with regard to telecommuting, electronic immigrants, and lone eagles. These shifts are quite large in scope and will involve a huge number of workers.

## WORK IN THE TWENTY-FIRST CENTURY

Clearly, lifestyle, work, careers, and much else about how we survive and hopefully prosper will change in the twenty-first century. The basic ideas of how we live our lives will shift. There will be very few life-long careers or safe jobs. There will be shrinking institutional sinecures as jobs in government, former monopolies, international organizations, and other life-long "job havens" will be streamlined, downsized, and "rightsized" with a vengeance. Even in Japan, the land of lifetime job security, there are major organizational restructurings and downsizings occurring at Sony, NEC, Nissan, and dozens of other major firms. The reform move to cut 1,000 high-level executive and management jobs even from the staff of the United Nations is a bellwether of the future.

There will, likewise, no longer be a one-time and final "completing" of a college education, or of advanced degrees, either. In the twenty-first century individuals with college degrees, especially those with advanced degrees, will have to be recertified to show they have a current knowledge of their field. Even going to work will shift in new and unfamiliar ways in the emerging flex-place environment of cyberspace.

In many instances, starting the workday will represent a shift in activities rather than a shift in location. A walk from the kitchen to the den and turning on a computer, fax, and modem will be the two-second commute of an electronic telework world. The traditional office space has long been recognized as a poor investment in productivity. Recent studies published in the *Harvard Business Review* found that executive and management offices are typically used only some 10 to 12 percent of the total hours in a year—sometimes much less than that at the highest corporate levels.

These various examples and the emerging trends of cyberspace-based jobs are only indicative of the coming chaos. The complex patterns of innovation and economic transitions that are just now beginning to take hold in the United States will soon spread to the entire world. The one central fact of a "plugged-in" world is that the best talent at the best competitive wages can be recruited from anywhere.

It used to be that immigration quotas and restrictions against employment of foreigners stopped free and open global recruitment.

The old rules no longer apply. New regional trade pacts allow more open movement of labor across international borders, but in the age of electronic immigrants the worker stays put and goes to work via a modem. In some cases the commute may be a few miles across town and in others it might be a 12,000-mile commute across many time zones.

## OVERALL TREND REVIEW

### Challenges and Pitfalls

- Increasing gap between consumers and producers.
- Workers not trained to meet e-commerce job-market needs.
- Social costs of technological unemployment and collapse of conventional retailing.
- Deskilling, information overload, and drop out of "burned-out" cyber-workers.
- Negative social implications that result from a broader range of routine (and professional jobs) being automated or devaluated.
- E-gap between infosocieties and developing countries.

### Opportunities

- Increased economic productivity and reduced production and service costs.
- Improved management through dis-intermediation and networking.
- Improved globally networked corporations that can leverage the power of teleworkers and cybermanagement.
- Environmental greening through the moving of ideas rather than people and resources.
- Stimulating ideas and thoughts arising from life-long learning.
- World peace and enterprise through e-commerce and globalization.

## CHAPTER 7

# Cybermanagement

Lots of folks confuse bad management with destiny.
                                            Frank McKinney

## GIVING CYBERMANAGERS AN EDGE

There are no magic answers. Good management is good management, period. Smart, motivated, and competent people managing smart, motivated, and competent people can be a formula for success in any enterprise. And yet somehow the world of cyberspace does make a difference. There are skills and insights that are essential for cybermanagers to know. Conventional approaches to management used in manufacturing, mining, agriculture, and energy may not work well (in fact, almost always do not work well) in the world of cyberspace. The pace, flexibility, skill set, and marketing systems, among other factors, are quite a bit different in the world of information technology.

Perhaps even more important, the special techniques born of cyberspace are awaiting their creative application to the traditional economic sectors. One of many possible examples of effective cybermanagement is the early access and use of the latest strategic information. There is, of course, a great deal of live news and interactive information available on the Internet, but there are emerging special financial and business information subscription nets that offer a special edge. In fact, one of these services is indeed known as "The Edge." This fairly pricey entry into the strategic-management electronic news service world offers three streams of traffic simultaneously: breaking news, focused news on selected topic areas, and headlines of business news of the day. It also provides (hours before the actual published editions) the full contents of the *Wall Street Journal*, the *New York Times*, and other key publications.

## WEB-POWERED CORPORATE SYSTEMS

There are other information providers, such as the database management corporation Oracle, that suggest that just being informed is simply not enough. These prophets of the cybercorporation are promoting what they call "customer-centric" enterprises. Their ideas about the corporation of the future are structured around how to maximize Web-based sales and Web-leveraged access to distributed employees and suppliers and places. The idea that Oracle, Microsoft, Novell, and others are promoting under such names as "Customer Relationship Management" is to provide immediate and highly interactive responses to customers. Alan Anderson, president of the Quintus Corporation, suggests that a typical on-line customer interaction to buy a product or service can be efficiently achieved within about twenty seconds with a highly responsive Internet-based system. Too much longer is too bad for the impatient Gen-X consumer.

Building on the experience of Amazon.com, eBay, and others, it seems that if the interaction can be accurate, reliable, time efficient, and responsive, then one can keep and indeed attract new customers. Further, if inventory control, warehousing, distribution, warranty and maintenance, production, and so forth are built around this system, lots of other good things will follow. This is, in essence, something we have known for a long time: Good, effective, and accurate communication is the key to good management.

The problem is defining good communications within the e-Sphere. In many systems, from merchandise retailers to newspapers, from banks to doctors' offices, the excessive use of automated communications can actually provide more frustration than communication. Bad voice-mail systems provide stress rather than efficient transactions.

Yet, consumer trends studies conducted by Nielson Research found an increasing number of people under thirty saying they would rather interact with a machine or an anonymous voice than with a person face to face when buying gasoline or airline tickets or withdrawing money from an ATM. This phenonema must be carefully researched and understood. The number one objective seems to be speed and accuracy.

Everywhere one looks we see runaway growth in e-commerce, automated sales, just-in-time supply, and inventory control. The generation that grew up with electronic games, voice mail, and computers are extremely time-sensitive and anonymous consumers. Managers who ignore these realities may have tough days ahead.

These cyberspace management trends seem to spell the end for neighborhood hardware, grocery, toy, or appliance stores. Likewise, they portend that in the most advanced and Internet-intensive countries only high-end, highly personalized service operations will likely survive in the cyberspace world of the twenty-first century. In all this it is the traditional middle manager who will become the most obsolete management concept of all.

These trends strongly suggest the continued spread of "electronically optimized" megacorporations that exploit economies of scale and technology on one end of the spectrum. Yet on the other end there appears to be a need for smaller, personalized, and high-service corporations. The mid-size manufacturer, supplier, or retailer had thus better have some special weapon, such as a patented product, a super location or ambiance, or something else in reserve, lest its days be numbered. The implications that flow from new cybermanagement techniques now extend beyond conventional businesses to almost everywhere—even to the farms and the hinterlands.

## SMART MANAGERS IN "CYBERDIRT" ENTERPRISES

The use of cyberspace as a strategic management tool or solution in farming, industry, or harnessing natural resources is a huge potential benefit of this technology that is sometimes overlooked. There are many rich examples of how smart managers in virtually all economic sectors are now using cyberspace technology to expand their market, increase their productivity, or develop better products and services.

### Delta, Colorado

In rural Colorado, fifty miles from the closest ski slope and sixty miles from the dinosaur pits, there has been a remarkable resurgence in specialized agriculture. Local farmers are growing broccoli and spinach and asparagus and whatever their Internet market index tells them to grow. Each day the cyberfarmers of Delta, Colorado, are surfing the Web and shipping their fresh produce in dry ice by air freight around the world. "Broccoli is today 2,795 yen a kilo in Tokyo and the shipment is on the way." "White asparagus spears are now 140 francs a kilo in Paris and the shipment will be in your warehouse freezer tomorrow." The cyberfarmers of Delta are so convinced that this is the wave of the future that they agreed to equip all the local secondary schools with personal computers and Internet modem connections out of their own pockets.

### Raleigh, North Carolina

If you can use high tech to sell your farm products, you can use it to make your yield better as well. University of North Carolina professor Scott Madry is working with local farmers on a new concept in cyberfarming called precision agriculture. This is a system that will use the new high-resolution (0.8 meters per pixel) remote sensing satellites to let analysts understand soil content, irrigation needs, and fertilizer needs on an amazingly detailed basis.

The point is to create a computer-controlled distribution system for micromanaged farmland. With such a system it is possible to give each small unit exactly the right amount of water, fertilizer, and tillage. As a result, very good things can happen. Crop yield per acre increases some 30 percent or more, and the use of water and fertilizer drops. Professor Madry is a cultural anthropologist turned space-based cyberfarmer who also plays a mean blues guitar. He is seen as a maverick by some, but has a good deal of data to back up his belief that remote-sensing-based precision farming will be a multibillion-dollar industry in twenty years and will also be the norm for the majority of U.S. farms.

## CYBERMANAGERS WHO ARE DRILLING AND MINING THE RICHES OF CYBERSPACE

The smart managers of mining and oil production have learned that they need to use the tools of cyberspace as well.

### Madagascar, Indonesia, and the High Seas

When it comes to high-tech image, the petroleum industry is usually not seen as being at the top of the list. Yet oil companies have learned that the key to their global operations are effective communications. The need to know exists at all levels. There is a voracious appetite for information on the status of drilling operations, pumping production, pipeline flow (or leakage), tanker location and logistics, instantaneous prices for crude on the global market, and much, much more.

There is even the need to provide telehealth services to offshore drilling rigs. Today, there are high-tech, very small aperture terminals or earth stations (called VSATs) that connect oil fields in remote locations in Madagascar and Indonesia directly to corporate headquarters. There are pipeline monitors in Siberia and Alaska that relay data via the new Orbcomm satellite system. These low Earth orbit, store and forward satellites, can relay a byte or so of data as often as every thirty minutes to indicate that the oil is flowing downstream A-okay. By the end of 2001, more than a million satellite messaging terminals will be in operation.

One of the more demanding cyberrequirements of the oil industry is the need to link to offshore drilling rigs off the coast of Nigeria, Malaysia, and Canada. Dr. Maxwell House of Memorial Hospital in Newfoundland was among the first to show how satellite links could be used to provide critical telemedicine services to help set broken legs, diagnose rare medical conditions, and react to emergency medical needs. Today broadband telemedicine links and cyberspace links to offshore rigs are the norm. The success of this program has been so great that Dr. House moved on to become governor general of the province.

### Boulder, Colorado

Another industry that is seen as low tech and lacking in astute cybermanagement capabilities is the field of mining. This also is changing. Today a start-up satellite service company is planning integrated networks that provide a full range of teleremote services for industries that range from heavy-equipment manufacturers to precious-metal mines. These turnkey systems include a T-1 Earth station, a full rate Internet interconnection, an Intel-based full-motion videoconference, and voice and data links as well. From their Colorado headquarters a full-service cybernetwork can be planned for the most remote locations on earth. The biggest problem is not the technology but the administrative procedures to allow the VSAT terminals to be installed and operated.

The message of these mini–case studies is a simple one. No modern manager in any economic enterprise can ignore the powerful boost that cyberspace technologies can provide. Cyberassistance can boost production, reduce expenses, allow better environmental practices, increase market reach or impact, or provide vital support services (i.e., remote telemedicine care).

It would be misleading, pretentious, and unrealistic to suggest that a quick read of this chapter, or even this book, is going to create instant insight. It is not possible in a few hours to transform someone without good computer skills, some knowledge of fiber and satellite transmission systems, and some Internet experience into an expert cybermanager. A careful read of the appendixes to this book, a few courses in cybertechnologies, and some good management courses at a local university or via a telecourse can begin to make a good impact. The following guidelines for incipient cybermanagers are not intended to be taken as a panacea for all management issues, but as the start of a new and fresh thought process.

## CYBERMANAGING NINTENDO WARFARE

Ever since the Gulf War the character of how wars are waged has been changing. Although the traditional concept of "lines-of-supply" warfare with the need to establish communications, roadways, and munition depots in hostile environments is still the predominant paradigm, the shift toward cybermanagement of "Nintendo warfare" is unmistakable. By 2010 the new infotechnology available to advanced warfighting units will be truly right out of *Star Wars*. In the Kosovo engagement only three soldiers were actually ever in enemy territory during the hostilities and they were there by accident. Cyberwarriors maintained their home base as nearby as Italy and as far away as Missouri in carrying out air-based attacks against Serb soldiers.

By 2010 the space and telecommunications capabilities available to carry on hostilities by "remote control" will be even more incredible. The cyber-war arsenal available will include new very broadband millimeter-wave satellites, various types of land mobile satellite systems in both low Earth and geosynchronous orbit, and stratospheric platforms in "proto-space" that can provide communications, surveillance, or even mount remote-controlled attacks. Unattended Autonomous Vehicles (UAVs), high-altitude platforms, robotically controlled tanks and air systems, and so on will allow distant field generals to pinpoint targets, mount offensives, and put only smart machines rather than human lives at risk.

In the age of Nintendo warfare there may no longer be a need to establish complex logistics to create the shelters, hospitals, roads, power, and communications required to deploy troops in hostile territories. Just-in-time warfare will make information and communications the critical element in mounting a foreign campaign. This just-in-time warfare will restructure the size, shape, form, and nature of the United States and its allies' warfighting capabilities. It could even result in the creation of new units, such as a "space and subspace force" and an "information, surveillance, and communications command."

The whole concept of training, equipping, and managing armies in the age of the World-Wide Mind and Nintendo warfare will thus need to be largely reinvented in the next decade. Access to radio and optical spectrums, ability to communicate via broadband systems that are flexible, secure, reliable, and mobile, and other such measures will be the yardstick for military efficiency and capability in the twenty-first century.

## CYBERTIPS FOR THE TWENTY-FIRST CENTURY MANAGER

### Redefine Distance

In the new age of cyberspace, distance has new meaning. In the new age distance should be calculated not in miles or kilometers, but in terms of instantaneous broadband communications. A person 1,000 miles away who can be reached at a cost of a penny per second on a broadband two megabit (E-1) channel is in cyberspace terms "very close." If there is a gigabit/second LAN in place, halfway around the world is virtually next door. On the other hand, someone that is ten miles away but whose telecommunications access costs are two cents per second and restricted to a 9.6 kilobit/second pipeline is in the cyberhinterlands. In essence, if one has electronic access (especially low-cost, broadband multimedia access) then actual distance is less and less important.

Studies conducted by the TeleGeographic group have shown that, in terms of communications efficiency, industrial traders in Singapore are ten times "closer" to San Francisco than Vietnam when measuring information throughput. Lab tests just conducted by Deutsch Telekom in Germany sent eighty different light channels at varying optical wavelengths though a single optical channel. Since each light channel represented 40 million bits of data per second, the total transmission rate was 3.2 trillion bits per second. This is enough capability to relay the Library of Congress several times a minute. This is also about the estimated capacity of Bill Gates's new Teledesic satellite system. By 2010 the rates will be up in the tens of terabits per second range, and distance in communications terms will have virtually no meaning left.

Good employees or consultants need not be physically next door in the world of cyberspace. Think in terms of talent and accessibility, rather than in terms of physical proximity.

### Take the Value-Added Challenge

The global communications systems represented by the Internet, enterprise networks, broadband fiber-optic and satellite systems, and the public switched telecommunications system can and does allow access to a lot of data and information. A megabit of information (the equivalent of thirty pages of information) can be zapped around the world for somewhere between a penny to 1/100th of penny on a dedicated network. The point is simple. Basic information and data are cheap. Not having the right information when you need it is expensive. People are increasingly willing to pay good money for targeted, specific, and desired value-added products, on-demand services, or individualized solutions. Along with these will also come information services that are charged on a bandwidth and throughput on-demand basis. This will result in a new type of tariffing that some are calling "e-streaming." In the world of the World-Wide Mind, basic information and communications start to look, act, and feel like electric power—they are instantly accessible and low-cost raw commodities. The actual worth is in the content and the value added.

Fishermen do not want a high-resolution, multispectral satellite image of the ocean. They want to know where the fish are or soon will be. Bookkeepers do not want a high-performance computer with advanced system-simulation programs. Rather, they want a form in which to enter accounting data quickly, cheaply, and with an absence of errors. The entrepreneur's ability to invent new solutions from basic cyberspace technologies is the most difficult challenge—not getting raw data.

### Exploit the Full Powers of a Commercial Web Site

An outstanding Web site with good graphics, frequent updating, and a system for selling products and services is a sine qua non of today's business world. The best strategies for commercial exploitation of Web sites just keep evolving. Many techniques can be used in parallel. Some are innovative, cute, and sophisticated. Several others are illegal or soon will be so. (A word of warning to hackers who have devised methods to electronically capture a Web page and send unsuspecting e-consumers to porno Web sites: Beware. This electronic kidnapping designed to boost the "cookie catcher" numbers and thus to increase advertiser sales is illegal in a number of states and soon will be a federal offense.) Likewise, we will soon see new laws against selling prescription drugs on the Internet.

On the legitimate side of e-commerce, there are lots of options. You can provide information and products or services on a free Web page and then sell access to more detailed information via an electronic code and the use of a credit card. (In this case the consumer should use "Zip mail" or other encoded systems to avoid security problems, such as having your credit card number stolen.) An e-commerce provider can also provide "free" access to his or her value-added database, but only after customers view a sequence of five ads sponsored by paying advertisers. Or you can just ask advertisers to post their ads on your Web site or on the access page of your friendly ISP. If you are advertising in cyberspace you can hope it gets you the exposure you want and need. You can always shift to other pages, and indeed the "churn rate" of advertising seeking the best exposure is very high. Advertising rates at the big ISPs, such as MSN, AOL, Compuserve, and Dellnet, are getting extremely pricey and skepticism about recorded hits are now becoming suspect. The possibility of manipulation or fraud is increasingly clear.

You can also have Web site visitors leave e-mail, or telephone or fax numbers in exchange for getting certain information and then have telemarketers make calls on your behalf. Many consumers are now fearful of visiting sites because of the misuse that can come from having your cookie or URL address captured without your having a say in the matter.

A number of organizations, such as IBM, MPRG, Anderson Consulting, Euroconsult, and dozens more consulting firms, specialize in providing information on how to sell products and services over the Internet.

### Global Reach via Public Telecommunications Access Plus the Internet Can Be an Even More Powerful Combination

As strong as the potential of the Internet now is for commercial uses, other media still have stronger and broader reach. Travel agencies, catalog order sales, and a host of other companies know that the Internet gives you the ability to access about 150 to 200 million potential customers. In contrast, spokespersons for the new Worldspace global radio satellite system claim their three satellites provide coverage that could potentially reach 4.6 billion people. There are about 2 to 3 billion people worldwide who are accessible via one or more radio and television channels. The largest interactive cybersystem is actually the public switched telecommunications network. Organizations as diverse as Lands' End catalog sales, Aetna Insurance, United Airlines, and Merrill Lynch have very high-tech customer interaction systems called call centers that still rely heavily on public telephone networks.

These systems are electronically sophisticated. They use artificially intelligent automatic call-distribution techniques and "once and done" record entry. They tie the incoming caller ID information to customer database access. When the customers call, they don't have a chance. The sales rep at the other end knows your buying habits, your credit card numbers, and probably the name of your dog and your lover.

Some major cyberspace retailers still consider the Internet to be a security risk and a limiting customer base. They thus maintain 800 and 888 toll-free-number call centers in synch with their Internet operations.

Organizations such as Intel and IBM have found new cybermarketing systems beyond the Internet. In the case of IBM, the solution was to contract with the DirecTV home satellite network to distribute software to customers. Intel has likewise contracted with the Astra direct broadcast system in Europe to do the same. Customers place their orders and pay for their new software via telephone. The customer, armed with the right code, cannot only download the software over their satellite terminal, but automatically get free upgrades over time via their satellite dish. The heavily encrypted software is felt to be much more secure than if the Internet were the distribution mode. Software worth billions of dollars is not something that Microsoft, IBM, or Intel want pirated.

### Avoid the "Over Hype" of the Internet

As suggested, some companies consider the Internet to be only one of several options. Most major corporations are inclined to operate their own private Intranet via a WAN to achieve broad levels of corporate interconnectivity. The Internet is a wild and wonderful electronic environment that is totally and "irritatingly" democratic. Everyone is invited to the dance: entrepreneur, entertainment, CEO, fascist, pornographer, telecriminal, and John Q. Public. It is a natural watering hole for infonuts, technotwits, and cybernerds. The result is that much of the information accessible on the Internet is weird, wacko, inane, or flawed. One can find favorite television shows or radio stations on-line along with scads of porno and gambling sites. One can find extremist propaganda from far left to far right. One can find perfectly respectable Web sites, but loaded with out-of-date data.

Graduate students at the International Space University who were recently putting together a report on satellite systems missed seventeen new multimedia satellites worth over $50 billion, simply because the relevant Internet Web site had not been updated. The Internet is an information source and not a "thinking" World-Wide Mind, nor necessarily an accurate source of knowledge. Books, journals, newspapers, specialized electronic news sources, and more are still crucial. The key is to be able to go to experts who accurately know when the Internet is out of date or inaccurate or in-complete. The use of special Internet guides and navigators such as Magellan and specialized information portals are only a start to finding what does and does not exist on the Net.

Certainly, the Internet is filled with infohazards, cyberpotholes, and really freaky information, such as the amazing "spam cam" Web site and the "pop-tart toaster flame thrower." There are other amazing creations, such as the "exploding whale" Web site that shows an eight-ton whale being dynamited or the "reverse speech" Web site where a cultist tries to analyze key officials' statements backward to search for hidden messages. There are guides that can help you avoid such pitfalls. Alternatively, if you wish to mine the most obscure and quirkiest of Web sites for hidden gold, there are "weirdness guides" as well. There is a Web site known as the "Center for the Easily Amused" and there is a newly published book called *The Weird Wide Web* whose author recently confessed that the Web is the natural gathering place for "fruitcakes" and disen-franchised extremists. In short, recognize the limitations of the Internet and that it is not a panacea but merely another tool.

### Use the Best Telemanagement Techniques

Cybermanagement in many cases will involve managing people at a distance. For some, this means creating an elaborate monitoring system to measure employment production on an hourly basis. The GE corporation has created home work centers with electronic work monitoring for handicapped workers and measures their compensation by work units rather than in terms of time spend on the job. For some this is seen as much like a twenty-first-century version of an electronic sweat shop. To its champions it offers a niche in the information-society job market for people with varying degrees of proficiency and skill sets. The truth is probably somewhere in-between. The key point is that modern cyberspace-based telemanagement techniques hold both new promise and pitfalls.

The AT&T small-business support group in Atlanta, Georgia, allows its professionals to work out of suburban work centers and at home. In this case management is provided in the form of strategic goals and overall performance to gain more business revenues and the sale of services over a period of months. This type of management will increasingly replace micromanaging staff under conventional 9 A.M. to 5 P.M. labor oversight systems that measure productivity in terms of hours spent in the office.

Telemanagement can achieve remarkable things. It can be used both to manage and support planning. It can be used to gather market information or access public information. It can leverage and make more productive top management's impacts on its remotely located employees, suppliers, or even the news media. The power of telemanagement has been actually demonstrated in a variety of ways. The Boeing Corporation claims to have saved millions of dollars and months off its production schedule by linking its production sites and engineering centers together to produce its 767 and 777 jetliners. One does not need to be an executive of a multibillion-dollar corporation to utilize telemanagement effectively. The National Technological University (NTU) is using dedicated digital satellite channels to expand its tele-education programs into the Asia-Pacific region using highly efficient new MPEG digital video channels that are more than five times cheaper than old analog video. NTU's key problems to date have not been proximity, but increased communications cost and market development in a new cultural environment.

Margot Wallstrom, a mother of two school-age children in Konstad, Sweden, also happens to be a minister of social affairs in the Swedish government in Stockholm. Margot routinely uses dedicated videoconference channels and computer networks to discharge her official duties. Her telesites allow her to be with her children two out of five weekdays, as well as consult with constituents and diverse groups around the country quickly and efficiently. The net result in the case of Margot Wallstrom has been quite positive. She believes she has achieved better time management, linked into a much wider-ranging audience to obtain public input, and developed more effective management of a several-hundred-member staff that oversees a multibillion-krona budget.

Yet another type of telemanagement approach for small business can be seen in the person of Christine Maxwell. Christine is the daughter of the mysteriously deceased and highly notorious publishing tycoon Robert Maxwell. Ms. Maxwell heads the McKinley Publishing Group and manages her business on two continents. Her offices are located in Sausalito, California, near San Francisco, and at her European home in the south of France.

Instead of a full-motion videoconferencing network, Christine exploits a high-speed Internet link to cyber-commute to work. She uses cyberspace to ship manuscripts to publishers, contact editors, and stay in touch with her husband and children. Some days she may even work a twelve- to fourteen-hour day based on the nine time zones that separate California and the Côte d'Azur. She and her astronomer husband Robert Malina, a professor at the University of California, collaborate on projects between France and the United States as a matter of routine.

The following are the connecting links among all these applications of telemanagement:

- Clear strategic objectives that cannot be achieved by conventional work practices based on "everybody-in-the-same office" concepts.
- Amplified communications to keep a distributed team better informed.
- Effective matching of information needs to adaptive electronic telemanagement channels (e.g., e-streaming).

### Exploit Global Partnering Opportunities

The creation of an electronic global economy has several large implications. It means more active and constant sharing of technology. It means that international trade will move more and more toward services. And it means that omnipresent digital technology plus the merging of ICEE-age markets will create an ongoing and powerful set of relationships that virtually dictate new forms of partnering. These new forms of relationships will come in many shapes and sizes:

- Corporate mergers.
- Acquisitions.
- Joint ventures.
- Alliances with options for future investment or acquisition.
- Cross investment (stock swaps for minority ownership by two or more partnering firms).
- Acquisition of brands, subscriber base, or specific products or services.
- Virtual firms based on loose and flexible telepartnerships that are organized on a project-by-project basis.
- Cross-licensing.
- Assigned intellectual properties on a variety of bases (e.g., cash, equity, percentage of future revenues, etc.).
- A host of other affiliate or alliance relationships.

Today there are several hundred thousand telecommunications and information-technology firms of note and several hundred thousand alliance arrangements among these same commercial entities.

The field of telecommunications seems to be moving toward there being fewer than ten global-scale supercarriers that control some 70 percent of the global telecommunications market. Every day the force toward consolidation seems to intensify, whether it is Concert that partners AT&T and British Telecom, MCI Worldcom and Sprint, or Deutsche Telecom and one of the major regional Telcos in United States. This is indeed the pattern for all high-tech enterprises. The aerospace industry in the United States has seen Lockheed Martin and the Boeing Corporation absorb most of their rivals as these manufacturing giants look to enter the global telecom and information markets themselves. In Europe, consolidation in France, the United Kingdom, and Germany will likely end with only two or three aerospace giants. The latest Daimler–Chrysler move to acquire their French aerospace rivals is only the latest indication of this trend.

The merging of markets, the merging of technology, and the need for global reach and distribution will fuel the interest in consolidation. Cyberspace technologies will make this increasingly feasible and in many cases more profitable as well. As the dividing lines continue to disappear between telecommunications and IP-based networking and evaporate between and among aerospace, networking, and telecommunications firms, the pace of merger and alliance will only accelerate. It is remarkable that we see more and more new start-up firms being capitalized and capturing new market share from the bottom of the market. Meanwhile, giants are mating at the top of the food chain to broaden their market and strengthen their economies of scale. The middle-size corporations are thus being "eaten" from above and below.

### Build on Principles of TQM and TBM

Two modern management concepts have been broadly applied in the high-tech industry in recent years and both are highly compatible with cyberindustry in the age of the World-Wide Mind. These are known respectively as Total Quality Management (TQM) and Time-Based Management (TBM). These management concepts each have their strengths and weaknesses but share many common principles.

There are several ways in which these strategic systems coincide. They include putting the customer and quality first, educating and upgrading the skills of employees, empowerment of teams and workers, working smarter rather than faster or harder, and emphasizing effective communications and information systems. Improved communications and artificial intelligence in information systems both allow improved real-time sharing of knowledge and reduction of middle managers who are often barriers to innovation and effectiveness. This is especially true in high-tech companies working in the innovation business.

In modern global corporations the management words of the decade have included "downsizing," "rightsizing," and "streamlining." Common to all these concepts have been: reduction in the number of middle managers, improved intracorporate communications, and flattening the corporate hierarchy so that communication from worker to management and vice versa can be more effective. This process of reducing and streamlining middle management has been called "disintermediation."

This process of streamlining corporate communications and management will only accelerate. Other management changes will happen in parallel. These changes will include the following:

- Emphasis on telework.
- Use of the best talent available globally via worldwide "plug-in" of electronic immigrants.
- Development of new global corporate structures and Customer Relationship Management (CRM). These "cyberspace-smart" and "customer-centric" corporate structures will facilitate more computer-based teamwork via Group Support Systems (GSS). These new corporations will facilitate quick and quality interchange with customers and self-management and self-motivation on the part of professional workers and teams. These "cyberteams" will not only have excellent computer skills but also work toward strategic goals and objectives that do not require a large degree of management intervention after training.

### Learn From the Mistakes of Others

The cybermanagement concepts mentioned are not easy to implement, especially in old and established firms. There are a number of high-tech industries and government agencies who have set out to conquer the world of cyberspace and embark on providing new cyberproducts and services. A number of corporations with well-known brand names have already tried and failed.

Case studies reveal that cyberspace is not immune to inept management. There are numerous problems to look out for.

*Overcompensation of Top Management Plus*
*Overconcentration on Control and Design Authority*

While some high-tech corporations have experienced setbacks or stagnant growth, their top executives have in many cases not experienced repercussions or been relieved of command. In fact, they may even have received record compensation. Examples such as IBM (in the early 1990s), Comsat (for decades), and TRW (for all of the 1990s) are just a few instances of dismal performance being rewarded with top salaries and golden parachutes.

In the mid-1990s, AT&T Chairman Bob Allen was sacked but with a huge settlement. AT&T also had other key and talented management jump ship to found new competitors, including the new infopowerhouse Qwest. Comsat has consistently rewarded a chain of unsuccessful CEOs with multimillion-dollar payoffs.

### Avoid Mixing Suppliers and Selecting Contractors, Especially for Political Reasons

The classic case study is that of the development of the first European space launcher by the European Launcher Development Organization (ELDO). The launcher's multiple stages were rigidly apportioned—one each among the key member nations. All the stages worked—at some point. But after a dozen launches none of them worked altogether.

Political division of suppliers for a large-scale project hardly ever works. Many feel that the international space station with its politically divided subsystems has run overbudget, behind schedule, and ended with few clearly defined scientific or industrial goals largely because it is based on politically apportioned suppliership. The latest problems in the Russian production process has already resulted in at least a two-year delay in the overall assembly process. This $100-billion project is a stunning technological achievement that is still in search of a clearly defined mission.

### Avoid Ultra-Caution

Overcentralization, ultra-cautious product development, and overstandardization are to be scrupulously avoided. It is almost always a mistake to force hardware- and software-defined projects and services to adhere to an overly complex and inflexible master plan. IBM remains rather rigidly a mainframe-oriented computer company in an age of personal computers and businesses that headed in a different direction. IBM and the emerging World-Wide Mind are definitely not yet in sync.

This "centralism" seldom produces innovation, excellence of design, or timely access to markets. Almost all flexibility can be lost. Anyone attempting to create a global cyberspace venture needs to beware both overly centralized control and excessive management review of new programs and products.

### Lack of Multidisciplinary Input to the Design Process

There is often a tendency to have a limited number of engineers design systems without a broader range of inputs from many different disciplines. We are moving toward cyberspace and information products that are more value-added and can produce more user-seductive solutions. The key concepts in adapting to this new environment are to use flexible and multidisciplinary design talents, to design updatable and improvable software-defined equipment. In the age of the World-Wide Mind the importance of multidisciplinary design teams will become more and more important. Most high-tech companies are today very slow to recognize the importance of this key point.

It will often be best to pursue services or products that are oriented to mass consumption. This is to say that one might consider the mainframe computer as the antithesis of most design objectives. Alternatively, one might think of a chicken in every pot and dozens of microprocessors in every house, car, and wardrobe.

## THE FUTURE OF INTERNATIONAL CYBERMANAGEMENT

Our global patterns of economic interaction will likely move away from industrial trade among nation states with more and more emphasis being put on the global-services market. International trade will expand more than threefold over the next five years.

We will see a new model of global-service interactions that can best be compared to the operation of the human brain. As we learn more and more about the brain we find it is highly flexible, adaptive, and fuzzy rather than digital in format. The brain operates differently in concept from digital computers, digital communications systems, and most modern software packages.

The future of cybermanagement has fascinating potential. There are a host of possibilities hovering on the horizon. One real possibility is some powerful new telemanagement tools that today may look almost like toys. This new type of digital equipment could provide almost complete mobility to workers and management with swift cyberconnectivity at modest cost. Already a visual display on specially equipped dark glasses has been demonstrated. The next step could well be a new technology known as visual retinal display (VRD). It could allow smart and small computers in the form of PDAs or smart cell phones to have a visual and perhaps an audio interface with the user. The VRD technology projects light (much softer than a flashlight) so that the user can see high-resolution images from a hand-held unit (from pictures to charts, graphs, and text). This or similar advanced-technology "eye-glass video cameras" give promise of "no-hands" and "total eye and voice" mobility. This technology, coupled with wireless and advanced, multimedia high-data-rate satellites could in time let a telemanager and his or

**Figure 7.1**
**Evolution of the Personal Terminal**

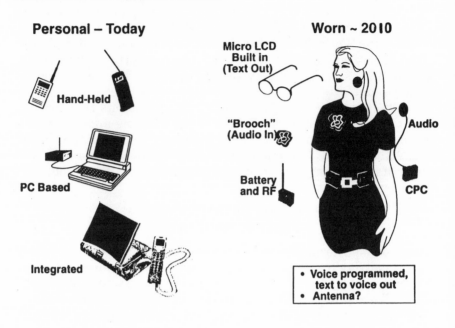

Personal – Today                    Worn ~ 2010

Hand-Held

PC Based

Integrated

Micro LCD Built in (Text Out)

"Brooch" (Audio In)

Audio

Battery and RF

CPC

• Voice programmed, text to voice out
• Antenna?

her staff be instantly in touch with each other, anytime and anywhere. In this new VRD era, the tele-office is wherever you are.

Figure 7.1 shows a concept drawing of this new "wearable office environment" as developed by engineers at the Mitre Corporation for a recent NASA study. The productive gains to be derived from total mobility and voice-driven information systems are today both extremely powerful and greatly underestimated. These gains, plus effective telecommuting and the use of electronic immigrants, may be able to double corporate productivity by 2010.

## OVERALL TREND REVIEW

### Challenges and Pitfalls

• Avoid the temptation to respond to cyberspace fads and staying on the "bleeding edge" of digital technologies.

• Do not abandon proven management techniques but adapt them to networking systems.

• Keep basic rules of communications, employee motivation, training, quality, and integrity.

## Opportunities

- Use on-line information services and breaking-news sources to cope with the 168-hour work week and a global economy.

- Apply the power of cyberspace to exploit the value-added challenge and to maintain access to the best employees over time and distance barriers.

- Use the power of customer-relationship services in designing management concepts, employ multidisciplinary design teams, and use electronic networking to maximum advantage.

- Use cyberspace and TBM or TQM techniques to speed communications and approvals, streamline middle management, reform obsolete practices and corporate structures, reward quality, and reach customers effectively.

- Exploit the power of cyberspace to redefine distance and global reach.

## CHAPTER 8

# Global Enterprise and the e-Sphere

> No man and no nation is an island entire to itself. Here, I be-
> lieve, is the great chance for the world. We must see the present
> in terms of the future, not of the past.
> John J. Powers, Jr., Chairman, Pfizer & Co.

Cyberbusiness and e-commerce will become unremittingly global
in impact in another decade or two. But, it will not be easy. Social
and cultural integration to create a true e-Sphere may consume all
of the twenty-first century. Those companies whose approach to
business markets cannot easily adjust to globalism and e-commerce
are potentially in for big trouble. We are talking about much more
than selling projects via the Internet. This also involves organizing
for electronic billing, servicing and maintenance, design and engineering, telecommuting, and global cultural and political agility.

In general, much of Europe is particularly at risk, with France
extremely well-positioned to crash and burn. Global markets ultimately must be transparent to cultural clashes. The smart Internet
marketers will give consumers information in the language of their
choice and not that of the product provider. In contrast, much of
Asia (especially the "tigers" and "dragons") are highly adaptable
and well-positioned to exploit cyberbusiness opportunities to best
advantage. The Americas, and especially the United States, are
uncomfortably in the middle. In short, those U.S. cyberbusinesses
that are looking to partner with Europe face a much greater chal-

lenge than those who are looking to team across the ocean of the future—the Pacific.

Meanwhile, South America, where Internet use is growing some 125 percent per annum, is well positioned to start catching up, even though per capita usage is still almost 100 times less than in the United States. But life in the e-Sphere involves much more than business; it involves multiculturalism, supranationalism, and adaptability at all forms of cultural, social, religious, and economic interaction.

Analysts such as Stephen Rosenfeld and Robert Samuelson have argued that the end of the Cold War–era helped to fuel a new form of international confrontation. This is the so-called economic nationalism. Certainly, we have seen the force of national separatism in Bosnia, Kosovo, Chechnya, Dagestan, East Timor, Kashmir, southern Mexico, and other hot spots around the world. In contrast to this trend, however, cyberspace networks make global commercial expansion easier to achieve. National economies trapped in the past, such as France, Germany, and other European countries, are ripe for cyber-invasion.

Cybernetic invasions of national service economies, if carried to an extreme, can be dangerous and ultimately counterproductive because of the backlash responses they can stimulate. Ironically, the countries that have the highest level of cyberspace capabilities are most vulnerable to attack by so-called info-war attacks. Banks, social security systems, stock markets, retailing systems, transportation networks, and power systems, among others, are today potential "technoterrorist" targets. In the e-Sphere opponents and electronic attacks can come from any location.

The most extreme cases of economic nationalism are promoted by ultranationalists and "jingoistic populists." These leaders see danger in the free flow of information that increases worldwide cooperation. These extremists and totalitarians correctly see a threat in ongoing movement toward globalism. In Iraq there is Saddam Hussein, in Libya there is Qaddaffi, and in Iran there is still a group of high-level leaders who provide terrorists with support. If only it were a few highly visible bad guys; the problem goes well beyond these known Islamist extremists. It even goes well beyond religious fundamentalism. In France there is Jean-Marie Pen, in Austria Joerg Haider, and in Russia Vladimir Jerinovsky. In the United States there are a number of vociferous but fortunately often ineffectual economic nationalists with rather extreme views and overbearing personalities. These include press commentator turned continuous presidential candidate Patrick Buchanan, political operative and fundraiser Lyndon Larouche, and, the most annoying political maverick, billionaire H. Ross Perot.

These neonationalists have a common theme. It is "national interests" that must be put first and those of "foreigners" somewhere between second and last. These nationalistic zealots are variously promoting strict trade barriers, restrictions on international trade and commerce, rejection of regional trade alliances, blocking of immigration, and basic "gut level" appeals to nationalistic intolerance that verge on early twentieth-century jingoism and racism. The people to whom such super-nationalist appeals are made are not only the consumers, but also workers and producers, who often see international competition and immigrating workers as threats to their jobs. (It is as if the intellectual poverty of Cold War thinking that reduced itself to "us" versus "them" has never been thoroughly analyzed and understood. Humanity seems determined to invent an enemy to work against rather than noble and lofty goals to which it can aspire. This type of systematic abuse of cyberspace to promote local hatred and bigotry will be explored in Chapter 9.)

The legacy of the Industrial Revolution is the systematic separation of the industrial producers from the mass consumer. The best and most profound legacy of the age of cyberbusiness could be to move production and consumption closer together again—ultimately on a global scale. With the right software and cyberspace connections people could start to become their own travel agents, their own stockbrokers, their own tutors and educators, and even partially their own health-care givers. The second most common use of the Internet after seeking pornography is actually acquiring health-care information (see Bibliography).

In short, cyberspace, by giving direct and low-cost information to people on a mass scale, can circumvent many service providers. If local or national service providers are expensive and difficult to deal with, or their office hours are limited, the local consumer is no longer constrained by geography. If you need to buy food, you must be able to physically acquire it at a shop or have it locally delivered. International services are not so constrained.

Two cyberspace trends may thus be linked together:

1. Consumer self-help. In the twenty-first century, cyberspace consumers will be increasingly able to provide part or all of their services (especially information services) through cable TV or satellite networks, the telephone network, or some other electronic or optical system.

2. International consumer bypass. In the future consumers who find more user-friendly, self-help, and lower-cost information services in the international electronic marketplace can and will bypass local or national systems. Transnationalism and the e-Sphere will ultimately prevail—maybe not today, maybe not tomorrow, but maybe by the end of the twenty-first century.

Ironically, at the time that international communications experts and international business enterprises are creating an unsurpassed global network and international electronic information services are growing, there is a reverse trend as well. Strong signs of both nationalistic and religious intolerance are everywhere. There are those that would seek to wall off nations, races, or cultures one from another. Centuries of experience involving Japan, China, the Inca and Mayan civilizations, and a number of other Asian, African, and Arabic empires have shown that walled-off societies become stagnant over time. Isolated societies tend to wither intellectually and economically. In some cases these societies have been literally shut off by walls or oceans (such as in the cases of China and Japan), or just figuratively closed off to outside ideas (some claim this is what has happened to Washington, D.C.).

We now live in a world in which an increasing number of people can communicate with everyone via the public switched network as well as the Internet . Given such a remarkable new capability, isolationism seems to many world citizens and multinational corporations somewhere between incongruous and absurd. The number of international electronic funds transactions has rapidly mounted in the last two decades. The World Bank tells us that such electronic transfers now involve over $3 trillion per day and an amazing $1 quadrillion in global electronic exchanges per year. These communications transactions sometimes occur by international phone calls, faxes, or e-mail, but most commonly it is by electronic data interchanges (EDI). Many of these transactions take place on a dedicated network such as SWIFT (Society for Worldwide Interbank Funds Transfer).

The huge volume represented by the current global electronic circulation of funds is best comprehended for its staggering size in relation to the actual worldwide production of goods and services. Electronic Funds Transfer (EFT) is twenty times the entire annual economic product of all the countries of the world: It will be around $80 trillion per month for the year 2000, and may reach $200 trillion per month by 2005.

The amount of international trade has soared into many trillions of dollars each year. In the post–World War II period international trade was largely a function of exchange of products and goods. The Global Agreement on Tariffs and Trade (GATT), now replaced by the World Trade Organization, in fact once addressed only trade in tangible goods and focused on tariffs and import duties for products. This international trade environment has changed a great deal over the last fifty years. International trade in services will increasingly exceed the value of international trade in goods and products in the twenty-first century.

The most fundamental point on global trade has perhaps been made by Dr. Robert Reich in his book *The Work of Nations*. In this book he notes that "national economies" really no longer exist. Multinational corporations like IBM, Procter and Gamble, ICI, DuPont, Dow, Ford, NEC, Toyota, Honda, Mitsubishi, News Inc., Matra-Marconi, MBB, Sony, Sunkyong, Hyundai, Ericsson, Siemens, Alcatel, and others may have a world headquarters in a so-called home country, but after that, national identities are increasingly hard to verify. Even the so-called big-six U.S. consulting and accounting firms typically each have more employees overseas than in America. Start-up companies that have U.S. management and U.S. capital but operate entirely in overseas markets are increasingly common.

There is a European-based telecommunications company that started over as a start-up firm over a decade ago. Its goal was to become the MCI of Europe. It was then known as Esprit Telecom. Most of its employees are European, and most of its investment capital has come from European banks and investors. In the past two years its start-up management, two American entrepreneurs, have been unceremoniously ousted by British managers and investors. The result of this British takeover was to facilitate a takeover by another American firm based in Fairfax County, Virginia. Its staff is recruited from all over Europe and the "connecting" link among its employees is not language or nationality but actually entrepreneurial spirit.

The company that was created in Canada as Northern Telecom and is now known simply as NorTel Networks is another case in point. Most of its employees and its research facilities and manufacturing units are in the United States, Europe, and Asia. Its headquarters is still in Canada, but its name change is obviously designed to create a globally neutral name. Is it a Canadian firm or not? Not really.

Every major player in the age of the World-Wide Mind is obviously seeking a global presence. Acquistions, alliances, technology licensing, partnership, and even name changes will move more and more high-tech corporations to a global stage. Meanwhile, Enterprise networks, LANs, voiceover IP, and the Internet will only accelerate that trend.

In short, it is increasingly hard to know exactly what nationality truly means anymore. Is it the country of birth, country of citizenship, country of residence, or by the national identity of the company one works for. If someone lives in a country four weeks out of a year and is traveling the other forty-eight weeks, where does that person live and what does home mean?

Many U.S. computer manufacturers actually produce their devices in Southeast Asia. It is really not surprising to note, for instance, that after jewelry exports the number-two category of international production and export for Thailand is electronic and telecommunications equipment. Nor is Thailand an isolated and unique case. The number-three export of Malaysia is also computer and communications equipment. So-called offshore production by U.S., European, and Japanese countries among the so-called Asian dragon and tiger nations continues to grow apace.

Thus, world trade involves much more than changing patterns of exporting products. Someday Microsoft, IBM, and others may distribute and sell their software simply by broadcasting it (under code protection, of course) to the world. The other big change is the swift movement toward "localized" global production. Many would interpret the phrase "offshore production" to mean that industrialized countries like the United States and Japan are moving their factories to overseas countries in order to benefit from low-cost labor forces. Although this move offshore will continue to happen, its benefits in the age of the World-Wide Mind will continue to shrink. The meaning of offshore production in the future may have much more to do with accessing markets (Japan building cars in the United States) than reduced labor costs. This will become particularly true as automated and robotic production costs continue to fall.

Some of the most popular and well-made "American" cars now manufactured and sold in the United States reflect this new trend toward localized global production. These cars are the products of Japanese and German car manufacturers. Yet they are produced in the United States and rely on domestic labor forces in states like Tennessee, South Carolina, Ohio, and Texas. These "American" automobiles are actually "offshore" products that are locally manufactured in the United States by Honda and Toyota. More recently, BMW built a plant in South Carolina. Other global automobile manufacturers will follow, just as Ford and GM are building their own plants or acquiring other global companies around the world, including Volvo, Jaguar, Opel, and others.

Some of the Ford and GM plants are to produce cars for foreign local markets. Other plants are producing parts that are assembled to be sold in the United States. There are already many "American" cars that have less than 50 percent of their overall parts locally produced in the United States. An increasing percentage of the manufactured content of "American" cars are produced in the merchardillos of Mexico. Other key components are produced in Korea, Malaysia, Hong Kong, and a number of other newly industrializing countries around the world. Global corporations, for reasons that range from tariffs, shipping expenses, local labor rates, management, marketing, and distribution costs, are moving toward the concept of localized global services and production.

The modern world of manufacturing can be distributed on a global basis. The key to this being done well and effectively is global information systems. For every bit that flies through the Internet worldwide, another five bits will operate through private corporate networks.

Today, telecommunications, computers, banking, insurance, and other services claim an ever-growing percentage of the total global economy. Further, the percentage of international trade in such services is surging upward. In such an environment, the idea of creating "national trade fortresses" makes less and less sense, and, in fact, become less and less feasible under the World Trade Organization's enforcement of the Global Agreement in Trade in Services (GATS).

Politically, the zealot who claims he or she will create trade barriers and save jobs being lost to illegal immigrants and cheap overseas labor is blowing smoke. As reported recently in the *Futurist,* the number of industrial jobs in the United States has decreased from about 25 million in 1980 to about 14 million in 1999 and will hit the 10-million level in 2000. This loss or redefinition of jobs is much more than 90 percent related to automation, changes in corporate structure through reengineering, and shifting market demands. Less than 10 percent has to do with illegal immigrants or other alleged problems related to global trade. Specifically, of the 12 million jobs lost in industrial production in the United States over the last twenty-five years, perhaps 11 million jobs have been lost to automation and industrial streamlining, while offshore locations or illegal immigrants have impacted perhaps a million. The numbers and percentages have been much the same in Europe and other developed countries.

Even in so-called heavy industries today the majority of new jobs are in marketing, sales, accounting, and billing. There are thus limited opportunities in industrial production, not because of shifts offshore but because of fundamental shifts in technology and markets. In a decade or two so-called offshore industrializing countries will find that industrial manufacturing jobs will erode there as well. This is because automation will soon begin to replace jobs even in Thailand, Malaysia, Korea, Taiwan, Hong Kong, Indonesia, the Philippines, India, and China. In ten to fifteen years robots will be cheaper than human labor even in these industrializing countries.

Industrial manufacturing jobs on the assembly line are quickly becoming a thing of the past in developed nations and will be decreasing very soon in a growing number of newly industrializing countries (NICs) as well.

## CASE STUDIES IN GLOBAL TRADE IN THE AGE OF CYBERSPACE

A decade ago the rural agricultural regions around Montrose, Colorado, were far from being booming economies. Prices in local and regional farming markets were largely stable or down. Some local farmers were shifting to other occupations or working part-time jobs to supplement their income. Today the economy in this remote and artificially irrigated agrarian southwestern Colorado region has changed for the better. Farming is a growth industry and more people are seeing agriculture as an exciting opportunity. The prices that farmers are receiving for their specialty crops in spinach, artichokes, and mushrooms are at record highs.

What changed? Was it a new fertilizer? New hybrid seeds? Genetically designed crops? New tilling or harvesting processes? No, it was none of these. The key was the innovative market monitoring by a cyberfarmer who learned how to harvest record profits from the Internet and then went into business to support the farmers of the entire region. The "magic" transformation was simply the matching of specialized agricultural crops with the highest paying global markets. While spinach may sell for $1.19 a pound in Grand Junction, Colorado, the Tokyo market may be paying 2000 yen (or $19) per kilogram. With this kind of price differential it is highly profitable to pack the spinach in dry ice and air freight it to Tokyo.

The irrigated farms of the region were able to support a wide diversity of crops to serve the demands of a global economy. The diversity of crop plantings needed to serve the global consuming patterns matched the climate and soil in the region. Further, the ability to deliver key vegetable and fruit foodstuffs in synch with the highest market values turned out to be a rather easy process via cyberspace. Global produce quotes on the Internet are available on a real-time basis. New broadband satellite systems that update electronic caches for ISPs are now able to use digital video broadcast (DVB) technology to provide completely new quotes at forty-five megabits per second. Someone in Montrose, Colorado, can be closer to the market that someone on the floor of the Tokyo commodity exchange.

The ability to harvest, package, and air freight products in dry ice in a matter of hours allowed the farmers of Montrose to hit the hot agriculture markets dead center. The key to efficient cyberspace brokering and global ordering by these agricultural entrepreneurs is thus first and foremost information. Over time the trend has quite naturally spread. Local ranchers are now using the Internet to find out where to ship their beef to command the best prices.

## GLOBAL RADIO

Many people, particularly those who grew up with radio rather than television, have a sense of nostalgia for seemingly passe and old-fashioned technology. Today, however, radio is making a rapid comeback with a whole new character. In one reincarnation it is a direct broadcast satellite (DBS) service that sends signals directly to the home, a car, a truck, a bus, an airplane, or a train. It sends a signal that is equivalent to a CD disc in quality, and can broadcast data, software, or computer gains, or even track stolen vehicles or, on command, trigger an uplink signal that deploys emergency or public-safety personnel to an accident or crime location.

Using satellite technology, this DBS radio service will no longer be local or regional but can cover entire nations or the globe. In effect this technology is a step beyond Walkman technology that allows one to obtain quality music, entertainment, and personal security no matter where one roams on the planet. American Mobile Satellite Corporation, XM Radio, and Sirius are providing or will provide this type of service in North America, while the new Worldspace system will provide many dozens of channels to broadcasters in Africa, Asia, and South and Central America. Radio is still the most available telecommunications media in the world in its ability to reach some 4 billion-plus people via some 10 billion-plus radio receivers.

Another rendition of contemporary radio is what is now being called Internet radio. Radio stations can now digitize regular programming from a Web site and send out their programming on the Internet to the world. There are many dozens of radio stations already on the Internet, and the number is currently projected to grow into the thousands. According to FCC sources, the most popular stations in the United States that are being received on PCs have current listenership of around 250,000 people.

It is likely that within five years there could be stations with over 1,000,000 listeners. There are a host of questions about such Internet radio. If the radio station is largely supported by local advertisers, what are the commercial benefits that derive from having a huge global listening audience? Will they attract national and global sponsors? Should licensing fees and authorizations take Internet distribution into account? Many countries have strict copyright and international trade and tariff restrictions with regard to global commerce and transborder data flow.

Of course, one can also step beyond into the realm of global Internet television. Indeed, there are starting to be "supertelevision stations" that are available via the Internet. It is unclear whether these can and will compete with global direct broadcast television systems that are being contemplated by Astra of Luxembourg, the News Corporation, and others. Who knows what future possibilities lie with Internet television? But rest assured there are a host of regulatory, copyright, and other legal questions yet to be answered.

Many legal and regulatory questions already pertain. Do Internet radio and television stations have to pay copyright or royalty payments in every country where the Internet operates? Do these stations have to also pay tariffs for transborder data transmission systems that variously apply to broadcast or data services? Today the radio stations are simply putting the programming on the Internet and assuming that this is a completely open and largely unregulated electronic environment with few restrictions on anything from pornography to royalty payments. With almost every new application, from voiceover and multimedia IP to Internet radio and TV, the Internet seems to pose a new paradigm and new policy issues. The openness and unregulated nature of cyberspace continues to raise legal, regulatory, licensing and copyright issues around the globe. Once-protected national borders in terms of trade, information, or broadcasting are now an increasingly open sieve. China and others who have tried to control the flow have largely failed. The predictions of Arthur C. Clarke in the Foreword to this book are quickly becoming reality.

In time, however, treaty or trade agreements may explicitly address such issues and curtail the torrential flow of the Internet Niagara. Depending on the strictness and costs of such a new regulatory regime, the wildfire spread of Internet radio may be dramatically reduced. Perhaps a number of participating radio stations will be taken off the Net. Meanwhile, people traveling may be able to tune in the Internet from Austria to hear a Colorado Rockies game or from Japan to hear the broadcast of a soccer match between Brazil and Argentina. With television, of course, the stakes will only go upward from here.

## COPYRIGHTS, PATENTS, AND INTELLECTUAL PROPERTY IN CYBERSPACE

Prior to the twentieth century most people who sought patents, trademarks, or copyrights only pursued national protection. In special cases they may have applied for protection in perhaps a selected few other countries. The twentieth century was the century of globalization and the twenty-first century will make both global business and nonstop information systems an omnipresent reality. Today major inventions are registered and protected in dozens of countries. The investment in legal fees to obtain protection and then enforce it against infringement can now be many millions of dollars. Comprehensive worldwide protection of intellectual knowledge, information, and entertainment is very likely to be one of the most important new innovations of the new century. The question is whether this will come through global regulatory fiat or enormous costs in legal fees. At least we can see where patent and copyright attorneys' interests will lie.

Today world trade and global multinational corporations thrive on two powerful fuels. These are global electronic networks and new and innovative intellectual property. The "currency" of high-technology global enterprises is now, more than ever, intellectual property. There are copyrights, trademarks, patents, exclusive and nonexclusive licenses, joint license agreements, and much more. We have seen in the past decade a host of mergers, partnerships, strategic coalitions, and new international subsidiaries based on leveraging mutually owned and protected technical and intellectual knowledge.

Today an increasing number of airlines, electronics manufacturers, telecommunications organizations, and computer systems organizations have pursued what might be called intellectual and market coalitions. British Telecommunications (BT) and MCI have been one of the most successful coalitions, but have broken apart and now AT&T and BT are working in tandem through a partnership called concert. (Some believe that the new global mega-deal may lead to a merger of these two telecom giants.) Meanwhile, MCI, Worldcom, and Sprint seem set to merge as the Global One alliance of France Telecom, Deutsche Telecom, and Sprint have split apart. Several major telecommunications carriers are now in pursuit of the Japanese powerhouse NTT, which has just been allowed to go global.

One can argue that market entry and market share represent the primary motives for more and more mergers and strategic coalitions. The power of sharing key technologies, linking powerful digital and software-related patents, and accessing world-class brainpools also must not be overlooked. The cost of some new technical developments and R&D efforts can run anywhere from hundreds of thousands to billions of dollars. Intel has estimated that moving to the next level above the super-Pentium chip could cost over $100 billion. There are big problems with trying to etch chips down to the molecular level, and thus there are large research problems to solve. This is in part due to concern about the danger of errors in megamicrochips induced by natural radioactive decay.

The cost of chip-manufacturing technology and the massive research investments needed to pursue state-of-the-art designs are now so high that the future of this technology seems in question. The breakthroughs at Hewlett Packard and UCLA in their research on molecular computers, however, seem to open yet a new door to the future. Serious research has also now been started on so-called quantum communications and a quantum computer. All these technological pressures toward "giga-dollar" research projects push forward the idea of virtual integration, merger, or alliance within the industries of the emerging World-Wide Mind.

Recent critical financial reviews of the semiconductor industry have questioned whether the hundreds of billions of dollars involved in designing and producing the next two levels of computer chips needed to keep performance gains on track can be financially justified. In particular, these analysts have suggested that the famous "Moore's Law," named after the founder of Intel, may finally have run its course after twenty-five years. This law predicts the doubling of computer-chip performance every eighteen months. This analysis suggests that technological partnerships or coalitions may be necessary for continued technical advances while retaining profitability.

A careful inventory of high-technology start-up corporations in Silicon Valley, Route 128 in the Boston area, the Research Triangle in North Carolina, the greater Washington, D.C., areas, and the Denver–Boulder Silicon Mountain sites shows the same powerful global trends. The financial backers of these innovation enterprises and "technology farms" are no longer U.S.-centric. Venture capital investments into high-tech start-ups come from sources that ring the globe. New private global satellite systems and world-wide fiber projects like Oxygen, Flag, and Global Crossings obtain investment capital in locations like Brunei, Qatar, Luxembourg, and Liechtenstein.

Today there is a dizzying array of alliances in just the telecommunications industry. Beyond this "big-picture" overview of major multibillion-dollar deals and relations there are hundreds of thousands of technical, intellectual, and financial relations with smaller high-technology companies as well.

## THE REDEFINITION OF DISTANCE
## AND GLOBAL ECONOMICS

The image of a Global Village from Marshall McLuhan and the concept of a Global Brain and a World-Wide Mind from *Future Talk* may be interpreted to mean a future of close integration of local, national, regional, and global cultures and economics. A more accurate and precise analog would be that presented to us by the idea of global "open standards" for telecommunications and networking. This is a type of "connection architecture" that allows local differences and specialization but defines a process that can still achieve a harmony of linkages and world cooperation. These standards that allow a merger of different transmission technologies and protocols are at once instantaneous, reliable, and high quality, yet diverse and updateable. In terms of equipment these standards allow computers, electronic switches, and transmission systems to still be heterogeneous.

In the past, the image of world trade was largely restricted to multibillion-dollar megacorporations. With today's flexible and "democratic" communications network, even the farmers and ranchers of rural Colorado, jewelers of Thailand, or rug makers of Turkey can and likely will be cybermerchants trading across national boundaries.

Key cyberspace issues to probe, explore, and solve with regard to world trade thus include the following:

- Enforcement and interpretation of international and national regulations related to international trade in professional services, copyrights, patents, intellectual property, transborder data flow and international broadcasting, plus labor safety and employment rules.
- Effective global standards for open-system interconection and worldwide competition.
- Resolution and smoothing of the conflicts and hostilities that exist between global trading networks and corporations and outspoken national political, religious, and cultural leaders who resist the spread of globalism (at the core of this debate is employment and labor concerns on one hand and religious and racial differences on the other).
- Protection of the security, privacy, and due process rights of cyberspace citizens who wish to live in a global trading environment with a degree of confidence and uniformity of process and appeal procedures.
- Clear controls and fraud protection in global financial systems that protect against laundering of illicitly earned money, electronic extortion, embellishment, or stealing of assets, especially from electronic fund transfer systems.
- Active assessment of problems related to the issue of electronic immigrants, global technological unemployment and job retraining, and national versus international taxation systems.
- New treaties and international agreements to address such issues as protection of the legal rights of individuals and smaller corporations engaged in international trade, insurance and risk protection against international disasters, technoterrorism, revolutions, and property loss or seizures.

By the year 2010 the global economy may well reach $100 trillion a year in turnover, with 25 percent or more of the activity being in the category of international trade. The adequacy of the global information network to handle this challenge with such huge trading volumes is clearly in question. The issue is not primarily throughput or interconnect. Fiber-optic systems that can transmit three to ten terabits of information are now under development. No, the problems are more likely to be reliability, quality, interoperability of standards, international copyrights and patents, and tariffs and controls (nontariff barriers) on transborder data flow and broadcasting. The predicted "Pelton Merge" as set forth in 1993 is indeed now happening to fiber, satellite, and terrestrial wireless systems, to telecommunications and information systems, and to diverse digital services and applications, but it is still a decade or more away from full accomplishment.

The world of global trade in the twenty-first century will be dramatically different. More and more people, organizations, and institutions will become economically interdependent. Global interactions of all types, from airline travel, to fax, to telephone, to the Internet, will only increase. One of the key contributions that cyberspace technologies will make over the next decade or so is the very redefinition of distance and the further blending of global economics.

Governments with burdensome restrictions on international trade and a "rotten" international demeanor can, of course, choose not to change. They will likely be voting to reduce the standard of living of their citizenry and to move toward or retain a third-class national status.

But in an increasingly integrated world what is the difference intended by distinguishing the terms the "Global Village" and the "World-Wide Mind"? In terms of trade, communications and IT systems, and work, the significance of distance will slowly evaporate in a way that makes economics systems more and more like a Global Village. These economic moves toward the Global Village will be driven by telecommerce and telework.

It is in the realms of education, scientific research, and intellectual activity, however, that even closer relationships will form. These intellectual collaborations and joint thinking capabilities are what I see forming the World-Wide Mind. The use of NASA ACTS experimental communications satellites can now allow telescopes in Chile, Hawaii, California, Asia, and Europe to be seamlessly melded together as if they are a single gigantic viewing instrument. Nobel Prizes have now been awarded to scientific teams that exist on three continents and whose labs are linked together as if they are one. The use of "group support systems" software like Lotus

Notes can allow teams of researchers or students to be joined not at the hip but at the brain. We can now know and see via multimedia systems exactly what our colleagues around the world are thinking and doing. The intellectual power of this global ability to think and act in sync is only now beginning to be realized as we start the twenty-first century.

## OVERALL TREND REVIEW

### Challenges and Pitfalls

- Overly aggressive expansion within the global market and thus creating risk to environmental and economic systems (especially local retailers).
- Labor unrest, cultural impasses, inconsistent approaches to leave, benefits, and pay.
- National clashes over trade, competitive markets, health standards, sweat shops, and so forth.
- Unequal and incompatible approaches to intellectual property, patents, copyrights, and trademarking.
- Inconsistencies with regard to privacy and security legislation and juridical decisions.
- Global deskilling of jobs, information overload, and megatraining.

### Opportunities

- More cost-effective access to global markets and lowering of consumer prices worldwide.
- Ability to ride the wave of global deregulation and competition to more fair, equitable, and open worldwide economic, scientific, and social environments.
- Ability to exploit advantages of an emerging global framework for provision of services under the protection of the WTO, World Intellectual Property Organization (WIPO), and other supranational entities.
- Advantage of entering markets primed for new competition.
- Global increases in and equalization of worker compensation.

# CHAPTER 9

# Race, Gender, and Bias in the World of Cyberbusiness

For every problem science solves, it creates ten new ones.
George Bernard Shaw

## COPING WITH THE NEW CYBERVALUES IN A COMPLEX WORLD

You have heard it dozens of times: "Technology is neutral. It is only its application that makes it good or bad. Technology by itself is without preference or prejudice." The truth is contemporary technological systems and their developers do have a preference—especially in the Western European and North American cultural settings. The subjective value system predominantly expressed by technology (and so-called left-side-of-the-brain thinking processes) is represented in the following chart.

| "Objective" or Technical Values | "Subjective" or Artistic Values |
| --- | --- |
| Large-Scale Economies | Small Scale, Individualistic |
| Cost Optimization, Streamlining, and Elimination of Redundancy | Esthetics, Redundancy, and Survival Margin |
| "Rational" | Nonstructured and Artistic |
| Left Side of the Brain | Right Side of the Brain |
| Symmetric | Asymmetric |
| Digital and Precise | Fuzzy and Fractal-like |

| | |
|---|---|
| Expressed in Linear Math Form | Expressed in Nonlinear Math, Fractals, and Complexity |
| Systematic and Repeatable | Nonsystematic and Random |
| Empirical or Deductive | Intuitive |
| Ever-Increasing Economic Efficiency | Ever-More-Creative Expression |
| High Tech | High Touch |

It may well be that some of the social values we express today are a reflection of biases that come with modern Western logic systems. Attempts to optimize economic growth over survival of our biosphere and to place math- and engineering-oriented solutions at a higher level than artistic answers could prove to be quite "wrongminded" approaches to life in the twenty-first century. As we increasingly live in an era of information services and service innovation we need to give increased value to sustainable environmental objectives. In short, we may need to devise new values and skills to live in the age of the World-Wide Mind.

The key to using technology effectively in the twenty-first century must be found in careful and thoughtful balance. It may well be that we have overdosed on left-side-of-the-brain values or actually misunderstood what we know to be the limitations of "logical thinking" or linear math. We may indeed have ignored the importance of right-side-of-the-brain values and misunderstood the value of "complexity" and fractal-based logic systems.

The questions are clear: Do current high-tech logic systems compel us not only toward digital solutions found in traditional linear mathematics, but also toward rigidly linear thinking and even intolerance of diversity? Have contemporary technology and management systems bent our social values and made us overly "digital" in our thought processes? That is to say, have we been conditioned by Western linear thinking processes to become overly rigid in our thinking about what is desirable and undesirable or right and wrong? Are there "technological edges" to sexism and racism that have been unwittingly supported by aggressive and unthinking employment of contemporary digital logic systems where they do not apply? When we pursue cost minimization and design efficiency what are the tradeoffs in terms of esthetics, "survival margin," and cultural diversity? A new tolerance in social values may encourage new flexibility and versatility that may be more appropriate to many new management and information-technology systems.

There may be more "right answers" (as in the right side of the brain) than we think. It may be best for our long-term survival and world peace to come down more often on the side of artistic values, fuzzy logic, and nonlinear thinking systems. There may be fallacies in believing that the left side of the brain is consistently correct. If there is a link-up between maleness and left-brain thinking and femaleness and right-brain thinking, we may find that sexism is not only wrongminded, but highly counterproductive in the new world of cyberspace and its effective management.

The bottom line may be that we should be listening more to so-called artistic or intuitive values and logic as we move from an industrial economy to an information economy. There is, for instance, mounting evidence that women make better infotechnology managers than men.

The idea that there is only one optimum or "ideal" digital solution to apply to any problem is a bankrupt thought. The twenty-first century may prove to be the "Age of Fuzzy Thought." Reducing complex issues to "right" and "wrong" options is overly simplistic. This has become clear as we have learned how to apply fuzzy logic systems, complexity, and fractals to solving problems of weather prediction, topology, stock-market trends, and smart transportation networks. Old-fashioned linear math may help us design the best combustion chamber for an automobile engine, but not the best computer programs for designing transportation or weather prediction systems.

Digital logic, math, and science comes down to us first from the philosophical speculations of Plato. It then trickled down to us from St. Augustine's theologies in the *City of God.* The idea that there is a single, immutable "ideal" solution to all issues is a brittle intellectual concept that is a flaw in Western thought. Fortunately this is not duplicated in Eastern enlightenment and thus we still have flexible ways of viewing the nature of the world and future possibilities. Idealism as applied to human thought systems was wrong when Plato thought of it 2,500 years ago. It was even more wrong when St. Augustine adapted it to religion. And it is still wrong today. As we learn more and more about nonlinear mathematics, chaos theory, and fractals, the more "fuzzy" ultimate answers seem to become.

If all possible solutions to a complex puzzle are contained within a space that could be visualized as an "answers cube," then Western philosophic thought suggests that the answers must be the "exact corners" of the cube. It is either soft or hard, wet or dry, right or wrong. The same rigidity does not apply to Asian philosophy. Today we can think beyond the confines of digital logic of traditional Western thought. We can use nonlinear math and fuzzy logic to suggest that shades of black, gray, and white provide a more complex and subtle answer. We can use the whole cube to provide solutions rather than just its corners. As fuzzy-logic guru Mark Kosko explains it, we need to explore complexity to find answers for a complex world. It is probably better to have an infinite number of solutions rather than just the eight corners of the Buddha's Cube as shown in Figure 9.1.

The application of fuzzy logic systems has proven highly effective in control systems for air conditioners to washing machines. These fuzzy controls have shown us that the "best" answer is one that adapts to a changing environment on a gradual and continuous basis. One single or ultimate answer does not apply to realities in a world that is usually nondigital and constantly changing in its options. If complexity and chaos gives the best answers for simple devices like air conditioners and washing machines, why not elsewhere as well?

**Figure 9.1**
**Fuzzy versus Non-Fuzzy Logic Systems: The Limited Options of Western Digital Logic Systems versus the Infinite Choices of the Buddha's Cube**

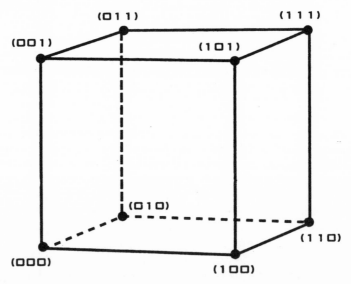

In Western logic there is the tendency to make all choices in the digital form of yes or no, on or off, positive or negative, or black or white. In Western thought, there are, using digital logic, only three decisions to be made among eight options as represented by the end points or corners of the cube. Within fuzzy logic systems all the available and infinite points within the cube serve as possible answers.

It may very well be true that the best solutions for problem solving and planning in human society can also be found in fuzzy rather than digital or hard-edge "idealistic" thinking. Black-and-white solutions and digital "on" or "off" answers may be wrong. They may, in fact, be as wrong in engineering as they are in cultural or social environments.

Studies of life's evolutionary patterns again show that nonlinear answers often seem to apply to both individual human intelligence and to society as a whole. If one looks at patterns of evolutionary change as being a dynamic numerical range where "one" represents virtually no change whatsoever and "five" means extremely rapid and chaotic change, then the formula of optimum evolution seems to be about "three." If change falls well below three then stagnation can lead to species extinction, and if it rises much above three then genetic chaos can also lead to extinction on the other end of the scale.

As we study the architecture of the brain further we find that too few or too many functioning pathways in the brain both lead to major problems. Again, the same kind of dynamic balance between too few and too many options seems to apply.

It is possible that many of the problems that have plagued Western society for literally thousands of years are a result of digital or "yes-versus-no" answers. Racism, sexism, religious bias, homophobia, and even discrimination based upon age, disabilities, or education are often founded upon the idea that there are fundamental rights and wrongs in society. This digital thinking system thus serves to divide the world into "holy" and "profane" and "superior" and "inferior."

The idealism that Plato and St. Augustine devised in fact has limited Western logic systems. It has reduced the infinite and constantly turbulent nature of the universe into simple questions of correct or not correct. Perhaps the pluralism of the Eastern philosophies of the Buddha may serve our future society somewhat better.

The fundamental message of George Orwell's *1984* was the potentially pernicious persuasive power of modern information networks. They not only can implant thoughts, perspectives, and values, but reduce them to almost childish "Newspeak" mottoes wherein virtually everything can be reduced to "good" and "un-good." In this horrific story, the ultimate instrument of control is to find each person's greatest fear or individual horror. From there it is possible through telehypnosis and video brainwashing to channel hatred along this key axis of individual frailty. If your greatest fear is rattlesnakes, your gender identity, or whatever, then your "hatreds" can be channeled and transferred by the "thought police" of Telepower tyrants to form an entire belief system.

On one hand this seems only a ridiculous fantasy. Yet in an age of technological complexity and information overload, is it undoubtedly true that more and more people are seeking simple answers. Fundamental religions, survivalists, and other simplifying formulas tell people how to employ natural beauty, internal auras, nudism, or pastel spandex to find their personal nirvanas. Is there a reason why we are seeing the rising popularity of horoscopes and astrology? One of the most popular uses of videotext systems and the Internet is to access horoscopes, and Dionne Warwick's Psychic Hotline is now making millions off of her phone-in astrological service. Why is there rapidly increasing attendance at evangelical churches and KKK rallies? Why have recent years seen the rising phenomena of extreme cultism, extreme conservatism within Islam, and the rise of neo-Nazis? Why have cult groups increasingly turned to terrorism, violence, and even mass suicide as a way of coping with their collective problems or at least perceived problems? Why are we continuing to experience rising backlash against women's liberation and minority recruitment programs? If an ever-increasing number of Web sites on the Internet pander to our worst prejudices of racism, sexism, pedophilia, or genocidal atrocities, what can or should we do about it?

Do these good-versus-bad thinking systems suggest a common theme? Is there indeed a global trend to reductionist, overly simplistic, and hate-filled thinking? Ironically, many of the organized groups using the most advanced satellite, computer, and CD-ROM distribution systems are employing them to convey the most simplistic, intolerant, and hateful right-versus-wrong messages. Ironically, it is here that the Christian Crusade, the KKK, and the American Nazi Party meet on a common cyberspace plane despite their greatly different messages.

In more and more cases these fundamentalistic religious, antigay, or bigoted groups are only a computer modem away from communicating with virtually anywhere else in the world. These groups are typified by ideologies that are most often steeped in a fundamental belief of "us" versus "them." These groups are very much based upon hating the digitally defined opposing group. They etch strong electronic images that define a group of the "desirable we" and an unwashed group of the "undesirable they." In short, it is really not a very long jump from sexism to racism, from religious intolerance to bigotry.

It is easy to get on the Net and find "cultural pornography." This is the most vile and hateful message of anti-Jewish and anti-Black neo-Nazi Klanners or dozens of other diverse cult groups based upon hatred, bigotry, and cultural bias. The speed, the reach, and the ease of access of our modern electronic networks often serve to amplify the spread and depth of cultural and social hatred.

Of course, it can also be much more subtle that simple racial bigotry. As reported in the Commission of the European Communities study *Eurofutures*, technological unemployment in Italy has led to some large layoffs in industrial areas. Here the we-versus-they bias has been directed from male workers toward female employees: "Women workers should be home with their families rather than taking jobs from men who really need them."

The power of the Internet can reinforce multivalue, interdisciplinary problem solving based on critical thinking skills, or it can magnify the worst of human bigotry. The Serbs can attack ethnic Albanians. The anti-abortionists can attack the clinics they oppose. Internet attacks on others can be anonymous, fast, easy, and low cost, and effortlessly reach a global audience. With sophisticated techniques of Web-page capture, spoofing, and other nefarious tricks, these Internet attacks can even reach an unsuspecting public audience.

Diagnosing the bigoted uses of cyberspace and noting the spread of undesirable applications is one thing. One estimate from the IDG group suggests that one-third to one-half of all Web sites are for pornography, gambling, or extreme social or political viewpoints. Solving this problem without impinging on the basic right of freedom of speech is quite another problem. It is perhaps easiest to note the least productive ways to proceed. Attempts at censorship, prohibition of hate groups, or definition of society morality will ultimately be destructive and lead to the same type of intolerant thinking that is essentially the core issue of concern. The key must be to create positive reinforcement of tolerance—in short, education.

Acceptance of the idea of diversity of opinion and alternative perspectives is critical. Intellectual tools that allow for clear thinking are not easily devised. Algorithms that allow for both clear comparative evaluation and fair cultural insights are even more challenging. Deep down, the "trick" to coping with a complex cybernetic world is to expose the poverty of digital thinking. The real world of the physical universe and the complexity of human society does not sharply and rigidly divide between rights and wrongs. To succeed in a fundamental and lasting way, learning in a cybernetic world must be carried out on an interdisciplinary and intercultural basis. Ethics cannot be digitized. The diversity of cyberspace and the rigidity of fundamentalism ultimately must be at odds with one another.

Educational programs (both public and industry based) in our evolving cybernetic world must confront and address a host of issues. They must confront the problems not only of bias, racism, sexism, and bigotry, but also the problems of ad hominem thinking, of absolutism, digital (or linear) thinking, and Western logic systems based exclusively on Boolean algebra. Rigid we-versus-they thinking gets us into trouble every time. Once one accepts gradient or gray-scale value systems, we can ascend beyond we-versus-they stereotypes. Once one accepts scaleable thought processes, then the futility of racism, sexism, and religious intolerance can follow. Cybernetic education and twenty-first-century logic systems must be able to connect the right and left sides of the brain. To realize the potential of our emerging global electronic network we must escape from the clutches of caveman clan mentality.

To evolve toward a planetary mentality and thus move toward the World-Wide Mind, we must escape from our past. We must escape from historical patterns of cultural bias and bigotry. These often come from the following:

- Instillation of racist, sexist, religious, and other biased values at childhood (this may be from parents, relatives, religious or ethnic community, etc.).
- Early social conditioning that separates values from critical logic and thus separates the left- and right-side functions of the brain.
- Little or no opportunity, especially at early ages, to have biases and intolerant views challenged by outside learning. Consider the cases of Kosovo, Serbia, Palestine, Bosnia, Iraq, Libya, Kashmir, and so on around the world. It is hard to escape social and cultural views that are steeped in inherited forms of bigotry and hatred of "other" peoples' ideas, races, or values that are inculcated in schools and other social institutions, as well as in the family.

One approach would be to enrich logic and thinking skills in both primary and secondary education (if not preschool). These logic exercises would be conducted in teams, with the students being challenged to solve complex problems that focus on ethics, religious tolerance, and philosophy. Further, such classes would explore the logic of digital versus infinitely variable decision-making systems. For instance, the Western tradition of a single precise answer versus the Eastern tradition of many competing solutions would be contrasted and compared.

This is but one example. There are dozens of others. Key examples of such diversity of thinking skills might include Paul and Percival Goodman's open-ended approach to urban planning and design in *Communitas*, a critical review and discussion of the Japanese play *Rashamon*, comparative religion classes, or political theory courses.

This may seem overly obscure and abstract. It really is not. The key "thinking-skill" objective would be to teach students how to reason. It would attempt on a synoptic basis to instill critical-thinking skills that transcend bias, bigotry, and religious intolerance. This new educational program carried out over the next thirty years would allow children and students to learn how to avoid ad hominem thinking. It will not be easy. Cultural and social education is always a political land mine. Yet the ability to evolve to higher thought processes and to devise a truly creative and powerful Internet for the twenty-first century may very well require such new approaches to educating our young. In short, if we do not attempt to address this issue we may find that the Internet becomes a major barrier to social, religious, and racial equality. Today, there are too many Internet Web sites devoted to the cause of racial injustice, to demeaning women's rights, to attacking gay rights, or to ultimately undermining world peace. The idea is not to instill the "right" values but to instill judgment. To succeed, such a program must aggressively demonstrate to students how to think, analyze, and reach informed value judgments. This may turn out to be the hardest task of all in distance education.

One does not lightly suggest that this problem of ad hominem thinking is growing in importance. The truth is, however, that the last twenty years has seen a downward trend in educational attainment and intellectual achievement. The pattern of non sequiturs and "emotional" decision making is everywhere. It can be seen in television commercials, where the use of logical presentation is in decline. It can also be seen in highly popular electronic and phone horoscopes. An occasional fortune cookie or a glance at a newspaper horoscope is one thing. When it becomes a multibillion-dollar business and controls peoples' lives it verges on becoming dangerous. The absurdity of the exploitation created by the Psychic Hotline once seemed a joke. Today, as it robs the poor and steers the actions of the weak, it seems more sinister.

From crackpot cults to New Age mysticism, it seems that modern society is coping with technological and societal complexity by means that are intellectually lazy, emotional, hateful, and selfish in their thinking. Modern educational systems around the world have for very good political and social reasons typically chosen the ostrichlike head-in-the-sand approach. Our current educational systems are just not working. We are not giving the right intellectual challenges and leadership to the generations of tomorrow to cope with the complexity of Telepower and Teleshock issues.

There is a fundamental need to revamp the educational system to force students to question, to challenge, and ultimately to think.

Some aspects of this educational reform to link critical thinking with more "objective" value formation can benefit from cyberspace technologies. One of the principal allies of intolerance is the separation of "us" and "them." This division must be dealt with so that biased opinions can be challenged. The use of all forms of communication, from e-mail to videoconferencing, from phone lines to interactive computer games, can help to break down the barriers.

Creative use of communications for learning about other people and societies can be quite powerful. Innovative programs such as Project Globe, which allows students around the world to talk about not only the weather but each other as well, are indicative of what can be done.

The use of new cyberspace techniques for intercultural understanding are only just now beginning to be explored. There is little doubt that something like universal and international e-mail connections, although this is still decades away, can help. We need to urge our leaders to develop a cultural cyberspace plan that acts to overcome hatred. It would be an integrated action agenda aimed at breaking down the barriers that separate races, ethnic groups, religion, and social sects in the community, the region, the nation, and indeed the global community.

Certainly one should not be naïve about the ease or speed with which success will come. The recent global experiences with racial and religious turmoil in terms of Israeli versus Palestinian, Bosnian versus Serb, tribal genocide in Rwanda, Tamil Tigers versus the Sinhalese in Sri Lanka, and even the racial tensions that surrounded the Rodney King and O. J. Simpson trials in the United States are not encouraging. The hope is in the use of cybereducation to instill critical-thinking skills in the young and to seek to overcome the poverty of tolerance that still affects the world.

Such progress will not be assured by the new tools of communications and education that cyberspace affords. As always, there is the flip side to how cyberspace could be used in a countercrusade to promote intolerance. It is incredibly easy for virtually anyone with a PC and modem to put wrong, scientifically incorrect, and emotionally charged slander and misinformation on the Net. Police in some jurisdictions are now allowing complaints and calls for assistance to be filed via the Internet.

The opportunity to file racist or hate-based erroneous crime reports with anonymity or even by "spoofing" your adversary's electronic identity is all too possible. The signaling and tracking capability known as caller ID makes the abuse of 911 much harder in the case of telephone calls. The decentralized, almost chaotic architecture of the Internet allows experienced hackers to hide or transfer their identities to others. It is, of course, possible to create with some ease (and little cost) multiple Web sites that spread messages of misinformation and hatred. These can be overt and obvious or disguised as to their intent and bigoted backers. There is no "truth in labeling" requirements on the Internet.

Certainly, every religious zealot, every hate group, and most entrenched power bases will see attempts to combine scientific, objective, or artistic values in education as an attempt to weaken morals. Fundamentalist religions in particular may see such "objective and multivalue" programs as a direct attack on their spiritual or cultural belief systems. If one assumes, however, that "God" directly or indirectly created humanity and allowed the human brain to evolve, then this seems a reasonable extension of "God's purpose." That is to say, a multivalued and critical-thinking approach to education has an internal or logical end: simply to let humanity achieve its intellectual potential.

## OVERCOMING TRIBAL AND RACIAL BIASES: REALIZING HUMANITY'S DESTINY?

Scholars of chaos theory and nonlinear math have tried to create a computer-based simulation of "artificial life" at a breakthrough institute in New Mexico. This is the Santa Fe Institute, where some of our brightest scholars, including several Nobel laureates, have taken up residence to ponder the implications of the new math, complexity, and fractals. Such a simulation should show us not only how life and intelligent beings might evolve, but also how civilization and moral thought might evolve in the twenty-first century. So far, evolutionary patterns shown in artificial life suggest that the "moral" and the "fair" approach to interspecies and intraspecies interaction is the most successful strategy. If so, there may indeed be a "natural morality" embedded or "wired" into intelligent lifeforms.

Certainly the findings of Nobel laureate researchers and their exotic colleagues at the Santa Fe Institute in trendy New Mexico are truly fascinating. They have worked in interdisciplinary teams, combining computer system analysts, mathematicians, biologists, economists, and physicists, to make some amazing discoveries. They are able to simulate and "visualize" patterns that characterize the evolution of life from the most basic organic molecule to higher forms. Recently they have seemingly discovered a "fourth root" law that explains why all mammals from mice to elephants live a billion heartbeats. Larger beings with more efficient circulatory systems and much slower heartbeat rates can live years longer. It could be that these basic laws of nature apply to plant life as well.

This collection of scientists and computer specialists has essentially developed a formula for the "life force." This formula expresses (just as Schrödinger's equation states the form of the hydrogen atom) the process that allows life to evolve. This nonlinear math simulation of the life force indicates that at every level of evolution the patterns of development are similar, equally chaotic, repeatable, and reflect an architecture that looks like the fractal chains generated from nonlinear equations on our computer screens. The chain of life, according to Santa Fe Institute theorists, consistently follows nonlinear formulas. The life force began with replicating biocarbonate molecular structures that then became single-cell organisms and then multiple-cell organisms, and so on up to humanity.

These same nonlinear formulas also depict a pattern of ever-more integrated complex systems. These fractal-like evolution patterns thus predict that the process of evolution does not stop with multi-cell, thinking mammals, but continues. Its "life-force formula" could be used to project the gradual development of clans, towns, cities, nations, a world society, and perhaps interstellar civilizations. There seems to be a real possibility of life having evolved on other planets. The 4-billion-year-old fossil remains of maggots from Mars, as found in rocks discovered in the Antarctic, has fueled our latest desire to go to explore the red planet in depth. Thus, the idea of life force—the idea that intelligent life and critical-thinking skills span galaxies—cannot be ruled out.

This may seem a stretch to some, but the conclusion can be reached from studying these life-force nonlinear formulas that humanity must overcome illogical thinking and cultural intolerance to evolve to the next stage of human development. The elimination of illiteracy, racism, sexism, religious intolerance, and political and social bigotry has been argued for decades as something we should do.

The findings of scholars studying artificial life and the formula of organic evolution, however, suggest this may be something we must do. This is still very speculative and theoretical. Yet there is increasing mathematical evidence that the future of homo sapiens is charted by the life-force formula. In order to achieve the next step of an integrated global social, economic, and political organism we must overcome primary barriers to advancement: bigotry, hatred, and all of the noxious "isms." The evolution toward the Global Village and then the World-Wide Mind may be actually "wired" into our genes and chromosomes.

For many centuries we have seen humanity ravaged by human slavery, the Spanish Inquisition, the Nazi holocaust, and so forth. Is it not time that we recognize that our aspirations to become a humane, just, and peaceful global society have fallen quite short? As with the Apollo 13 mission, "We have a problem." Yet we do not have a mission control center in Houston to call for helpful instructions.

The thought that higher levels of scientific knowledge, improved education, and objective forms of problem solving can also elevate us to a higher moral plane where avarice, discrimination, warfare, and bigotry fade away has to date unfortunately proven illusory. Objective and scientific knowledge does not make humanity better. The need to rely more on our artistic, intuitive, and left-brain skills may be a new and productive path to follow. Certainly, new evidence derived from fuzzy logic systems and nonlinear math now strongly suggests this is a productive path to pursue.

It is in our grasp to use new education and learning tools to address the problems of racism, sexism, religious bigotry, and discriminatory biases of all types. Why does it seem so impossible to do so in what we pretend is an enlightened and educated high-tech society? Why will hate and intolerance be such hard opponents to address and vanquish by the time the twenty-first century is complete? Are we masters of our fate or doomed to a predetermined destiny? If we do control our future, is it not time to act that way? The twenty-first century may be our last chance to succeed.

## OVERALL TREND REVIEW

### Challenges and Pitfalls

- Racial and gender biases retard and distort worker and management efficiency.
- Pink-collar bias and technological unemployment don't mix.
- Unintended reinforcement of hatred and social intolerance on the Internet.
- Continued exponential spread of pornography, gambling, racist, and similar sites on the Internet without a responsible educational and social response.

### Opportunities

- Broadbased primary education and worker education and training to overcome bias and prejudice will be increasingly important.
- Application of nonlinear math and fuzzy logic systems to management and discriminatory patterns of behavior can provide new insights and progress.
- The Internet can become a key element in developing new approaches to social justice by integrating it into early educational processes.
- A century-long cyberspace cultural plan.

# CHAPTER 10

# Education for the Age of the World-Wide Mind

There is only one good, knowledge, and only one evil, ignorance.
Socrates (469–399 B.C.)

## IF SCHOOLS AND UNIVERSITIES WERE BUSINESSES, THEY WOULD BE BANKRUPT

If *Homo sapiens* survives the twenty-first century, it may well be because he has finally learned how to learn. To date the scorecard for significant reform of late twentieth-century educational and professional training programs in the United States and abroad is dismal. Test scores continue to decline. Functional illiteracy is increasing on a global basis.

If cyberbusiness is to succeed and if the World-Wide Mind is to represent a "livable and rewarding" environment for humanity, education is where to start. Everyone will have to become proactively involved in developing better educational and training programs for the twenty-first century. Cyberbusiness and infotechnology enterprises will run on the minds of intelligent and well-trained workers—or not at all. This is a problem. If we are to believe outspoken social and education critics such as Lew Perlman (the author of *School's Out*), we are running on the reserve tank of intellectual capital. Currently, 17 percent of U.S. citizenry is functionally illiterate and the numbers are headed up, not down. The numbers for Japan and Korea are headed down.

A few people and some institutions and companies have caught on to some new ideas and are developing improved ways of learning. Unfortunately, these are the exceptions to the rule. The mainstream primary and secondary educational programs, the mainstream university programs, and the mainstream corporate training programs are largely headed in the wrong direction. The move to private vouchers for private schools is gathering support because many parents perceive that public education is declining rather than improving.

The noble traditions of higher education have been etched in stone for over a thousand years, but unfortunately the university of that tradition is better suited to the second and first millennia than the third. Everywhere across this six-sextillion-ton mudball we call Earth there are new educational and training possibilities open to us. They are largely being squandered. We are increasingly acquiring the right to plug into a global knowledge base that is based on worldwide humanistic and ecological values. Yet education and learning are in general not improving. Why not?

The creative and productive learning experience for the new millennium needs to be lifelong, self-directed, interactive, multidisciplinary, and self-paced—yet with team-based opportunities and even become enjoyable. Using the worst of our capabilities, it has great potential to be pornographic, idiotic, racist, and mindless.

Education in the age of the World-Wide Mind can be the best of times and the worst of times. Without any centralized quality control or obligation to be up to date or correct, the Internet is the "virtual anything for everybody network." It is the ultimate antithesis of the tabula rasa. It is a torrential gusher of information for creativity, plagiarism, and stolid "groupthink." Seldom in the history of our species have we invented a tool that can lift one's aspirations and knowledge to such heights and at the same instant mire someone else's intellect in the mud so thoroughly. We have to understand and exploit the enormous educational opportunity of the Internet and recognize the damage that mindless acceptance, copying, and application of information from the Internet can bring over the next twenty years. It is not a panacea but only another tool—at once of great potential and subject to dangerous abuse.

The key to this new environment is what may be called "network learning." This new approach to education depends more on fresh educational concepts than on the Internet or new digital-technology tools or software. It depends on the ability to achieve global sharing, to engage in both experiential and lifelong learning, and ten other basic reforms set forth later in the chapter. The key is to exploit and harness the power of on-line and interactive learning and multidisciplinary team synergies, and creating new educational systems for a new millennium. The single most important point is to create a clear and challenging framework within which learning can occur. Some reality checks need to be built into current educational practices to determine what is and what is not working.

The corporate world of cyberbusiness will have a large stake in this transformation, because if this dramatic change is not achieved there will be major failures among the info-enterprises. Critical workforce capabilities will not be available. The smart corporations of the twenty-first century will crumble or at least wither if a cyberliterate and well-educated workforce is largely absent. Already these corporations are borrowing intellectual capital by hiring cyberworkers from India, Pakistan, Korea, Russia, and elsewhere around the world.

Our educational institutions, our methods of teaching and learning, and especially our universities today appear ill-suited to their assigned tasks. Professor Eli Noam of Columbia University sums up the dilemma quite well in an article entitled, "The Dim Future of the University." Michael Saylor, the multibillionaire-founder of Micro Strategy, Inc., in March 2000 pledged $100 million to launch a "free-to-all" Cyber University. He is actually seeking to implement a twenty-first-century version of an idea that has many intellectual proponents that date back more than twenty years. Tele-education pioneers such as former BBC Education Secretary Jim Stevenson, CNN executive Sidney Pike, Japanese communications official Takashi Iida, Indian space leader Yash Pal, public television executive Lynn Fontana, Cook Islander and Peacesat advocate Stuart Kingan, relentless tele-education crusader Tak Utsumi, and Sir Arthur C. Clarke are just a few of those who have championed the idea of quality satellite and electronic education systems since the 1970s.

## BASIC CONCEPTS OF LEARNING

It is now nearly 2,500 years since the age of Socrates, Plato, and Aristotle. Since that time we have created rocket ships, biotechnology, genetic engineering, lasers, radio astronomy, nonlinear math, chaos theory, satellites, supercomputers, bungee jumping, spandex, talk-show television, and artificial intelligence.

Most of these innovations we would view as progress. But what about our educational process? Two-and-a-half millennia later we are putting students in a classroom with a presumably knowledgeable authority figure in front to teach. This person's defined job is to lecture or pose questions to the students for prescribed periods of time. This we call education.

Education in the United States and many other countries has been reduced to well-known but essentially effete formulas. We typically equate "education" in colleges and universities to completion of set "jail sentences." A three-credit-hour course is equivalent to "doing time" for some forty-five contact hours mandated by accrediting organizations. The teacher serves as the warden, while education is the punishment quantitatively measured by the time spent in the classroom or "cell." Seldom in the current formula for education is the idea put forth of measuring education on the basis of retained knowledge and actually acquired skills. Why is it so hard to accept that cyberlearning is best when a person is actually acquiring and applying new knowledge rather than being a passive listener? Glenn Jones, founder of Jones Intercable and the Mind Extension University, kindly acknowledges that my book *Global Talk* (1981) inspired him to try to create a dynamic new form of electronic learning systems. This was hard to do in the 1980s but is now increasingly possible.

In the old educational model, the swift and slow learners seemingly acquire the same amount of learning or knowledge by exposure to a more or less equal amount or quantum of information. We certainly have laboratory and design courses, and there are indeed some research activities associated with theses and dissertations. Except for a few modest testing mechanisms called Graduate Record Exams, LSATs, GMATs, we end up having little to go on to test acquired knowledge. It is actually difficult to find out exactly what a college graduate or a high school student has really learned from these standardized tests. Amazingly, when we have subjected high school teachers to basic competency tests in several states in the United States, one-third or more of them fail. The standards for some education degrees at some teachers' colleges are shockingly low.

Most college students with four years of residency within the halls of ivy are simply "more ripened" rather than necessarily "more learned." The "educated student" presumably emerges with adept reasoning abilities and a great deal of acquired knowledge. But very little in the current educational process guarantees that this will actually happen.

Some, such as Lewis Perlman, author of *School's Out*, would say that the modern, prepackaged, and standardized schooling process of the late twentieth century, which we call "formal" (as in straitjacketed and overly prescribed) education, is about 90-percent wrongminded. Perlman suggests that the predominant educational paradigms in the United States are intellectually bankrupt and highly cost inefficient to boot. Furthermore, Perlman would argue that the rest of the OECD countries are really not much better off when it comes to effective educational systems. A test of "functional literacy" measures ability to read basic instructions, perform simple math, use a map, or follow the plot of a graph or soap opera. UNESCO tests show that "functional literacy" stands at some 4 to 5 percent of the population in Japan and perhaps over 17 percent in the United States.

The problem with education is certainly not the ancient Greek scholars. They were innovators who were actively experimenting with the latest in learning technology. In a historical sense, the problem could probably be best laid at the feet of Saint Augustine. In the *City of God* he began by applying Plato's idealism to theology. He then also borrowed some from medieval scholars Ambrose and Gregory and came up with Divine Law. Presto—we had the form and structure of medieval intellectual thought. Within this framework, for better or worse, were born the medieval universities. This framework was rigid, woefully rigid, and it is time we get it off our backs.

The key was that the teacher had a monopoly on the right knowledge and the tutelage of the student was highly controlled. The student had to learn the correct or "ideal" knowledge. Most important, he or she (albeit precious few of the female gender were involved) must not learn the "incorrect" lessons. The student must not be allowed to think or learn "outside-of-the-box" thoughts, certainly in terms of religious orthodoxy, but a rigid intellectual orthodoxy as well. The basic idea in education for the last two thousand years has been that knowledge is defined from above. In this model wisdom must be stored in vats or bins and poured out in measured quantities. This elitist model of education with the teacher as the storer and dispenser of knowledge has survived in a very resilient way for a very long time. It has been quite a few centuries since St. Augustine told us the way to think, to pray, and to teach the uninitiated student. It is time for a change.

The current course of events in U.S. education is not likely to be effectively reformed in the near term or even the longer term. Nevertheless, the idea that the Internet can largely substitute for a complete educational system is no more plausible than to say that libraries or museums can substitute for a complete learning system. There are no simple answers here. The Cyber University is only a partial answer.

## WHAT IS THE SCOPE AND NATURE OF PROBLEM IN GLOBAL EDUCATIONAL REFORM?

The challenge of reforming, improving, and extending quality education and training to a global population is huge. The number of people to be educated in the next half century is much greater than all of the humans to be instructed since the beginning of human history. U.N. studies suggest that this is not only so, but by a large margin of a billion students or more (see Bibliography).

Nevertheless, educational reform is possible. Further, it is possible to address the needs of 2 billion people (out of our global population of 6 billion) that now have inadequate or no schooling, health care, or electrical power. The main issue to attack is not the obvious targets. Clearly we need better and more up-to-date educational materials and more and better-trained teachers. It is, however, institutional barriers and traditional images of education that are the largest roadblocks to reform. Using new networking technology and software is another key component. In essence it is the current structures, paradigms, and objectives of schools and universities that are the biggest obstacle to progress. Here are ten reforms for serious consideration.

Global reform of education to overcome the constraints of the medieval educational model and to extend adaptive learning systems throughout the planet is comparable to such human undertakings as the Apollo Moon Project, the Great Wall of China, or the Great Pyramid of Egypt. In this case the materials we must work with are not stone and steel and construction plans. Here we must work with people's minds, educational philosophies, historically formed values and biases, and just a touch of "intellectual snobbery." The following is a list of some of the problems that educational reform needs to address:

- Lack of self-paced learning systems and databases that augment "fixed-course" lectures and text materials.
- Lack of opportunity for independent learning and self-paced instruction.
- Absence of experiential or hands-on design exercises and problem-solving assignments to develop critical thinking and writing skills, especially within teams.
- Discouragement rather than encouragement of interdisciplinary and multidisciplinary learning exercises.
- Absence of processes to learn information acquisition and "screening" skills and ways of knowing when information may be incorrect or out-of-date.
- Few mechanisms to distribute high-quality information and educational programs through global satellite, fiber, the Internet, or other electronic networks that are culturally and linguistically "transparent" to students.
- Such high-tech distribution mechanisms now available for tele-education are typically based on content developed externally rather than by local educators.
- Few systematic requirements for education and skill sets to be periodically updated and modernized. More than just doctors, nurses, and engineers need to be recertified on a scheduled basis.

- Little recognition of the need for life-long learning and new-skill acquisition.
- Creation of a system to measure actual learning that is better than hours of incarceration. The current awarding of grades and degrees and the active disincentives for team learning all need to be rethought.
- The need to develop, in a period of increasing global prosperity, new methods of appraising the cost of providing education versus not providing education to everyone on our planet (e.g., population growth, spread of disease, etc.).
- Dangers of megatraining that can derive from automated learning or abuses of new tele-education techniques.

## TEN STEPS TO REINVENTING
## TWENTY-FIRST-CENTURY EDUCATION

The following ten steps are immodestly proposed to transform and revitalize global education and especially higher education and research in the twenty-first century. This is a blueprint that would allow us to address the problems mentioned and some possible approaches to reforms.

This new blueprint would allow us to educate more people more effectively by releasing the learning capacity of every individual. It would also allow us to exploit the power of team learning and interactive critical thinking. Amazingly, it can all be done with a potential savings of money if longer-term social and resource costs are considered. To accomplish all this does, however, require that we reinvent our schools and universities, institute life-long adaptive learning, and recognize that the status quo is the enemy of effective twenty-first-century education. Just as we should build "smart" buildings and cities and then measure life-cycle costs, we need to create "smart" education systems and then measure life-cycle costs of our planet.

### Reform 1: Deregulate Education and Stimulate Competitive Systems at the Institutional Level

Many would say they do not see the problem. They would say that there are both private and public schools and many different types of institutions ranging from community colleges to elite universities. This seemingly open and dynamic process, however, masks a number of problems. If education systems are working well, why do major corporations in the United States spend more on their training and learning programs (and even their own universities, in the cases of Andersen Consulting, IBM, Motorola, etc.) than is spent on higher education? Why, if one examines the research awards of U.S. federal agencies such as the annual reports of the

National Science Foundation (NSF), does one find that about 90 percent of major research awards are renewals of existing and previously funded R&D projects? Why does one also find that of the new research awards the great majority are to universities and institutions already with ongoing work? New research awards to new institutions are thus typically under 3 percent of the total. Why do we find that groundbreaking and truly innovative new ways of learning do not come from the "establishment"? We see high-cost and research-oriented education stemming from the elite. Yet new paradigms of learning and especially breakthroughs in tele-education, cyberspace interaction, life-long learning, and adaptive or experiential education seldom seem to come from the top of the hierarchy of prestigious learning centers, although Stanford University could be deemed a notable exception.

To be blunt, there are few incentives and a lot of disincentives for the elite educational institutions to reinvent themselves. This is true around the world. It does not matter whether one considers the University of Tokyo, or Harvard, or Yale, or the Sorbonne, or Oxford, or Cambridge. Large endowments, large campuses, and sprawling research labs at major universities around the world are based on hierarchical tiers and the accumulation of academic wealth at the top. Most educational systems of the world, to use an economic theory as an analogy, are based on "trickle-down."

Thus it is not surprising that new models and paradigms of learning seem to emerge not from the elite but from new and experimental groups. We see the main source of innovation coming from groups and institutions such as the National Technological University, the Open Universities, EUROPACE, TV Ontario, KNOW, the Mind Extension University, the University of Phoenix, and Internet-based educational programs. Michael Saylor's Cyber University is seen as a threat rather than an opportunity to many.

No one would deny that in the United States and many other countries there is what might be called an educational establishment that is based on a hierarchy of institutions. Although the evidence is anecdotal, the ability to evolve new twenty-first-century educational programs from the status quo seems in doubt. The size of the endowments and levels of prestige of universities is seemingly inversely proportional to the perceived need to reform educational process.

The prestigious universities have certainly not been recent leaders in deploying new educational processes in such areas as tele-education, interactive CD-ROM learning systems, educational networking, life-long learning, TQM, or quality learning techniques, and so forth. The recent trend is to have the academic president assume the role of "ceremonial leader and administrator," with the prime responsibility being that of chief fundraiser, rather than being the intellectual leader and top scholar. This trend seems very likely to perpetuate rather than reverse itself.

Nothing could do more to spur new innovations in education and university research than new and vital competition from new sources. Withdrawing the sense of complacency from the elite university establishment could trigger major changes. This should be encouraged through the following:

- New financial incentives and awards.
- New competition for public resources from a host of new educational players.
- New emphasis on networking and cyberspace technologies.
- New approaches to quality tele-education through sponsored competions.
- Creation of a level playing field for educational competition and research awards.
- Corporate-based educational systems being encouraged to compete with university teaching and research methods, with the results appearing on network TV and the Internet.

### Reform 2: Instill Concepts of Teamwork, Critical Thinking, and Continual Learning at the Student Level

If universities and especially elite universities are not challenged by competition to innovate more rapidly, the students of these institutions may be hampered by outmoded concepts of education. Most educational systems today create barriers to team-based learning. In most aspects of modern industrial and service industries, teamwork is critical to success. Modern management concepts of Total Quality Management or Time-Based Management emphasize teamwork, communication, and efficient administrative practices (such practices are seldom observable within universities).

The crux of improved performance, innovation, and better results in education is likely to depend on improved communications, interactive learning, and critical analysis. At the root of these are teamwork, whether in a classroom or on an interactive network. Ironically, competition among academic and learning centers to develop new learning programs might actually foster better teamwork among students.

There are a host of barriers to improved learning within schools, colleges, and universities. These include an absence of creative teamwork, an emphasis on rote memorization rather than problem solving, the confusion between "sitting in classrooms" and "learning," and a lack of critical-thinking exercises. Further, there are problems with not viewing education as a life-long and continuing exercise in a time of explosive information growth. Simply put, education of the future must emphasize learning how to learn. Adaptive learning and critical thinking are key to educating people for an environment wherein information grows 200,000 to 1 million times faster than human population. My estimate is that the global information base will be doubling every three years by 2005 and maybe every year by 2010.

The world's best educators need to work on new computer software, on new interactive CD-ROMs, and on Internet-based systems to develop new interactive systems to teach critical thinking, life-long learning, and teaming skills. These, of course, need to be reinforced in classroom exercises and interpersonal activities, but the same activities can also be accomplished on cyberspace networks.

### Reform 3: Experiment with New Global Educational Systems Such as Interdisciplinary and Multidisciplinary Centers of Excellence

As the world's information expands exponentially, global access to all information within the human knowledge system can but erode. Since the time of ancient Greece the accumulated information of our world has increased an estimated 10 million times. Within the next century it will likely increase another 20 million times. We will use intelligent agents and "knobots" to acquire and filter information for us as the scope of global data systems expand beyond our individual brain processing capabilities. Some believe that this can only mean ever higher levels of specialization and the death of the concept of a Renaissance person.

Others are concerned about the runaway growth of "passive information," which is on an exponential growth curve. This is the unwanted junk information that is spewed at us, from advertisements and infomercials to useless factoids. Passive information, as first defined by Yasumasa Tanaka of Japan, will make it increasingly difficult to get "active" information that we really want. Indeed, some fear, perhaps with good reason, that the Internet, much like British Telecom's ill-fated Prestel service, will ultimately break down under the weight of too much passive information unless some form of control is developed. (In this respect, commercial software developers who build high-quality and accurate databases on the Internet may prove to be its saviors.) The price, however, is unrelenting commercialism and a lack of educational and cultural goals.

The fear of massive growth of information systems is a real concern in terms of how humans individually cope with growing "information overload." Organizations like Oracle, IBM, and Microsoft are now routinely supporting so-called terabyte data systems.

One education strategy that can perhaps cope with information overload is that of using interdisciplinary teams. This educational strategy for the age of the World-Wide Mind allows for comprehensive learning and research in the best tradition of Renaissance thinking. In basic concept, it is the new small, interactive, networked, and interdisciplinary university or school that has both focus and multidisciplinary team participation. One specific example is that of the International Space University (ISU) with a central hub campus in Strasbourg, France, and another two dozen interactive or satellite campuses linked up electronically around the world. Within the umbrella of outer-space studies and research, the following disciplines are explored: space engineering and propulsion, life sciences, policy and law, the humanities, space applications, space physical sciences and astrophysics, manufacturing, resources and robotics, information sciences, and business and economics. The students and faculty of the ISU work in teams, conduct interdisciplinary design studies, and even contemplate future space missions through electronic ganglia of collaboration. These students and faculty create an early twenty-first-century approximation of a "interdisciplinary and multidisciplinary interactive brain" focused on space exploration, application, and research. If individuals cannot know everything as individuals, then sophisticated teams of people can interact to create better solutions by pooling their knowledge and experience. Such institutions would seem to need the right scale. If these institutions grow overly large, the "collective brain" concept will tend to break down. The ISU, for instance, has capped its summer study programs at around 100 students and it then divides the students into two design study teams. A new and parallel project, devoted to interactive and interdisciplinary problem-solving projects that are to be carried out on a global scale, is the new global virtual research project at the Arthur C. Clarke Institute for Telecommunications and Information (CITI). The seeds of a World-Wide Mind are thus being planted around the world.

### Reform 4: We Need New Ways of Keeping Score in Education— Credit Hours and Degrees Are Increasingly Passé

Possibly the worst invention in education is individual achievement grades, and a close second is the idea of a permanent award of advanced academic degrees. In many fields an advanced degree is often out of date in a matter of five to ten years. Soon it may be only two or three years. Students who cram for exams and make good grades often actually retain little of what they learn. Some of the best entrepreneurs and businesspeople did poorly in their academic programs. Those in a course of study who are asked to solve problems in a hands-on and experiential format usually retain more knowledge than those who are asked to recall facts for an exam. Experts with narrowly focused Ph.D.s are often poor at overall analysis and synoptic reviews aimed at system optimization. The challenge here is as much for instructors as it is for students.

The gap between real-world "smarts" and academic programs seems to have grown, particularly in theoretical and research-oriented studies. The idea of increasing specialization and the awarding of degrees in ever-narrowing areas of expertise ultimately seems self-defeating. Massive computer databases and expert programs are better specialists than humans. The key is to recognize that data storage and thinking and synthesis of knowledge are two quite separate skills. Every educator should read the book *Godel, Escher, Bach* (Hofstadter 1980) at least once before devising a course for twenty-first-century students.

Our smart machines equipped with artificial intelligence, expert systems, and ever-greater memory banks are well suited to become the "quasi-Ph.D." experts of the twenty-first century. In terms of retrieving ever-greater amounts of specialized information in a particular area, it is hard to see how humans will compete effectively with seventh- and eighth-generation computers. It is on the reasoning, judgment, and critical-analysis scale and the ability to make connections that humans still seem to have an edge. It seems that more Ph.D.s specializing in eighteenth-century Boston architecture or migratory habits of Australian wombats is really not the answer. Instead, we need to have more rigorous and challenging multidisciplinary and interdisciplinary studies, while reinvigorating our current disciplines as well.

It also seems that team-based design studies, critical thinking, and problem-solving skills sessions based on actual or simulated experience would teach more. If such exercises were to be carried out as group competitions under real-time constraints this might result in higher levels of learning than midterm exams. The truth is that the forms, structures, and processes of education have been built up over many centuries and well-established traditions are often hard to question and even harder to change.

### Reform 5: Reinvent Academic Research and Especially Reform the "Publish or Perish" Paradigm

One of the more powerful reasons that higher education is hard to change is that the current academic process feeds a large research-and-development complex. The most prestigious and largest research universities are locked into a system that is self-sustaining. Masters-level teaching and research assistants, Ph.D. candidates, professors, government research agencies, and even industry have created an "industry" of specialized information generation that has less and less to do with the instructional process.

Ironically, this process has become increasingly like navel contemplation worthy of a Marcel Proust novel. A study sponsored by the *Chronicle of Higher Education* of research monographs, academic journals, and in-depth studies has shown that the average number of references to academic publications has decreased from over five times per article or publication to well under one. Self-citations are increasingly the most common of practices. The Ph.D.s of tomorrow stand in danger of knowing what they know and sharing this information with their computers and perhaps one or two other colleagues.

Again, the problem is more apparent than the solution. Clearly, interdisciplinary and multidisciplinary research programs can and will be part of the answer. A system of life-long learning and recertification of one's academic capabilities may also become necessary. Training and certification may challenge the prestige and importance of college degrees. Colleges and universities may reinvent themselves to offer a wider panoply of courses in a wider range of formats. Meanwhile, commercial establishments may well intrude into areas of instruction and learning that colleges and universities have considered their exclusive preserve. Such competition, if constructively structured to adopt the best results from all programs, could well be highly productive. Educational programs around the world have for too long not been adequately challenged to innovate and improve.

### Reform 6: Emphasize Experiential Learning and Rethink the Classroom Lecture as a Measure of Acquired Knowledge

An ancient Chinese proverb explains that there are three basic ways to learn. These are to hear, to see, and to do. Of these three, the "doing" is the educational process that truly works. There is truth to the joke about the instructor who drones on about fishing and does not let the student experience how to troll. Experiential learning is the fundamental challenge to cyberspace learning. Innovative commercial educational programs such as the Mind Extension University have concluded that a mixture of videotapes, readings, interactions with CD-ROMS or Internet Web sites, and e-mail chat groups can teach more than a lecturer in a classroom. Students can learn better, faster, and at their own pace with cyberspace learning systems. Educational labs and interactive Web sites are essential tools for the future.

These electronic learning systems can be used not only in OECD countries but also around the world. If current cumulative aggregate growth rates (CAGRs) in Internet use continue in the developing world (i.e., 87% per year in Africa, 110% per year in Asia, and 125% per year in South America), the potential of cyberspace-based interactive learning can become enormous by 2050.

### Reform 7: Exploit the Best New Educational Technologies and Applications

The new information and network technologies and applications on the horizon are impressive. These include such capabilities as the electronic tutor and smart and interactive satellite and local wireless loop networks. There are also such ideas as the Internet-lite personal terminal for under $100, and interactive multimedia educational systems that operate both in the classroom and at a distance. The electronic tutor has the potential to become a global mass-consumption product that could rival the personal computer in sales volume. The key to developing this user-friendly, satellite-accessible, dense memory storage, and simple computing system may well be through the advent of the electronic newspaper. Such a device developed for twenty-first-century distributions of newspapers and magazines could easily be adapted to the distance-education market as well.

The prototype for the so-called electronic tutor may well be the stripped-down computer designed for the purpose of providing low-cost Internet access. The so-called Internet-lite line of World Wide Web access devices was introduced in 1996 at a market price of about $500. The latest versions are now under $100. Add some more memory and upgrade the disc drive and the electronic tutor is largely invented. A classroom model only needs to add interactive connections with satellite and local loop wireless communications systems. In many villages solar-cell electric power and light technology will also need to be added, but this is increasingly economic for even very poor countries. Annual reports of the Solar Electric Light Foundation (SELF) indicate that this can be accomplished for nearly the same cost as candles.

The true key to cyberspace education is the Internet of today and the Internet of tomorrow that will inevitably follow. The Internet is indeed a very powerful and flexible teaching tool. Why upgrade and retrofit CD-ROMs when you can put the same information on the Internet and update it as you like? Why build huge computing power into terminal devices at high cost when you can get computing power, high-speed simulations, and much more on the Internet? The problem, of course, is to get low-cost T-1 access to the Internet. This can and will come. Time-Warner has started to offer T-1 service (1.5 megabits per second) on an operational basis in selected parts of the United States at a rate near $25 per month. The broadband Internet 2 system that now links only U.S. research institutes will expand to embrace more and more consumers.

Other options will be interactive satellites with narrow-band return channels and even exotic High Altitude Long Endurance (HALE) platforms or Unattended Autonomous Vehicles. These systems could in theory provide very broadband educational and broadcast services from eighteen- to twenty-one-kilometer-high robot airplane radio platforms. The cost of such platforms can be much lower than satellites, even though the maximum coverage would be for countries the size of Taiwan or South Korea.

Certainly within a decade there will be a host of new cyberspace technologies and applications that will make conventional universities look somewhere between stodgy and archaic by comparison. Many of today's endangered universities need crash courses on the new technologies and perhaps even more so on interactive multimedia applications. Under Eli Noam and Lewis Perlman, I do have faith that creative changes will ultimately occur and that the reconstituted university will still endure.

### Reform 8: Beware the Danger of Megatraining

Some are greatly impressed by Internet chat groups, World Wide Web information centers, interactive CD-ROM discs, direct-broadcast educational systems, and the other trappings of modern electronic educational systems. Some zealots, like Lewis Perlman, suggest that we should shut down the schools and universities and just let the new technology do the teaching. Certainly, automated training systems such as those developed by the innovative IXION corporation of Seattle suggest that remarkably effective personal and interactive training systems can be developed. These systems are best for repetitive processes, whether it is for mass training in CPR techniques or for doctors to practice surgical operations.

Many large corporations are more inclined to invest in automated training systems than in public education and universities. There is great danger concealed here. A system that trains by rote and repetition and does not provide underlying knowledge and understanding of the overall field is dangerous. What might be called "megatraining," as opposed to tele-education, is dangerous to democratic processes, self-esteem, and longer-term commitment to corporate success. It creates the agenda of "deskilling," corporate indifference, and insensitivity upon which new types of service-based labor unions might well be built. It helps to separate production from consumption to the extent that no one cares about their job or quality.

In short, our new technologies contain the ability to educate rather than to megatrain, but abuse of these capabilities is quite possible. It would be unwise for large corporations pursuing short-term profits to contemplate the idea of training employees for narrow niches or job-specific skills. The image of what might follow has been provided in the frightening images of the future as offered by Kurt Vonnegut, Jr. in *Player Piano*.

### Reform 9: Higher Education Offerings Need to be Relevant to Current Societal Needs and Not Just Academic Standards of the Past

If any modern enterprise looks to the future through a rearview mirror it is higher education. Many university educators are proud of the fact that they are among the oldest, the most stable, and the most unchanged institutions in the world. Each time new fields of study or fundamental concepts (such as nonlinear math and fractals) emerge, there is an almost ritualistic process whereby the newcomer discipline is viewed with contempt, then skepticism, then begrudging acceptance, and finally anointed by the "true believers" who only "pretended" to be skeptics. Computer sciences represent such a newcomer that took some forty years to complete this tortuous path of obeisance, homage, atonement, and enlightenment.

If anything, cyberspace-based education will serve to change a great deal about the academic process within schools, colleges, and universities. Institutions that ignore social relevance, avoid new technologies and applications, and neglect the power of educational networking will find that their base of support will erode. The elite universities that do not see the warning signs will begin to fade away.

Only if public action is taken to restructure and shake up the educational establishment (i.e., the moral equivalent in education of the divestiture of AT&T) will this process happen quickly. You can be generally assured that this is the most unlikely scenario. For historical and financial reasons today's elite institutions will last for many decades to come and coopt the educational tools of current educational innovators. Most revolutions do not happen dramatically, with royal beheadings, but gradually over a generation or two.

### Reform 10: Adapt to Globalization of Education, Interactive Networking, and the Coming Era of the World-Wide Mind

The power and economics of global networking and worldwide education will be hard to deny. Nevertheless, the issues of language, culture, and societal norms will pose major challenges. Just because new technologies and applications will make global education more plausible and cost effective, one should not assume that the problems of content, software, and educational process can easily be solved. Certainly, one can assume that the problems of language, culture, and religion will create major problems in even the best approaches to global or even regional education reforms. The most successful programs under the Intelsat organization's global experiments with tele-education under their Project SHARE came in countries like China, which insisted on developing its own educational programming. The Chinese National TV Satellite University, which started with only a few thousand students, now supports over 4 million students. India's homegrown satellite tele-education program offers instruction to over 1 million students. The most successful and extensive tele-education programs are not in the most economically advanced countries, but those who felt the most need for these programs.

Although the problems of creating global distribution networks and accessible user terminals around the world will remain great, the problems of software and the content of learning systems will be much greater. Even so, the potential use of Internet, satellite, and wireless communications technology to reach the 2 billion people now dramatically underserved by effective educational systems remains brighter than ever. Then again, as noted earlier, U.N. studies have concluded that there will be more people to be educated in the coming decades than have ever been educated in the recorded history of humankind (see Bibliography).

### THE CYBERSPACE UNIVERSITY: A NEW MODEL FOR TWENTY-FIRST-CENTURY TRAINING AND EDUCATION

For a very long time schools and universities have been defined as buildings with teachers, classrooms, and students. In the coming age of cyberspace education, interactive learning, and globalization of the learning process, the rules will change. Bricks and mortar cost money and require the consumption of energy and complicated transport systems to shuttle students about. The idea of schools without walls, universities webbed together by electronics, and learning systems based on new academic paradigms will not be easily denied in the twenty-first century.

Cracks in the barriers to tele-education are now occurring. Stanford University, for instance, has embraced distance learning and is offering its courses via satellite across the United States. The National Technological University has found financing to expand its satellite distribution across the Pacific Ocean. Today's prototypes, such as the Knowledge Network of the West (KNOW), the International Space University, or the University of the West Indies will become tomorrow's mainstream of educational procedures.

Generations from now, a new elite and a new university establishment will rise to the top of cyberspace educational institutions. A new Internet will have greater controls, greater security, and massive information storage, processing, sorting, and distribution capabilities. At this time new reformers will begin to call for a new order. That is, however, decades away. The reforms of today's system will begin in earnest by the start of the twenty-first century. If the so-called information highway ever comes to mean something in a societal sense, it will mean the increasing triumph of cyberspace learning systems over traditional schools and universities.

The future of the university need not be dim, for the university is still the entity with the best capabilities to evolve into the cyberspace learning system of tomorrow. The keys are simple. In order to develop and implement the new electronic technologies and applications, it is essential to be extremely sensitive to key cultural, social, legal, and political issues. It is necessary to experiment with the best of the systems and adapt them as necessary to the needs of both the academic community and the economic marketplace of tomorrow. Certainly, new types of corporate universities, such as the University of Phoenix, may be able to tell the traditional university a good deal about how to train the workforce of tomorrow better, faster, and cheaper.

The time to begin prototyping and perfecting these systems for both the developed and developing world is certainly now. The endangered university is just that. In its current form it may have twenty to forty years left, but the medieval university is starting to lose its resilience to change, and quickly. The "University of the World-Wide Mind" already has its seeds in such projects as the Global University System headed by Tapio Varis of the University of Tampere in Finland and backed by such pioneers as Tak Utsumi of Columbia University. Michael Saylor's initiative seems to hold much promise although its global implementation may have serious challenges to overcome.

The importance of these changes should not be neglected. These reforms are needed to create a global educational system of information exchange. They are needed for environmental and social reasons as well. Most important, they are essential because today's schools, colleges, and universities are not meeting the needs of society.

## OVERALL TREND REVIEW

### Challenges and Pitfalls

· Rapid obsolescence of knowledge after graduation from courses of study.

· Rising functional illiteracy in most western nations.

· Lack of international teamwork training.

· Lack of interdisciplinary and integrated or systems-oriented educational programs.

· Lack of self-directed, on-line, experiential, and interactive learning programs.

· Elitist programs are not responsive to bridging the gap between consumers and producers in the cybernetic information age.

· The needs of most rural and remote areas of the globe are largely ignored.

### Opportunities

· Life-long learning and flexible adult retraining programs.

· On-line, on-demand interactive learning programs and interactive Website learning labs that promote experiential learning.

· Interdisciplinary team-development programs that capture the power of World-Wide Mind networking.

· Effective use of the latest electronic tools to provide global and regional tele-education.

· Recertification of professionals and, in time, of academic degrees as well.

# CHAPTER 11

# Telewar, Info-Espionage, and Electronic Crime

Technological Progress is like an axe in the hands of a pathological criminal.

Albert Einstein

There are more instances of the abridgment of the freedom of the people by gradual and silent encroachments of those in power than of violent and sudden usurpation.

James Madison

By the start of the 1980s there were whispers around the edges of the "spook" community about a new era. This was not only about electronic and satellite spying and surveillance, but actual electronic warfare. Cryptic references were made to computer viruses, databombs, info-warfare, and even RF death rays. Certainly during the 1980s some of the top-secret "star wars" research focused on computer and communications technology, but largely in the context of how to make instruments of destruction work where and when they should—not to make them offensive weapons themselves.

With the publishing of *The Puzzle Palace* in 1982, however, the general public began to realize that the ultimate weapon in the information age could well become information itself. If anyone understood this megatrend of the future it was military planners and organized crime. Today more and more military organizations are creating units specifically devoted to defense against and offensive use of telewar techniques. If anything, electronic criminals are even more active. According to an IEC study (see Bibliography), credit-card crime now represents somewhere between 3 and 5 percent of the net operating expenses for credit-card companies and the percentage is rising all the time. In some areas over 10 percent of cellular telephone revenues are lost to fraud. Drug dealers rip off cars, but their motive in stealing a vehicle is simply to use the cell phone for a few minutes to complete a drug transaction somewhere across the world. Business losses due to various forms of telecrime are now measured in tens of billions of dollars, and unless proactive steps are taken by cybersmart managers the problems will escalate sharply in the next decade. Those providing electronic services and operating on a global scale will be particularly vulnerable.

The first and simplest way to utilize cyberspace for an illegal purpose is what has been called Class-One information warfare. It is characterized as Class One because the targeted victim is at the most basic level, the individual. Class-Two activities, in contrast, are targeted against banks, department stores, car dealerships, and, in general, businesses. Class-Three attacks are against nations, military groups, and political entities. Such Class-Three attacks are thus political or military acts of terrorism or of national aggression. There are groups, however, such as the so-called Russian mafia, that are not unwilling to extort money or profits from any entity, including national governments. Attacks on governments can bring major losses to business, and thus should not be lightly ignored as threats by a cybermanager.

Any person with a credit card, a bank account, or any form of electronic identity is susceptible to electronic fraud, embezzlement, extortion, or theft. A typical person in today's cyberspace environment has five to ten credit cards, three bank or savings accounts, and over twenty financial records related to insurance, social security, stocks or bonds, retirement accounts, benefit programs, and so forth (see Bibliography). Any person using the Internet to buy something or to transfer funds without Zip mail or some form of encryption is taking a chance of having their credit-card number electronically stolen.

Vulnerability, however, does not have to be high tech. In truth, anyone carelessly posting a bill can have mail stolen. A clerk in a bank, store, or restaurant can steal a credit-card number and expiration date with ease. A sensitive recording device or a $150 scanner can capture electronic tones to learn telephone numbers, credit numbers, or whatever.

One of the newer and more disturbing techniques used for Class-One cyberattacks against individuals is the tactic known as "spoofing." In this case a cybercriminal or terrorist assumes another person's identity for sabotage, smearing, planting of evidence, theft, extortion, or financial attack. Electronic criminals can plant highly incriminating evidence against wealthy targets and then extort money not to expose the "fraudulent" information. Wealthy politicians and CEOs of major corporations can be particularly vulnerable in this respect. In the global business environment such tactics and more are currently in use.

A Class-Two attack involves corporate cyberattacks. In this case a sinister technique called "sniffing" may be employed. The attacker typically accesses a corporate enterprise network or banking system to extract corporate intelligence, financial transactions, or the like. This can then be used to attack a corporation or a corporation's clientele. In extreme cases it can be used to disable or cripple a defense-related corporation or other strategic industry, to attack a government, or to extort money from both a corporation and a government.

Class-One and -Two cyberattacks can be used simply to acquire some cash quickly (albeit criminally), or they can be used to strategically attack rival businesses or rival criminal organizations, or most sinister of all, for terrorist or military/political purposes.

Cyberattacks now available to cybercriminals for telecrime or for info-espionage can range very broadly. The spectrum of telecrime includes extracting, distorting, or misdirecting information, creating scandals at the low end, or real technoterrorist acts, such as disabling transportation systems or energy grids.

We have seen a growing number of demonstrations of cyberattacks and telecrimes at work in recent years. A hacker at Cornell University, the son of a professor, virtually shut down a national-defense computer network in the mid-1990s. We have also seen how an East German spy financed his espionage operations by adding a few cents onto the telephone bills of tens of thousands of unsuspecting consumers and small businesses.

As long ago as 1995 there was a cover article in *Time* that described a range of cyberattacks that could be used against an unprepared adversary. This article, almost like a do-it-yourself manual, itemized how to attack an individual, a corporation, or even a warring nation. These cyberattacks are at once diverse and hard to anticipate or forestall. They can, at very low cost, be highly effective and potentially quite destructive. The arsenal of cyberattacks against which more cybermanagers must be prepared to defend include the following.

### Viruses

Releasing a virulent computer virus throughout an opponent's entire computer communications network can largely incapacitate it within hours. Valuable records, financial assets, intellectual property, genetic information, and more can be lost—forever. Backing up systems, at least daily, and archived records are essential to info-based corporations. Such systems are vital to protect against fire, earthquake, and natural disasters, as well as computer viruses.

### Switching Systems

Spurious electronic commands or defective software could be given to corporate LANs, Public Branch Exchanges, street and highway traffic signaling systems, or even railway signaling systems to disable communications or transportation networks or to throw them into chaos. A random survey conducted by a major consulting firm in 1998 found that some 90 percent of all communications switches currently in operation in the public and private networks in the United States has the original access code that the manufacturer originally assigned. Disgruntled former employees of Lucent Technologies, Siemens, Ericsson, Northern Telecom, NEC, or Alcatel could create havoc in a large corporate enterprise network before anyone recognized that there was any danger. Another source of concern comes from a recent vulnerability survey conducted by persons from a branch of AT&T that focuses on security. At the request of a major airline, they conducted a "war dialing" campaign against this airline's worldwide telecommunications modem network that is accessible via the public switched network. After a massive campaign conducted against 80,000 "code protected" access lines, connections were actually established in nearly 1,200 instances. Numerous other examples of security vulnerability have been found in corporate, academic, and government computer networks. A concerted program to improve security and update security access codes and software control for all types of communications and transportation systems is urgently needed.

### Air Traffic Control

Air traffic control systems could be disabled through both computer and communications networks to the extent that most aircraft would be grounded or destroyed in crashes. This would more likely be the result of a cyberterrorist or military attack, but its commercial consequences on industry could still be devastating. Here, security systems such as those used on command antenna systems for satellites are needed. This means that activation, command, or system reconfiguration must be dependent on two coded commands received from two independent sources—with one source well removed from the ground control site.

## Bank Chaos

The possibilities here are almost countless: random withdrawals, filtering out all legitimate records of deposits, databombs that on command erase or reverse records, and so forth. This could be used not only against banks, but against companies with large accounts in a banking system. Here, the protections must include increased encryption and frequent code updates, off-site backup and archiving, and improved computer auditing of accounts with artificial intelligence programs.

## Raids on Key Databases and Financial Records

Just as bank records can be infiltrated, so can the records of insurance companies, social security and health records, and benefits databases. Someone with the right information extracted from databases about executives of a major corporation or critical business transactions could virtually destroy a company and its managers in an afternoon. Further, a skillful attacker could silently vanish before it was even known that an attack had been made.

## Energy Grids

Among the most devastating acts would be to disable and disrupt national energy grids. Generators can be shut off, or power can be misrouted to overload one area and starve another. Again, as in the case of air traffic control, this is more likely to be a terrorist attack, but the commercial implications and losses would still be huge. This means that similar protections to those recommended for air traffic control facilities should apply here as well.

These cyberattacks need not destroy infrastructure or hardware to be effective. If you can seize control or disable information systems at will, you do not have to destroy any equipment or facility. You only need to substitute your infodominance over your adversary. Further, you can often do this without your opponent being aware of your actions—at least until too late—and without them knowing your identity.

The sinister subtlety of the telecrime and info-espionage techniques comes from the fact that there are dozens of different weapons that can be used. A skillful cyberwarrior can enter a network in almost an infinite number of ways. The attack can vary from psychological to actual destruction of physical or human resources. One may attack decisively with a major if not crushing blow that disables a national air traffic or railway control system. Alternatively, an attack can be used almost as a negotiating tool by exercising a series of escalating strikes that represent "warnings" of what may come next. In short, with access to modern telecommunications and information systems, the technoterrorist or cyberattacker can exercise almost any amount of pressure. The psychological interventions can start with "cyberpranks" that announce you are there, but capable of doing much, much more.

The world of conventional crime, terrorism, or warfare almost always has to follow certain patterns and logistical staging mechanisms. To launch a full-scale attack you must have lines of supply, air support, artillery, and a huge support system in place. In the world of telecrime and info-espionage, it only takes strategic intelligence and tiny amounts of electronic equipment to launch what could be a devastating physical attack or to steal critical information that may not even be detected as missing.

The concerns are not limited to terrorists. Word leaked out in 1999 that Russian intelligence agents had obtained U.S. military codes "at the most sensitive level." This led to a massive process of recoding the entire U.S. military system. Ultimately info-war is the greatest concern.

The following quotation from Michael Crichton's *Congo* is a frightening scenario. It represents a realistic description of not only the potential of cyberwarfare, but the type of "double-think" military logic that might actually occur in this new information age that we call the twenty-first century. Here, a fictional General Martin outlines for a congressional committee why automated warfare is the only option for the future:

But given diversified tactical warfare, the number of weapons and "systems elements" begin to increase astronomically. Modern estimates imagine 400 million computers or micro-processors in the field, with total weapons interactions at more than 15 billion in the first half hour of war. This means there would be 8 million weapons interactions could occur in every second in a bewildering ultra fast conflict of aircraft, missiles, tanks and ground troops. Such a war will be only manageable by machines. Human response times are simply too slow. World War III will not be a push button war because it takes too long for a man to push the button—at least 1.8 seconds, which is an eternity in modern warfare.

For instance, if one were to seek only a mild set of cyberwar pressures, one might start by a simple action. This might be to capture and liquidate all but one dollar from a strongman's numbered Swiss bank account as a first step against an adversary nation. The next step might be to create an electronically morphed video image that seems to show a leader and his top aides on a television broadcast undertaking a raid on the national treasury or accepting previously undisclosed bribe money from overseas interests. In this case the digitally created artificial image might portray real events and actual crimes or the infractions could be completely spurious but seemingly in character with the actions of a dictatorial leader.

These types of "morphed-reality" info-war techniques under U.S. control are supposedly committed to truth. This means that only actual events based on solid intelligence would be depicted with "complete accuracy." In the heat of actual hostility or all-out warfare, who knows where truth and reality might part company. The temptation might be to say, "The ends justify the means." The concern is that opponents of all types and with widely varying morality systems will in time develop such capabilities.

There is no agreed-upon code of international conduct for info-warfare. Yet its power can be devastating. The toll in terms of national infrastructure and human life can in the most extreme circumstances directly equate to nuclear weapons or nerve gas or biological weapons. In fact, one can use thermonuclear devices to create an EMP (Electromagnetic Pulse) of an intensity that is capable of wiping out computer and communications networks over a huge sector of the planet's surface.

Also, the line between recordings of real events and digitally morphed images will become harder and harder to detect through objective tests. A leader of a country could be convinced that his nation had been wiped out by a nuclear holocaust or a chemical-bacteriological attack that never existed.

## TECHNOTERRORISM

There is no reason to think that the use of electronic technology as a weapon will somehow be restricted to conflicts between warring nations. In fact, the most likely scenario is that techniques developed for potential future application in an info-war will somehow be transferred to one or more terrorist or criminal groups. The potentially devastating impact of these technoterrorist activities could be used to extort political or financial concessions from governments, international organizations, banks, or other entities. Just consider the possibilities.

A cyberspace gang of criminals can covertly install an "invisible filter" that creates the illusion of normal operations. This might, for instance, allow what seem to be routine banking transactions and electronic records to flow through to the bank's permanent records without any indication of an irregularity. After three weeks, however, a specially inserted virus makes all banking records and their back-up copies either disappear or become hopelessly scrambled.

The bank checks back with its customers but finds that half of some $158 billion in transactions are neither clearly recoverable nor assignable. What does a bank do under such circumstances? Perhaps a ransom of $5 million to recover the information seems reasonable, rather than disclosing how vulnerable the banking information system actually was. If the bank is a federal bank, perhaps the release of two political prisoners seems a necessary albeit highly repugnant tradeoff that must be made.

In recent years the range of technoterrorist attacks has clearly broadened and become more virulent. The pattern is a lack of pattern. There are the Japanese subway terrorists who unleashed virulent World War II nerve gases on commuters. There are the really low-tech extremist car bombers from Beirut, to the not much more sophisticated "militiamen" fertilizer-bomb attack on the U.S. Federal Building in Oklahoma City. And then there are the teenage hackers who took over and commanded a national security satellite in the United States and another group that took over the U.K. Skynet military satellite in 1998 and demanded ransom for not destroying the satellite. These are just a few examples of the possibilities of relatively unsophisticated technoterrorists at work. They may be high tech or low tech and they may be pranksters or ruthless killers, but they are potentially highly dangerous.

Certainly a much more sophisticated group of cyberterrorists could derail trains, crash planes, poison or pollute water supplies, infect food and beverages, taint medicines, and possibly even totally disable national security networks and the armaments under their control. Not only is the range of possibilities broad and unpredictable, but so too are the possible demands that might be made.

To prevent these technoterrorists from carrying through with their threats, high-stake ransoms could be demanded. These might be cash payments, the supply of arms or highly specialized electronic equipment, or the release of convicted criminals or terrorists. The worst thing is that attempts to prevent or mitigate such attacks could be almost worse than the cyberspace attacks themselves. Individual liberties and high levels of surveillance could be the price that might be paid to alleviate the possibility of unauthorized use of cyberspace powers.

Business attempts to curtail telecrime, extortion, or terrorist cyberattacks need to focus on the top threats but also balance security and surveillance so that it does not stifle or thwart its own staff creativity. Codes need to be regularly updated. Dual- or triple-code matching from multiple site locations is needed to protect key information and maintain fire walls at maximum efficiency. Prison-like surveillance systems and rigid controls on staff members will ultimately be self-defeating. A recent AT&T survey shows that 70 percent of the incursions against protected networks come from insiders with access to security codes.

The most disturbing aspect of telecrime and the threat of technoterrorists is the ranks of those trained in such skills. Paid mercenaries who have crossed over from previous military service or corporate security to become hired "hit men" are becoming more numerous each year. They represent a wide range of nationalities, political philosophies, and backgrounds. There is nothing to suggest that some percentage of individuals trained in info-warfare techniques will not over time succumb to financial, political, or other enticements and agree to use their skills for terrorist or criminal purposes. Further, experts in telecommunications networks, computer technology, transportation systems, and power grids could devise, without any previous military training or instruction in electronic sabotage, their own highly destructive techniques.

In the twenty-first century literally millions of computer-literate people with probably no more than a few weeks of training and experimentation could obtain sufficient information to become highly dangerous. It is likely that experiments in technoterrorism could be carried out quietly and with little chance of detection. Most momentary difficulties or "blips" in electronic systems are likely to be dismissed as temporary aberrations or human errors. Most corporate and government security systems in virtually every country in the world are highly vulnerable, and adequate protection systems are very hard to devise and can be expensive as well.

## CONCLUSION

The world of Telepower, and particularly the international world of cyberbusiness, enterprise networks, intranet systems, and electronic networks, are, in general, fast, efficient, and rapidly accessible. Despite our complaints about computers and information networks, they are generally accurate and today almost indispensable to airlines, insurance companies, global retailers, credit card companies, and so forth. The convenience factor represented by automatic teller machines, telephone-based banking, electronic bill and tax paying, and a host of other electronic conveniences are enormous. We have become comfortable with letting our fingers do the walking and are not likely to surrender this convenience lightly. It was thought that Y2K concerns would present a wake-up call with regard to computer vulnerability, but it has had the reverse effect. Young people revealed in surveys that they like computer and automated transactions. They would rather deal with a computer terminal like an ATM at a bank or an automated gas pump because it is "faster," "more reliable," and less "hassle."

Almost all attempts to address the issues of telecrime, info-espionage, and various forms of cyberattacks tend to focus on technical solutions. There are advocates of ideas such as the "clipper chip" (fortunately now a quite dead proposal, but subject to resurrection) that would allow the government to check up on subversives but protect commercial secrets. The general public, Internet users, and businesses have yet to be convinced that the solution is worse than the disease. The problem is the clipper chip could become a Trojan horse in the hands of a skilled tele-criminal or technoterrorist. There are also new technical concepts, such as "time-slot interchange," that are virtually impossible to decode, particularly if the code system is changed at frequent intervals.

The problem is that the weaknesses in systems that criminals, terrorists, and cyberwarriors can most easily and effectively exploit are usually not at the technical level at all. If such systems are to operate, there have to be trained users. The easiest way to break through codes or encrypted systems is thus simply to get the authorized users to disclose the secret information.

This security breach may involve a bribe, blackmail, or a trick or ruse. People give up critical secrets much more easily and frequently than through the effort of hackers using supercomputers to break computer codes via covert password-invasive calculating systems. Any traffic control system, any power grid with computer control, any missile launching system, any banking or commodity trading system, or indeed any record system is vulnerable as long as authorized users are operating them. As noted previously, for every security breach successfully attacked through technological manipulation, there will be more than two that are created due to human frailty, error, or trick.

The real problem is that the "info-risk potential" for OECD countries will just continue to get worse. The United States, Japan, and Europe, among others, will become more not less dependent upon advanced information networks that operate on a global basis, twenty-four hours a day, and are thus automated and code protected.

Some possible strategies do come to mind. Distributed and redundant systems for information exchange and control with multiple-codes correlation systems make a great deal of sense. It short, we should avoid putting all of our eggs in one basket. This means recognizing the danger of overcentralization of Internets, intranets, or computer storage and the advantages of backup and off-site archiving.

The idea of cybersecurity must start at a very fundamental level of distributed and decentralized networking with high levels of protection. We would do well to avoid megalomania-driven Telepower fantasies of megacommunities with overly centralized utility, energy, and information systems.

The growth dynamic of modern telesocieties has pushed us more and more toward development models based on rapid expansion and economic efficiency. In this environment the objective measures of efficiency are placed in direct competition with so-called subjective measures of beauty or survival margin. In a modern technological society we need to design our cities, business complexes, and transportation and power systems with survival margins and humanely conceived security systems in mind.

The dangers of overcentralization and nonredundancy of control and recovery mechanisms are not to be found just in spy novels or the journals of confessed tele-criminals. In fact, the great danger may be in thinking we are smart enough to design "fail-safe" systems. The human cell design and the operation of the human brain are not optimized in an economic sense, but they both allocate a good deal of resources to survival margins and multiple control and recovery systems. As a final thought on this subject, one might note the very wise words of one of the original founders of the British Interplanetary Society, *Christian Science Monitor* columnist Eric Burgess:

Bio-systems which evolution has produced by billions of years of trial and error are generally survival-oriented. Once a species errs it becomes a fossil. Others more worthy take over its eco-niche. The human industrialized system is not survival-oriented but growth-oriented and tries to maximize yields at the expense of survival. The two goals are incompatible. Unrestrained growth always results in non-survival, whereas survival demands restricted growth.

If Eric Burgess is right, the dangers of telecrime and info-espionage are endemic to our current industrial-based economic society. The lack of survival margin is thus more and more likely to become a crucial problem. The more information oriented and industrial based society becomes, according to Burgess, the greater the danger becomes. From Biosphere 2 to the Chernobyl and Japanese nuclear energy disasters, from genetic engineering to organized technoterrorists, the warnings to our survival in our fragile econiche are clear.

The ill-fated summit meeting on terrorism held in July 1996 in Europe was notable in its lack of significant results. Aside from various nations being able to share information on certain antiterrorist measures they had developed, there were few new ideas on what could be done. The most specific actions concentrated on imposing more security restrictions at airports. Systematic international attempts to introduce tracer elements in explosives such as black powder, extended use of wire-tapping techniques, and other countermeasures are not likely to solve the problems, even if implemented. Absolutely no effective means for controlling the spread of telecrime and info-espionage for commercial or political purposes were identified or agreed upon.

In fact, attempts to adopt new legislation to control telecrime, info-espionage, or technoterrorism at the national level in the United States have also been unsuccessful. Most antiterrorist techniques under active consideration are of limited value. They tend to restrict democratic freedoms and are often ineffectual against the professional while handicapping the ordinary citizen or business-person. They are subject to circumvention by sophisticated (and even not so sophisticated) tele-criminals and cult groups, as shown by the so-called Identity Christian cult groups like the Freemen and Branch Davidians. The religious or pseudoreligious character of cult groups when mixed with high-tech computer and communications skills can be a dangerous combination. New banking laws in the United States will make financial institutions larger, more integrated, and more vulnerable, and consumers will lose additional privacy protection. It is time for new legislation to take electronic crime and technoterrorism more seriously.

## OVERALL TREND REVIEW

### Challenges and Pitfalls

- High-level vulnerability for confidential files stored on computer systems.
- Keeping ahead of competitors in accessing strategic information.
- Need to filter out passive and spurious information.
- Losses due to telecrime and information-based terrorism.
- Inadequate protections against privacy abuse with regard to critical private and government databases and few effective legal and criminalization safeguards against electronic crimes, technoterrorism, and telewar attacks.

### Opportunities

- Use of advanced encryption and coding technologies to reduce telecrime and credit-card fraud, and to allow rapid tracing of electronic criminals.
- Development of less intrusive and user-friendly security systems.
- Creation of new international and national regulations and uniform laws concerning the control, operation, and criminalizaton of computer fraud, and illegal access to satellite networks.
- Treaties and sanctions against technoterrorists and nations that harbor such criminals and terrorists.

# CHAPTER 12

# Cyberentertainment and Virtual Reality

Television is a medium because anything well done is rare.
Fred Allen

Virtual reality, or, as the in-crowd would say, VR, is coming. This new technology will produce a dramatic multibillion-dollar megashift in entertainment, tele-education, telehealth, and computer-based television over the next decade. At the same time the VR revolution is occurring, other changes will come as well. In general, entertainment will become more mobile, more personalized, more interactive, and more pervasive. These technologically driven changes will bring a host of economic and social problems in their wake.

## THE NEXT STEP IN CYBERENTERTAINMENT

Sony, Sega, Blockbuster, Disney, and others will pump billions into huge virtual reality game arcades alone. Sony profitability currently stands almost exclusively on PlayStation 2. During 1999 and 2000 Disney opened a string of VR arcades that let everyone on the planet go to Disneyworld just by shelling out a few dollars and putting on some VR goggles. It will actually be a bargain. Disney is putting over $2 billion into its Disneyworld Japan and only $1 billion into fifty VR arcades around the planet. In case you wonder why this is happening, it is the bottom line. Many of the companies like Sony and Disney are now making more money off of computer games and amusement parks than they make off of their movies. It is only a slight exaggeration to state that so-called blockbuster adventure movies are today just ads for theme parks and electronic games—the areas where "real" money is made.

In a business sense info-entertainment will continue to experience monster growth by expanding into new and almost mysterious sectors. The boundaries that separate entertainment, information, news, education, interactive games, and even normal perceptions of reality will increasingly blur and become intermingled. This will be particularly so as virtual reality becomes more prevalent in the world of info-entertainment. Indeed, the next step beyond current high-tech info-entertainment systems may very well be a form of "virtual life," where superb visualization systems and tetherless, hands-free wireless communications make it increasingly hard to distinguish illusion and reality.

Despite the move toward personalization and interactivity, the mass-market and mass-cultural aspects of television and computers will not only survive but even expand. In fact, in the twenty-first century the negative effects of the massification of entertainment media may reach their peak—a result of technological amplification via cyberspace.

To some there is an implied contradiction here. Won't interactive systems be more individualized and therefore demassified? The answer is not necessarily. New fuzzy logic systems can be mass produced to give consumers individualized responses. These logic systems can, for instance, follow a set of rules such as "tit for tat," "merciless preemptive strikes," or "sympathetic kindness" rules. These fuzzy logic systems can thus allow mass-produced software packages to interact and to simulate new modes of response with different types of players. It is as basic as employing different combinations and permutations with various kinds of people who use a defensive, impulsive, offensive, or random mode of strategy. This can be done without actually personalizing anything on an individual-by-individual basis, but it strongly creates the illusion of individual response and reaction. The power of programming languages like C++ or object-oriented languages are that they can substitute or plug in sets of information or strategies in such a way so as to mimic individual response. This is not necessarily new technology. It is only the VR application that is innovative. The subtle practice of these arts has been the stock-in-trade of fortune tellers and horoscope artists for many years.

Millions of people can be served by a single powerful set of software. Yet this complex software can make each consumer feel he or she is having a unique experience. In fact, the complex results are still within the bounds of maybe a dozen fuzzy logic rules embedded in the software. Oddly enough, individualized and interactive entertainment can still end up as a mass-media phenomenon, and a dangerous one at that.

Its impact on society and global culture will be even larger than its multibillion-dollar business impact. As the line between entertainment and information becomes grayer, the possibility of negative impacts on societal learning and cultural norms certainly seems to increase.

This change in the areas of entertainment and leisure will, in part, come from the merger of information, communications, and computer industries and services. The evolving of new hardware and software that allows the mature development of computerized television (or televised computers) will be another critical dimension of the future. Finally, the development of ever-more sophisticated types of virtual reality will complete this picture of cyberspace-based entertainment and its migration into advanced business, education, and training applications as well.

Recently a group of us from George Washington University (GWU) traveled to Blacksburg, Virginia, to play with the new VR "toys" that Ron Kriz and Robert Schubert have created along with some willing accomplices in the form of graduate students at Virginia Tech. Here we could travel through yet-to-be-built monuments and buildings in Jerusaleum, and through thunderstorms and low pressure fronts as sharp winds crossed the Rockies into the Great Plains with an eerie sense of truly being there. We could soar up nearly forty stories into the air and float over historic cities of the Middle East with incredible ease. The potential of these supercomputer-driven VR applications to become powerful tools of instruction as well as just plain fun was undeniable. But for every professor and every dollar that backs the development of VR-immersion technologies for tele-education at Virginia Tech, or GWU, or some other college there will be a hundred that back escapist games and entertainment. The educational applications will almost surely end up as trickle-down software.

Remarkable changes are coming and VR entertainment will lead the way. It will redefine where and when entertainment and leisure activities begin and end. In fact, the changes are sufficiently large that our basic measures of economic activity and employment will be redefined to accommodate the coming revolution in the entertainment industries.

In economic terms there are three basic divisions for all global activities. All economies are dividing into the primary sector (agriculture and mining), the secondary sector (manufacturing), and the tertiary sector (service). For the United States such a division of the labor force is really not all that helpful. This is because only 3 percent of all workers in the United States today are in farming and mining and only about 10 percent are in manufacturing.

It has been suggested that for the twenty-first century we define a fourth sector. This fourth sector of the economy would be those services that support sports, leisure, and entertainment (including theme parks, movie/television/electronic games/VR, and the hotel and restaurant industries). The economic logic of such a suggestion in terms of dollars and employment is well founded. But it is also, in a sense, disturbing. Exploding information at a fourth-order exponential and more creation of wealth from information does not necessarily mean more knowledge, wisdom, or education. The World-Wide Mind implies as much an age of entertainment and fantasy as it does wisdom or research. It also probably implies a time of deskilling and idleness as much as it implies the accumulation of knowledge or intellectual development. The importance to humanity of real challenge as opposed to psuedo-thrills must not be overlooked. One can at least hope for the future. Perhaps we could actually seek to create a biosphere on Mars or educate all of humanity rather than define our species destiny in terms of conquering electronic opponents in VR fantasy worlds. What should we choose? Will it be real challenges to create a sustainable biosphere and save the species or to devise better 3D computer games with gigantic pterodactyls?

The world of entertainment versus serious objectives for the World-Wide Mind are thus on a collision course. The patterns are already clear. Most would assume that the execs at Universal Studios had more than met their expectations when the movie *The Lost World* became the top grossing movie of the year. The truth is *The Lost World* turned out to be a very slick, very expensive, rather mundane but highly profitable commercial for Universal's theme-park ride through dinosaur land. In 1999 Disney, Universal, and several other movie studios will make more profit on their theme parks than on celluloid. People plunk down $7 to $10 to see a movie. Families pay $500 to $1,000 per day to escape into the fantasyland of their choice.

Universal Studios has renamed its 840-acre Florida complex Universal City. And why not? It is investing billions of dollars in hotels, restaurants, buildings, amusement rides, and service industries of all shapes and forms. More than 1,000 set designers, art directors, illustrators, and architects are currently employed in Los Angeles, but not on a blockbuster movie. They are hard at work designing an unbelievably huge and expensive mega-entertainment center for Tokyo. We are talking billions and billions of dollars to create a completely escapist fantasy world where vacationers willingly part with large amounts of cash. Here they can hope to escape from the humdrum and the ordinary and feel it is somehow real.

At the superficial level you could say that top Hollywood moguls are reshaping the movie industry. Certainly many of these companies are selling escapism, whether it be by means of big-budget movies, electronic games, or theme-park fantasies. At a more fundamental level, you could observe that the challenge of the entertainment industry is to capture larger and larger client bases with experiences that are increasingly real, exciting, perilous, and totally absorbing. Seen this way, you might envision a spiral toward experiences that are more and more fantastic, exotic, erotic, and thrilling. Yet because there are "virtually real," they are still safe.

The same trend can be seen in different forms almost everywhere. The Venice and the New York, New York resorts in Las Vegas are merging entertainment, gambling, escapism, and risk taking. Houston's gentleman's clubs like the Ritz (which feature twenty-four-foot projection screens for sports, show girls, and gaming) are on one hand just a grown-up and expensive version of the old go-go bars. These and other such offerings are thus on the retro side of this fantasy-world megashift.

Today most of the major cities of the world have elaborate, high-tech theme parks, exotic gambling casinos, and other appealing adult and child-based entertainment centers that feature amusing animal or show-biz robots, dancing bimbettes, or fantasy landscapes or jungles. The same trend is featured in a growing number of themed chain restaurants. Recent Chapter 11 filings by entities like the Hard Rock Cafe and the Super Model clubs suggest that glitz does not mandate success. The concept of "theme it and they will come" apparently has it limits.

The next frontiers are not difficult to project. Interactive films and games where you become a part of the virtual landscape are certainly coming. A full-motion cage with full mobility and virtual reality goggles, boots, and gloves, plus surround sound, may be designed to let you fight dinosaurs or act out a seduction of your "ultimate conquest." The VR cage for dinosaur slaying is indeed already here. Next there may be escape entertainment centers where you can attempt to woo (or perhaps molest) a courtesan in the electronic form of a "really bad Apache-type" gigolo, or perhaps enter the arena to have your ear bitten off by an ersatz Mike Tyson. These scenarios and more are not improbable virtual reality fantasy-park fodder for the next generation of interactive theme parks. Virtual reality entertainment systems, 3D and multiple-rastered image-projection systems, heat, cold, and aroma-dispensing devices, and more are certainly all happening. There will be customized electronic games that allow you to enter the action. In these interactive VR-based cybergames you will not just see the action, but feel the pain and stress your muscles. In order to add interest, you will begin to play only after a brief profile of your personality and a digitization of your body profile has been scanned into the interactive software. It will all be designed to make you feel connected. You are there! The risk is real! The joy of success or the dangers of failure will seem up close and personal. The desire to continue and to overcome defeat will be urgent, vivid, and—for the consumer—dangerous. All this will be accomplished with the high-tech version of personalization.

There are some steps beyond the high-tech interactive theme parks of Disney and Universal that are even now in research and development. These steps beyond conventional VR are increasingly possible from a technical viewpoint. This is why the social and legal implications of these near-term prospects need to be considered now.

Arthur C. Clarke and Mick McQuay's book *Richter 10* is just one version of a possible future world inhabited by the escapist or fantasy seeker. In *Richter 10* a growing percentage of the population have chip implants and a direct communications port to the brain that allows people to have virtual lovers, virtual entertainment, virtual trips, and even virtual sex. The line between reality and chip-induced virtual reality experiences in *Richter 10* becomes so confused that many of the "chippies" become dysfunctional, including the vice president of the United States.

Today chip implants are being studied for medical purposes, to automatically control hormone dozes, control serious eating disorders, and even to increase intelligence or overcome memory loss. Once this technology is installed and connected to the brain, where does it logically (or legally) stop?

The virtual reality environment will by itself not have to be based on reality. It can be peopled with characters that lived centuries and continents apart, such as Hitler or Atilla the Hun, Buddha or Hirohito, Henry VIII or John Kennedy, Florence Nightingale or Mata Hari, or perhaps Marilyn Monroe or Mother Theresa. Or it could be populated with virtual characters generated by a ten-gigahertz supercomputer out of a viewer's visual profile of their most exotic romantic interest or perhaps their favorite male stripper at Chippendales. As computers become faster they will become smaller and require less power and thus will increasingly become implantable as well.

For others, the desired experience will not be romantic or sexual but perhaps to perform a heroic deed. One player might wish to match wits with a villain in a gothic castle or wrestle and overcome a super hero. Virtual reality images that perform individualized fantasies do not have to be paid a salary or royalties and can be commanded to do things that an actor or actress may not wish to do. Movie makers are even trying to devise completely synthetic movie actors for the silver screen using Cray supercomputers. They could be a whole lot cheaper than Sean Penn or Bruce Willis or Demi Moore and would read their scripts perfectly the first time through.

Another way that virtual entertainment might go is in the direction of the so-called sexbot. This would be a robotic device with artificial skin, sensors, recorded voice, and other programmable features that would allow a personalized sexbot to interact with a human friend. Over fifteen years ago a Marilyn Monroe robot capable of singing and movement was developed at the MITI labs in Japan. As fantastic as it may all sound, there are similar types of experimental robots under development in several laboratories around the world. Legislatures around the world will soon face specific issues such as whether chip implants for sensory stimulation will be legally sanctioned or not. Similarly, they may need to regulate the use of robots and their interactions with humans.

## THE ECONOMIC IMPORTANCE OF VR
## AND ENTERTAINMENT

Some tend to dismiss entertainment and leisure as something to think about after everything important and serious has been addressed and resolved. Do not be misled. As noted, entertainment, leisure, and sports are today mega-industries and collectively they promise to become the hottest growth sector in the early years of the third millennium. In the process, the Internet may become the prime media for connecting these new interactive and VR entertainment offerings to consumers. Over half of today's Web sites can in one sense or another already be considered entertainment or leisure.

Nearly 20 percent of the French economy represents leisure activity in the form of hotels, restaurants, tourism, entertainment, or sports activities. Even in "serious" countries such as Germany it is some 12 to 15 percent of Gross Domestic Product. Within the economically advanced countries, broadly defined "services" are anywhere from 60 to nearly 90 percent of all jobs and economic activities. It is not surprising that some economists have started to think in terms of basic services on one hand and leisure and entertainment services on the other. These basic services (i.e., the third sector of the economy) would include information, communications, retailers and wholesalers, transportation and energy, banking, insurance, education, training, health services, and so forth. The fourth or quaternary sector would include leisure, cultural recreation, hotels, restaurant and tourist services, gambling, electronic entertainment of all sorts, sports, fitness, and what might be discreetly called "adult services." These leisure and entertainment services have been suggested as a logical way of understanding the nature of twenty-first-century economic trends. Universal, Disney, Sony, Microsoft, and others have targeted this sector as the golden goose or growth industry of the cyber age. The limits of where this trend might go are underscored by a recent *Washington Post* article that suggested that Rupert Murdoch, CEO of the News Corporation, and John Malone, CEO of Liberty Media, might try to take over General Motors in order to acquire GM's DirecTV subsidiary.

The size of this quaternary sector of the economy is already quite large and is rising. This sector in terms of dollar turnover and employment is already five times larger than agriculture and mining. It is a good thing, too, since farming and mining now represent only 3 percent of jobs. Automation, productivity gains, and other changes in the economy are now requiring some basic restructuring of the economy. The conventional view of economics is that fresh approaches and new economic growth are needed in order to create new jobs and new patterns of consumption. Entertainment, leisure, tourism, fitness, and sports are, for better or worse, some of the more important answers.

Exactly what does the future hold? Different people have different answers. The cable television industry is deploying massive amounts of information and entertainment-carrying capacity via fiber-optic cable. TCI magnate John Malone contended that the answer is a lot of television channels—as in 500 or more channels. AT&T has agreed so strongly that they bought John Malone and TCI out, lock, stock, and barrel.

The DBS systems have begun to pose alternative, broadband and multichannel answers. Already there is Primestar, General Motors' Hughes, DirecTV (previously noted), Hubbard Broadcasting, and Echostar (or as it is popularly known, the Dish Network) in the United States. These direct-to-the-home satellite systems collectively offer nearly 1,000 television channels and dozens of CD-quality audio channels in the U.S. market alone. Around the world there are the NHK, JSAT, and SCC systems in Japan, TV-Sat in Germany, and TDF in France. For all of Europe there are the Astra, BSB, and EUTELSAT's Hotbird systems. Ruppert Murdoch's News Corporation has now planned a direct-to-the-home service that could ultimately reach 80 percent of the world's population. This nearly global collection of DBS systems already covers Asia, Europe, South

America, and the United States. If the News Corporation and Liberty Media link-up could actually overcome antitrust objections and obtain control of DirecTV (with control of the Astrolink, Primestar, AsiaSat, BSB, and a South American DTH system via INTELSAT already in hand), Rupert Murdoch and John Malone would become candidates for being the most powerful media czars in the world. These advanced entertainment satellite systems with large channel capacities, however, have heretofore tended to follow the pattern of the cable television industry. This is simply to bombard consumers with megachannel TV systems. The only difference is that the DBS systems are also seeking to provide a more exotic or higher-value mix of services as well. Nevertheless, cable and DBS satellite systems today are largely one-way maxichannel systems. If and when they convert to interactive services, these systems will have enormous potential to be part of the new global information highway and an essential part of the World-Wide Mind.

The various conventional telecommunications carriers, stuck with huge amounts of copper wire, have limited channel capacity. Yet they also have lots of switching technology at their command. These corporations have suggested that one only needs one or two broadband channels to the home to have many choices. Their solution is to switch to whatever channel of information or entertainment or sports that is desired. Again, the residual Baby Bell corporations (i.e., Bell South, SBC, Global Crossings/US WEST, Bell Atlantic) have chosen to offer essentially the only option they currently have. This, of course, is enhanced copper wire that can be upgraded to provide a few television channels over short distances by using a transmission technology known as DSL or XDSL. This is, however, only a short-term strategy that cannot succeed in the long run. This is not to count the Bellcos out but rather to see how they link up as partners with others to get the fiber, broadband wireless, or satellite capacity they need.

The trouble with all these alternative approaches (whether it is the offerings of cable TV by coax or fiber, direct-to-the-home satellites, or Baby Bell copper-wire pair services) is that the consumers' wants and needs are not driving the bus. Rather, it is the installed technical plant and the planned networks of various would-be competitors that are seeking to define the market. There are now dozens of would-be providers of broadband, multimedia services, but are they paying sufficient attention to their customers, or perhaps concentrating too much on the technology and the delivery systems?

A number of different companies have come up with test beds to let customers decide. In Orlando, Florida, Time-Warner, together with Anderson Consulting, installed a complete, full-service interactive information highway to several hundred homes. Everything was available. They offered movies; local, national, and international news; stock market and financial reports; electronic catalogs; and menu guides from restaurants to carry-out pizza orders. The results have been mixed. The ultragimmicky "navigator" or video master of ceremonies was too cute and cumbersome for most consumers. Some learned that they could order a pizza by phone in thirty seconds, but that it took about two minutes to order by full-color multimedia cable television.

Several years ago, US West (before it was acquired by Global Crossing and Frontier) announced an upgrade to their wire-based network in Omaha, Nebraska, to move megabits of information for video, voice, and data over short distances represented by the local loop. Even before this system could be installed and tested, however, US West executives decided to pull the plug and go for an even better product and service. Bell Atlantic, with similar plans in its service districts, decided to retreat from equally ambitious plans. A joint undertaking of AT&T, US West, and TCI to test 500-channel television in the suburbs of Denver, Colorado, produced little definitive information on what the consumer really wanted.

There is great confusion about what the consumer wants and, perhaps more important, about what they are willing to pay. Overall it seems that many consumers want broadband multimedia access (i.e., T-1 data rates) to the Internet, but—and this is a significant but—they do not want to pay a whole lot for it. After numerous exhaustive market studies few new "killer" applications have been found. Entertainment, interactive entertainment, and the Internet lead the list, and after that applications are hard to find except for home telecommuting. Consumers, in fact, would like to have more communications capacity, but pay less. This is a mentality that has developed as a result of continuing computer performance increases and the public sees no reason why this should not be true of telecommunications as well. At a time when long-distance rates in the United States are falling from $0.15 a minute to $0.05 a minute, the public is saying this is the kind of performance gains or cost reductions they want. Meanwhile, consumers in Japan and Europe are saying they want cheaper rates for Internet access and will give their business to someone who will respond to their demands for better and lower-cost local service.

This confusion over what the consumer wants and will pay for in the United States, Europe, and Japan will likely remain for some time. In talking to an executive (who wishes to remain anonymous) from Scientific Atlanta, a major supplier to cable television, DBS, and the satellite industry, the degree of the current confusion becomes clear: "I talked to one of the big five consulting firm and they told me that the 'typical consuming family' was willing to spend up to $300 a month for entertainment, voice, data, security and other information related services. Yet I talk to another respected firm and they say perhaps only half that much or less. Who am I to believe? This is about as scientific as using the entrails of wild bats to forecast the future. No one knows."

The ever-present optimism of Moore's Law and the efficiency of the consumer electronic industry have certainly helped to condition the consumer to expect better for less. There is also a desire among consumers for greater mobility, flexibility, and speed of service, with less hassle.

Of course, hassle is in the eye of the behassled. The remote control certainly was thought to eliminate hassle. This innovation, however, created a new hassle in the form of disputes over the control of home entertainment. Families (i.e., men and women) are still fighting for control. Of course, as we move to two- or three-person homes with three or four television sets and VCRs, this issue may resolve itself, but life will be a lot lonelier with this solution. What then do consumers really want?

First of all, mobility is clearly in. We will see an amazing range of mobile products. These will include mobile cell phones, personal communications devices, mobile TV sets, projection television inside of dark glasses, palm-top computers, and personal data assistants. These and more will be high-growth markets for some time to come. Mobile multimedia services in totally hands-free formats are clearly attractive to consumers. This is why wireless is here to stay and Americans are not yet willing to go on a completely "high-fiber" telecommunications diet.

In the area of cost, the data are fairly convincing. Most cable television subscribers would rather pay a flat monthly rate for entertainment services simply because they like the cost containment and believe that they will spend less money under this approach. The so-called pay per revolution has yet to happen. Less than 15 percent of cable subscribers have been lured into purchasing "pay per" services. The home-delivered pay-per-view movie apparently will need to significantly undercut the price of video rental services like Blockbuster to succeed. The convenience factor is apparently not enough to command a cost premium. The only interactive service that has turned out to be highly successful is the QVC channel for home sales of jewelry, knick-knacks, and virtually everything else.

Cable television can probably undercut telephone companies for phone and data service, but the issue of reliability and service availability may well stop a number of consumers from switching unless they see a clear advantage. This would need to be a lower-cost combined cable television and telephone service or improved multimedia service and Internet access. Further, they will have to be convinced that a legitimate telecommunications company such as AT&T has invested the billions of dollars needed to turn cable TV into a reliable, effective, and quality broadband information network. Some of the major business analysts on Wall Street believe that AT&T will have to spend too much money and will take too long to make their broadband cable-modem approach succeed.

In the area of speed, the issue is not necessarily the speed of a data link, but rather how quickly a movie, a financial report, or a particular service can actually be provided after it has been requested. Consumers will soon expect to be able to access broadband service routinely (i.e., 2 megabit/second in Europe and 1.5 megabits in the United States and Japan). This will become the normal expectation in OECD countries within the decade and the speeds will only continue to go up. Further, the expectation will be that this megabit/second service will be provided in an openly competitive environment at not much higher cost than today's telephone service.

Again, Moore's Law is looming large over the cyberspace world that now includes telecommunications. Moore's Law is saying, "If you want to succeed, then increase performance a lot and increase costs just a little." Meanwhile, the new Internet law is saying, "Give them IP anywhere, anytime, to anybody." Ultimately, one should note that the big money is not to be made in providing the links to the home. Programming, entertainment, and software are where the real money is. Content is the name of the game. If you are not sure, just ask Bill Gates, or if you can't reach him ask how much Bill Gates is worth today.

Lots of bets are currently being placed on the big info-entertainment roulette table. One of the biggest bets has been made by cable television giant TCI, now owned by AT&T. They are engaged in one of the most massive digitization programs in the entertainment world ever undertaken. Every movie, sports film, newscast, or other form of programming that is now owned by TCI is being converted from analog to digital format at their headquarters in Englewood, Colorado. Certainly this helps distribute materials more efficiently and exploits the potential of digital compression techniques as well.

There is, however, a key added value that comes with this process. It is possible to edit this digital material electronically so that you can obtain specialized or customized programs. This huge digital database can be manipulated so that you can order very simple things like the last two weeks of your favorite soap. You can also order the best touchdown passes of Bronco quarterback John Elway or Dolphin Dan Marino. Alternatively, you might order the best goals of soccer great Pelé. Someone might seek the best ice-dancing programs of Torville and Dean. Other programming requests may well be more mundane or scandalous. Suddenly, from a finite database an almost infinite amount of "new" programming can be created. Again, time will tell if the consumer responds to these possibilities and whether they are willing to pay dollars or cents for such options. So far, there seems to be little consumer support for the much-ballyhooed "pay per" revolution.

Others are betting in other directions. The Knight-Ridder newspaper chain thought that the consumer would invest more leisure time in electronic news and hopes that the right combination of television news editing and detail will score big on the information highway. Knight-Ridder envisioned that mobile links to a portable electronic newspaper terminal rather than static living-room-based cable television sets would be key to selling their video-format news. After spending millions of dollars and promoting their concepts with lots of high-tech hype, Knight-Ridder folded the tent on this ambitious product. Once again, we witness a victim of technology push without clearly defined market pull.

Other cable television operators, such as Glenn Jones, have consistently held that the consumer who is worried about his current or perhaps his new job will invest time and dollars in tele-education programming. In the info-entertainment world, only Glenn Jones, founder of Jones Intercable, has the chutzpah to bet on the "interactive info" part of the market. The good news is that the Jones Mind Extension University is providing outstanding educational programming to well over 20 million homes in the United States. The bad news is that only a few thousand students are actually enrolled for credit in the electronic telecourses and the effort is at best breaking even.

At this point info-entertainment executives are wildly guessing what the key market areas will be and whether the profits will lie in Web casting. Dozens of scenarios—plausible and not so plausible—are under consideration. If the Playboy channel were to link up with TCI's digital entertainment bank, what could happen? Would the latest in interactive virtual reality and the possibility of offering at least some consumers the ultimate "Fantasy Island" result in some very high value-added and profitable services. Perhaps the Chippendales could link with up with Steven Spielberg's Dreamworks to create the obvious alternative product. Certainly the sleaze factor cannot be discounted. Some estimates say 25 percent of all Internet transactions and 35 percent of all Web sites are sex, pornography, or gambling based. The most-visited Web sites in the world are educational in only the ironic sense of the word. Are the keys to the future success of info-entertainment based on interactivity, virtual reality, escapism, originality, the latest news, inside business information, sexuality, or what?

## VIRTUAL REALITY, MEGA-TELEVISION, AND CYBERSPACE ESCAPISM

Escapism has been with us for quite a few centuries. Hieronymus Bosch, Salvador Dali, Jules Verne, H. G. Wells, Aldous Huxley, George Orwell, and many others have shown us in words and vivid images ways to escape. They have provided vision beyond humdrum reality and sights into worlds and places previously unknown. In some cases these visionaries have shown us possible fiery hells that we would desperately seek to avoid. Others have depicted futures that scientists and technologists have aspired to achieve. The technical capabilities that represent today's operating virtual reality systems now suggest that we must choose how to apply the increasing power these systems provide.

To some the idea of virtual reality is as simple as a three-dimensional display of data. The most accurate descriptive term for this particular feat is actually "scientific visualization." The essence of virtual reality is the creation of an artificial but very realistic electronic environment with which people can interact. Part of the confusion over virtual reality is that it can be created on several different layers. There are three progressive levels of virtual reality and each level is increasingly sophisticated and interactive.

To discuss virtual reality with some precision, one must begin by understanding the three levels that now exist or will soon be available. The first level of virtual reality is now most commonly found in kiosk systems and is the least sophisticated. The Atlanta Summer Olympics of 1996 successfully featured a number of Georgia Tech developed kiosks throughout the city. Here visitors were able to take virtual tours of the city and the Olympics facilities. In this case you could go only to those locations that had been filmed and digitized. With this type of Level-One virtual reality the user looks at a conventional television screen. It is virtual reality only in that you can control your itinerary and can see what you choose of the complex database in any order you wish.

This type of VR has been around for almost a decade. Among the first applications of this type of virtual reality was the BBC's "Doomsday" project. In this experimental undertaking they visually mapped virtually every aspect of a town so that a viewer could go, see, and do anything in the town by virtual reality. This was actually a rather sober-minded project. In the event of a doomsday destruction of the town or country, this virtual reality record of the former community would still remain. This first level of virtual reality allows one to control direction and steering within the VR environment, but little else. There is no pretense that one is doing anything other than viewing a controlled and limited set of images, yet one can still roam freely around inside of this artificial electronic video environment.

The applications of VR at this level can still be powerful and highly effective for education, training, or entertainment. One of the world centers of virtual reality is in Sausalito, California, just across the bay from San Francisco. Here, commercial applications are being developed, such as the virtual stock market. In this mode a stock-market analyst can look at how stocks are moving in dozens of market sectors and monitor developments in three dimensions for a host of technical indicators. The same data as before are available, but the ability to visually compare a host of complex variables is dramatically enhanced. Trends can be seen in a glance rather than laboriously deciphered from columns of raw data. Today most business users feel more comfortable and at ease relying on a joystick to navigate through the VR displays. Despite the ease and interest in this type of Level-One VR, it is neither absorbing nor captivating as an entertainment media.

The second level of virtual reality involves the use of a helmet or viewing device, such as a set of goggles, that creates the illusion that you have indeed entered another world or environment that is three dimensional. This illusion is created by "seeing" this electronic environment through 3D glasses. This is to say you simulate bipolar vision or depth of real three-dimensional objects. It also creates the illusion of being able to interact with this environment. One can improve upon the interactivity by adding electronic gloves that let you "feel" this environment. Likewise, one can climb into a free-wheeling three-axis sphere that allows participants to move with the VR environment. This type of VR can be (and in fact often is) found inside of an arcade game environment. Here you might try to shoot at flying raptors that can also attack back.

There are, of course, much more useful applications than raptor slaying. One might also use this technology for educational purposes. Such techniques can be used in understanding sheer wind conditions or structural flaws in buildings or bridges or in training a pilot for rapid interactions and avoidance techniques. This is particularly well suited to learning how to accomplish CPR or even for teaching a surgeon how to perform arthroscopic surgery. For these types of medical applications thousands of inputs from sensors must be stored and electronically modeled on a computer to coincide with the 3D projection or actual robotic model. Repetitious learning routines designed to perfect particular motor skills are where these simulation technologies stand out.

As the virtual reality at this level becomes more sophisticated, important new industrial applications will emerge. Today chemical engineers are devising systems that would allow users to look inside of a molecule in order to design new and unique substances. Mechanical engineers are using VR systems not only to design new machine parts, but to actually "go inside" and inspect for design flaws or devise design enhancements. Ultimately one might be able to "see" a nuclear chain reaction or even a nuclear fission process at one-billionth of a second stop-frame speed to understand the precise characteristics of these fundamental energy processes. Today the market is largely defined by video games available at arcades, but there are entrepreneurs who speculate about huge interactive entertainments as well as a training market for home-based systems.

The possibilities are almost limitless. One of the recurring proposals is a very exotic application—virtual sex. There have been other far-out proposals that range from virtual war to virtual novels and virtual soaps. Today there are many questions about the timing and nature of such products. Indeed, it is not clear whether some of these virtual reality applications would actually be kinky and self-absorbed parlor games or whether they would be useful training modules. Past history suggests that both results might indeed be expected. In any event, Level-Two virtual reality applications can span the range from pornography and voyeurism to "telepresence" games to training and therapy.

This Level-Two virtual reality gives access to an electronic environment that seems real, is highly interactive, and allows geographic mobility throughout the entire virtual reality world. This system still describes an environment that is premapped with a finite amount of information and a precisely defined set of options to be explored. Once the sensors are implanted in a training unit, they do not change or organically adapt. A new species of dinosaur cannot evolve. The number of CPR maneuvers and responses are specifically defined in terms of preset quantitative levels.

The third and highest level of virtual reality includes all the features of the previous levels, but includes increased abilities for mapping. It also allows exploration beyond the initially defined electronic environment. It allows the electronic environment to adapt and "learn" through the use of expert sensing systems or even true artificial intelligence. The latest applications of fuzzy logic systems could, for instance, allow the attacking dinosaurs in virtual reality games to become smarter and more deadly in response to being hunted.

Yet another dimension of Level-Three virtual reality is to allow a new type of cyberenvironment where two or more humans or computers can interact. The interactivity and the added new intelligence in the system can thus be provided by multiple participants who enter the virtual reality environment. The first application seems to be in computer games and escapist entertainment. There may be more practial uses in business and training.

## TELEPRESENCE: ECONOMIC BONANZA OR BUST?

The most immediately promising application of this type of VR is known as "telepresence." In terms of immediate commercial applications, telepresence is being promoted for medical applications such as tele-operations. It might also be used as a highly useful substitute for international business meetings or negotiations. A businessman in Tokyo, an architect in France, and a banker in Chicago could all enter an electronic conference room with high-quality visual displays. They could all hold an hour-long telepresence meeting without leaving their offices if they could simply agree on a common time to meet and develop the 3D environment that they would like to explore and modify on computer command. They would only need their virtual reality goggles, a dedicated international communications link, an adaptive computer, and a willingness to believe in the technology.

When videoconferencing first became a technical reality in the 1970s some experts predicted a massive impact on telecommunications on the basis of shifting airline travel to electronic meetings. At the time videoconference meant fairly wideband communications in the form of a three to six megabits/second data channel. Some marketing forecasters suggested that just a 7 percent shift in airline traffic would mean a fivefold increase in communications services. When this did not happen, the experts said that videoconferencing was too expensive. Then when digital compression drove down costs, a large impulse increase in telecommunications still did not occur. Not only did the foreseen traffic not materialize, but the decrease in transportation revenues did not occur either. Telepresence could conceivably overcome some of the limitations of conventional videoconferences, but its importance and effectiveness has still to be proven.

Elaborate predictions about how telepresence could eliminate the need for travel or at least greatly reduce travel must therefore be viewed with skepticism. This is based not on business trends, but rather human nature. It seems likely that telepresence will only replace undesirable or routine corporate travel. People are essentially social animals and like to travel. They may give up their weekly sales meetings during the winter months in Buffalo, New York, but they still want to go to conferences in Maui or Nice. The emerging mega-info-entertainment industry wants people to spend money on escapist entertainment, travel, restaurants, hotels, and sporting events. They clearly will not want to make telepresence and teletravel so appealing that consumers would be willing to give up either leisure travel or exotic business trips.

The actual symbiotic relationship between communications and transportation should nevertheless be clearly recognized. Researchers at M.I.T., like Richard Solomon, who studied the usage patterns of the Internet, found that e-mail and chat groups were, in a number of cases, used as a travel substitute. They also found that heavy users of the Internet actually met a large number of individuals in cyberspace as well. They also linked to a number of new organizations that they might not have encountered otherwise.

Thus, communications and especially surfing the Net can, in fact, generate new linkages that lead to new travel. This is travel that may well have not arisen except for the electronic communications hookups. The conclusion of media guru Richard Solomon is that savings in physical travel created by electronic networks are probably more than offset by new or augmented travel generated by a broader range of contacts made possible through the Internet and other systems. As the World-Wide Mind extends from local to national to international contacts and relationships, it is reasonable to project increased travel. This suggests that finding more environmentally gentle ways to travel, other than petrochemical propulsion, must remain a key mandate for the twenty-first century.

Another key aspect of the emerging world of info-entertainment is the collision between consumer electronic manufacturers who produce television sets and computer manufacturers. There is essentially a race to determine who controls the age of 3D Internet television, in which mass-entertainment programming, Internet visualization, and broadcasting become intertwined with interactive video production, electronic communications, and information systems. Predictions about how this will occur are probably dangerous, but the software and protocols will very likely be based on IP. The most-likely transmission media to develop these applications is the rapidly emerging Internet 2 broadband system. This new age of interactive and dimensional entertainment is just one of the likely ultimate outcomes of ICEE-age mergers.

Today, computers simulate full-motion video through CD-ROM presentations, but these actually only deliver a few million pixels per second, while full motion commercial television can still offer more pixels per second and HDTV digital systems provide the highest resolution systems of all. Laboratory display systems even have several-thousand-line display systems that require huge amounts of throughput to create their illusion of "superreality."

The desire for instantaneous and increasingly "real" virtual reality will push the current pixel race to higher rather than lower limits, despite the benefits of digital compression techniques. Even so, the extremely good digital image that can now be achieved by the 6 megabits/second MPEG 2 standard has certainly served to close the gap between television and digital computer display systems. In fact, manufacturers such as Sharp have already brought to the market a computer television that is also a television computer. At several thousand dollars per unit, it is still far from a mass-consumer item, but the prices keep falling. Moore's Law is lurking everywhere to tell us that faster, better, and cheaper is coming.

At the ultimate level of virtual reality with a true computer television, a game could be created and populated with players who had certain characteristics and were even imbued with personalities. The players in this game could be armed with fuzzy logic learning systems that would allow them to evolve and develop in new and perhaps unexpected ways. The prototype for this type of virtual reality game was in fact invented almost a decade ago. Chris Langton, a researcher at the exotic and Nobel Laureate-ridden Santa Fe Institute invented a computer program based upon chaos theory and genetic processes.

By changing only a few basic variables it is possible to create different artificial life forms that exhibit totally different behaviors and succeed or fail in different types of environments. In this rather strange world of Level-Three virtual reality you do not necessarily know what you are creating. Most important, however, you know that whatever you create will change and evolve into something different. We once thought that to create an environment with an infinite number of possibilities would require a computer with infinite memory. Now we know that only a few fuzzy logic rules can (as we see in fractal-generated designs) open up unlimited possibilities.

The more we learn about Level-Three virtual reality and the rules that govern open-ended artificial life, the more we may learn about life. This type of Level-Three VR could even help us explore evolutionary possibilities for humanity. Certainly we will learn how to create interactive entertainment forms that mirror the unexpected vagaries of life. Life and Level-Three VR are both essentially unpredictable and scary.

Once the doors of virtual reality are opened into the infinite complexity of Level-Three VR, some feel that we will have truly opened Pandora's box. There are already a number of sci-fi thrillers that portray the potential horrors of being trapped in some kind of perpetual virtual reality dreamworld where escape back to reality is impossible. These range from the rather upbeat or at least whimsical images of *Tron* and *Max Headroom* to the outrageous concepts of *Batman Forever* to the truly dark and brooding possibilities of *Brainstorm, Dreamscope,* and *Deathwatch.* In some of these movies the viewer is not able to separate image from reality.

Certainly what is so fascinating about this third level of virtual reality is that it can and often does become increasingly real. Since you are interacting with a sort of intelligence that could in fact map your own intelligence, the game becomes not only interactive and complex, but increasingly personal. It could very easily become like getting to know someone, and on a highly intimate and sensitive level. This kind of interaction could be challenging, skill enhancing, or even loving in nature. The appeal of escaping into this "virtual life" world could at least for some become more appealing than reality. In time we indeed might see virtual life addiction and even rehabilitation centers where "infodruggies" are taught the importance of eating and drinking, holding a productive job in society, and rationing their access to interactive entertainment. There are already fully operational Internet addiction centers in California. These, no doubt, will be coming soon to a city near you.

Although the level of technology for interactive chip implants does not exist yet, it probably will in a short period of time. The "chippies" of Arthur C. Clarke and Mike McQuay's *Richter 10* may indeed only be two or three decades away. The question arises as to whether we will reach a point at which the surgeon general will begin to label certain virtual reality products as being addictive, narcotic, or harmful to a citizen's health. This could be a warning label like that now used to warn consumers of the hazards of nicotine and smoking. Or perhaps certain products or services might be so very dangerous and habit forming that outright bans will be imposed, such as now apply to cocaine or heroin. The age of "total escape havens" may emerge in offshore island countries that can provide the full range of legal and illegal virtual life experiences. Just like with real drugs, such a habit might become extremely expensive to sustain.

Clearly there are major pitfalls here. Unlike heroin, infodrugs will contain specific information content. Any attempt to ban such offerings to the public in the United States or abroad would likely be protected under the First Amendment or its equivalent in other countries. There is also the issue of individual responses versus general responses to interactive virtual reality games. One VR offering might totally absorb one individual but have little effect on another. The chemical effects of drugs on individuals vary from person to person, but they are generally the same for all *homo sapiens*. The same is not true for infodrugs, where impact and effect will vary widely. In the case of chip implants we have no idea what the impacts might be. A lot must be learned before the regulatory environment for Level-Three virtual reality can be decided and reasonable laws placed into effect.

One might at least speculate that the producers of this type of programming would have a commercial interest in creating a product or service that is as entertaining, absorbing, or entrancing as possible, but stop short of making it completely addictive and health threatening. This, quite logically, is because they would want to see more products and improvements in the future. Further, they would wish to avoid regulation and lawsuits. Despite these incentives of producers to avoid total addiction, finding the right balance is difficult. There is a real possibility that the info-entertainment of the next decade or two could become so compelling that the user does not wish to retreat back to reality for such necessities as eating or earning a living.

This is not a hypothetical concern. A real patient at the California clinic for Internet stress, who we will call James Cyberspace for the sake of anonymity, is currently being brought back to health after complete physical collapse. He had gone more than four days without eating or sleeping when hospitalized . He had been virtually continuously on-line for 100 hours. He had already lost his wife and his job and almost his life because he could not go off-line. This is not an isolated case. Companies like Sun Microsystems, Microsoft, and others are hiring counselors to deal with such problems and terminating infojunkies who can no longer perform their jobs. These problems could well increase, and in the near future. As Arthur C. Clarke has said, "Any future reality we can clearly envision is likely to happen."

Predicting the future of info-entertainment is clearly difficult. Entertainment systems will become more interactive, more personalized, more vivid, more compelling, and more mobile. The form of the personalization may well be more illusory than real. The artificially intelligent and fuzzy logic programs will, in effect, be able to shape patterns of thoughts and images that will be quite similar within comparable socioeconomic and demographic groups.

Fifteen-year-old males will likely want similar but individualized entertainment packages. They will only answer a few preprogrammed questions and then await their mass-customized response.

## OVERALL TREND REVIEW

### Challenges and Pitfalls

- Virtual reality junkies incapable of being reliable workers or contributors to society.
- Entertainment-impoverished underclass (resembling drug and gambling addiction).
- International hostility or cultural intolerance to U.S.-dominated high-tech VR entertainment systems.

### Opportunities

- Achieving a high value-added entertainment business while avoiding the creation of socially dysfunctional environments.
- Leveraging the most powerful info-technologies to other cyberspace industries and creating important new business, health, and educational applications.
- Creating a whole new series of leisure/entertainment/sports/recreation industries that replace traditional industrial jobs and create new industries.
- Globally integrated direct broadcast entertainment with interactive entertainment and Internet-based systems.
- Effective legislative and regulatory action to curtail the potentially most destructive applications of the new VR technologies.

# CHAPTER 13

## The Next Billion Years

### CHALLENGES TO THE SURVIVAL OF HUMANITY

The so-called third millennium (at least in Western time concepts) will be a time of enormous challenge and change. How well we meet these challenges will decide how long the species *homo sapiens* will survive. These potential challenges to survival seem almost endless. The hurdles to be overcome in just the next century suggest that sustaining the species for even a thousand more years may be extremely difficult.

The problems to be met range from global warming and carbon dioxide and methane buildup to the darkening of the albedo (or reflectivity) of the polar ice caps. They also include global pollution, desertification, loss of the rain forests and arable land, depletion of petrochemical energy sources, inability to achieve and economically sustain a steady-state global population, inability to provide universal access to global education and health care, techno-terrorism, nuclear proliferation, and much more. We seem to have an endless array of new viruses attacking humanity's health.

Ironically, we have made little substantial progress in overcoming known dangers even as new technologically generated challenges are emerging at an exponentially increasing pace. We have even had difficulty vanquishing rampant computer viruses (now over 50,000 formally recorded and growing strong), or even fixing something as seemingly inconsequential as the millennium (or Y2K) bug.

Thus, it seems that the next century and most certainly the next millennium hold the key to whether humanity can survive as a species. To do this we will have to shift from a maximized economic-growth mentality to a maximized human-development and survival mentality. This means developing more wisdom rather than blindly developing more information or more technology.

Goal number one must be to sustain a livable biosphere. This is not something we can do quickly. The objective must be to improve the environment at least gradually over the next few centuries—a task easier said than done. If our global population hits 12 billion within the next century the challenge will become ever so much larger.

Consider this: So far we have lived at best some one-seventh as long as the giant dinosaurs that once ruled the earth, a fact that should put our current environmental dilemmas in clear perspective. As Sir Arthur Clarke has said, "The dinosaurs failed to survive due to the lack of an effective space program." The lesson to be learned from Sir Arthur's observation is not to pursue a space program (although this is certainly a good idea), but rather to plan ahead. It is possible that we may fail to survive because we developed high technology but failed to develop from it systems designed to evolve our species instead of simply expanding economic production.

The twenty-first century may thus spell "do or die" for humanity. Here are some of the issues to consider with regard to our aspirations to survive not just another millennium, but an entire eon.

### Coping with the Challenge of Future Compression

The rate of technological change is not accelerating but rather constitutes a state of jerk, an increasing rate of acceleration. The future is approaching us much faster than the past is receding. Technology is a one-way gate. We cannot easily "un-invent" our advanced technology or turn the clock back without catastrophic results. We are headed at astonishing speed toward the age of the World-Wide Mind and the question is whether we can survive our own intelligence. The spiral of technological advancement thus becomes an opportunity and a threat.

### Using the World-Wide Mind to Survive

Most of the great challenges to preserving a livable biosphere on our fragile planet will require not only new and enlightened social, economic, political, and cultural policies, but technological innovation as well. Significantly, most of the great global challenges in terms of pollution, global warming, clean energy, improved education and health care, and so forth depend on technology. In technology, particular space, telecommunications, and information technology. Social challenges, trade disputes, personal liberties, labor disputes, and ethnic and religious disputes will very much complicate the problems even more.

## CAN HUMANITY SURVIVE ANOTHER CENTURY?
## PERHAPS ANOTHER MILLENNIUM?
## OR DARE TO ASPIRE TO LAST AN EON?

Our greatest challenges to survival will likely come in the course of the twenty-first century. A host of key technical, economic, regulatory, and trade issues will need to be overcome in the course of the next century. The challenges are everywhere, but as the historian Barbara Tuchman observed, "The March of Humankind is largely the March of Folly." And yet we can hope. We can aspire to wisdom. We can start to build new institutions that can help design plans for survival rather than simple-minded economic growth. We can build new interdisciplinary research entities, such as the International Space University, the new Clarke Institute, or the Santa Fe Institute, that can provide us with key insights into the future.

We need such new educational and research institutions to help us better shape ways to foster cooperation between so-called advanced and developing economies—to realize not only increased global prosperity, but, more important, the survival of the species. We have begun to shape not a Global Village, but a World-Wide Mind to help us think more clearly and plan more synergistically and sometimes more serendipitously. In honor of Arthur C. Clarke and the ancient island of Serendib (the historic name of Sri Lanka and the root word for serendipity), let's explore the ambition of humanity to survive another billion years.

### Jerk

The pace of modern innovation and technological change has gone from swift to super-exponential. If one were to pretend that the entirety of human civilization were only one day long, we would see a rather remarkable image of the development of the species known as *homo sapiens*. The phase we would know as that of the hunter/gatherer would consume virtually the entire day, except for the last three minutes. These last three minutes, the time of a properly cooked egg, would represent the time of agriculture, towns and cities, and the birth of technology. The last nine seconds of our artificial "superday" would be the Renaissance. The last four seconds would be the industrial age. And what about the time of television, lasers, satellites, biotechnology, super computers, robotics, artificial intelligence, and spandex? This age of high technology, which consumes us so thoroughly in the late twentieth century, would occupy about 600 milliseconds of this superday of human existence. Within the next few superminutes of time—if we survive as a species—we could colonize and terraform planets, convert to clean and limitless energy, create von Neumann machines to search the universe for other intelligent life, and much, much more (to review a superspeed view of the universe, see the Next Billion Year Timeline at the end of this chapter).

Human development and the evolution of technology is not accurately represented by a steady series of progressive steps with continuous and steady evolution. We have managed to lurch both forward and backward. But now we increasingly live in a period of "future compression." In physics an increasing rate of acceleration is called "jerk," and this is what we are experiencing in contemporary times. Just since the time of Ancient Greece, human population has increased about sixty times from 100 million to 6 billion, but during this same time period global information has increased some 10 to 100 million times. Information is mushrooming at least 200,000 times faster than our population growth. This is like an agile turtle trying to catch the space shuttle.

In trying to catch up, our education and information systems have tried to speed up faster and faster on more and more specialized conveyor belts. The opportunity to become Renaissance people or solve complex problems in interdisciplinary teams has been increasingly lost. Ph.D. research has become so narrow and deep it has almost become invisible. The future challenge in telecommunications and information systems is not faster throughput. It is coping with information overload and creating new ways of learning and sharing information.

Humanity has been around, at most, only about 5 million years. This is much, much less than the 35 million years that represented the age of the giant dinosaurs, when they were the masters of the world. The survival of our species on Earth for the long haul is in question in part because of our exploding technology and a Niagara of specialized and unconnected data. The ability of *homo sapiens* to create not only an effective electronic Global Village, but to create humanized smart cities and ultimately a viable World-Wide Mind will require better telecommunications, information, and energy systems than today's experts are now planning.

The truth is that the twenty-first century can be one of two things. Either it can be a vital connecting link to the future in which we use our most advanced information, telecommunications, and education tools to create a viable economic, industrial, political, and ecological system for human survival, or it can be the end of us as a species. Not only will we not realize the unimaginable achievements that one billion years of continuous human culture could bring— we simply will not make it.

In the next century we have the potential to use our information and telecommunications technology and systems much too unwisely. We can indeed fail as a species. In the twenty-second century our planet will still be here, but we humans may not make it or we may find ourselves a dying breed. Already frogs may have started to mutate into oblivion due to the lack of adequate ozone-layer protection from radiation.

How can we fail in the crucial twenty-first century? There are a lot of choices:

- We can change the albedo of our polar caps through oil spills and pollution and flood our towns and cities. Once melted, the sea water will be enormously difficult to freeze again.
- We can create enormous holes in the ozone layer and mutate ourselves, like today's frogs, ultimately risking our very existence.
- We can develop a steady-state global population but not adapt our economic systems to such limited growth. The problems of the Japanese economy may well be sending us such a warning today.
- We can fail to use our best tele-education and telehealth systems to provide for global equity of learning and health care in our increasingly seamless worldwide economy.
- We can allow the process of desertification and destruction of our wetlands and rainforests to continue unabated. This will reduce our food supply and destroy other species while also raising the levels of carbon dioxide in our atmosphere to dangerous levels. To cope, our remote sensing and information-processing systems need major changes to become much smarter and user friendly.
- We can continue raising levels of energy consumption of hydrocarbon-based fuels to higher and higher levels until the cost of fuel reaches disastrous levels.

The experiment with Biosphere 2 in the Arizona desert proved that humankind is not yet smart enough to create a livable planet of our own design—even one a few city blocks in size. We don't need huge amounts of new technology as much as we need new and better ways to apply it to society in interdisciplinary and "knowledge-rich" ways. For the new millennium the challenge in developing and applying new technology is not to increase economic growth and material wealth, but rather to find ways to sustain our species within a recyclable biosphere as well as to move our species into

204 / e-Sphere: The Rise of the World-Wide Mind

the cosmos beyond our planet. This is a common mission for all humankind and must involve all countries and all people.

In rising to meet this new millennium challenge it will be increasingly clear that space-related technologies and applications, information and communications technologies, and effective use of artificial intelligence are the keys to human success or failure. Only these smart systems can allow us to think and act synoptically on a planetary scale and create the tools to establish global cooperative behavior. This I call the rise of a new e-Sphere and the start of a World-Wide Mind.

The primacy of space is both inwardly and outwardly directed. We must use our space tools to cope effectively and comprehensively with planetary problems such as pollution, education, health care, communications, smart transportation, and navigation. We can also use our most advanced space sciences to move outward into space. Perhaps over the next 50 million years we can explore, settle, and make livable vast parts of our galaxy as well. It is the estimate of Eric Burgess that in just that small amount of cosmic time (i.e., 50 million years) we can indeed build a Galactic Brain.

### Tele-Education and Telehealth as Critical Steps

At the opening session of the International Program for the Development of Communications, organized by UNESCO in the late 1970s, Sir Arthur C. Clarke explained that our emerging computer and communications technologies will eventually produce something he called the "electronic tutor." It would be portable, cheap in cost, and contain a vast encyclopedia of information that could be electronically updated or connected via satellite. When asked whether this electronic tutor was going to replace teachers, he sensibly replied, "No, of course not, we will always need teachers. But come to think about it," he continued, "any teacher that can be replaced by a machine probably ought to be."

Today this technology seems less than a decade away. Tomorrow's developments are with us ever faster. There are "anytime and anywhere" satellite handsets to be bought at under a thousand dollars. There will soon be fifty smart virtual reality arcades from Disney strewn about our globe. We can even buy Dragon and other software (this is a computer program that allows spoken words to be transferred into written text reasonably fast and accurately).

Infotechnology is sweeping us quickly ahead. The latest developments in Ka, Q, and V-band satellite communications promise us the ability to provide megabit/second messages to handheld tele-computers that can tell us where we are, access any library, and calculate in an instant any problem that Eniac would have taken hours to have solved. Soon, when we learn to cope with "rain fade" problems that affect extremely high frequency radio waves with tiny wave lengths the size of amoebas, we can have almost unlimited communications to portable electronic telecomputer units with memories many times the size of the *Encyclopedia Britannica*. Of course, in time these might become even more portable as they shrink to the size of implanted chips and "worn" phased-array antennas. Or maybe we will simply carry our pocket-sized electronic tutor units around with us and then plug them into the closest fiber-optic terminal for any necessary updates or language translation.

Such technology can revolutionize our global educational and health-care systems by making these services universally available and at much lower cost. Experiments carried out under the Intelsat Global Satellite System's Project SHARE in 1986 and 1987 showed the potential of space-based tele-education and telehealth in many dozens of countries. For instance, the Chinese National Television University started under the Project SHARE tests and demonstrations. This project that began with a few thousand students and a few dozen terminals has mushroomed in size. It now has over 4 million students and over 90,000 operational terminals. The SITE experiments that started with the NASA ATS-6 satellite experiments in India likewise stimulated a wide range of operational tele-education programs that are now carried on by the Indian government's INSAT satellites and provide service to over a million participants.

There is a phenomenal amount of new space-segment capacity planned for deployment over the next decade. These advanced satellites will have a combined global throughput capability of some five to seven terrabits/second in the new millimeter wavebands alone. These new satellite systems contain sufficient margin to create multichannel video, audio, and Internet multimedia education systems and health-care networks on a planetary basis. Fiber-optic systems (some with links capable of many terabits/second) will represent at least 10 to 100 times more raw transmission capability than these high-capacity satellites. The problem will not be throughput or the cost of telecommunications. No, the key will be to use our extraordinary new technical capabilities to achieve "better" rather than simply faster.

Even more challenging than new fiber and satellite hardware, therefore, is the issue of the content and the software we need to meet social needs. The concept of a single global health-care or educational system for the world is fatally flawed. The demands of language, culture, local economic and agricultural needs, and so forth suggest that we need a diverse and complex source of programming that responds to local needs. It is here that space cooperative ventures can combine strengths. Project SHARE showed that space-based tele-education and telehealth succeed not on the basis of sophisticated technology but on the basis of local initiated programming that respond to locally defined needs.

### Mission to Planet Earth

Another hope for the future is the practical application of space geomatics to saving the Earth's biosphere and more effective urban and transportation planning. Already one can see progress in using space to make our planet green again. The Indian province of Uttar Pradesh has, through the long-term application of space-based remote sensing, been transformed from semiarid desert to a green and agriculturally productive area. Amazingly, this process of replanting forests, rechanneling streams and rivers, and redevelopment of arable lands has also served to create new industries and jobs, empower women's cooperatives, and improve education and health-care systems as well. It is the only place on the planet where we can see from outer space significant progress toward the "regreening" of Earth.

There is no reason why the lessons learned in Uttar Pradesh cannot be repeated again and again in Sri Lanka, Burma, Bangladesh, Pakistan, China, Thailand, Indonesia, Vietnam, the Philippines, Malaysia, Ecuador, Bolivia, Nigeria, Ghana, Uganda, and so on throughout the developing world as well as in barren regions of the OECD countries. The powerful new information tools that emerge from the use of global information systems are only beginning to be understood.

Today there are plans for integrated development and modernization projects that combine solar electrification, information and telecommunications systems, tele-education and telehealth, microbanking, microenterprises, and more, to be coordinated through the World Bank, Intelsat, the Solar Electric Light Foundation, and the new Clarke Institute for Telecommunications and Information. The point of such as the Millennium Village project is to create a model that generates sufficient revenues to sustain capital investment and is also environmentally sound.

It is important to try to develop new economic and technological models for all countries of the world. We need new "e-Sphere models" that sustains  our best hope for the future. In these new e-Sphere models there should thus be projects to support, refine, and improve the following:

- tele-education.
- telemedicine.
- reduced air pollution programs—especially with regard to methane, carbon dioxide, and fluorocarbons.
- elimination of human-generated pollutants.
- sustained and productive fishing.
- preservation of diverse species on the planet.
- recycling of arable land.
- reversal of desertification.
- conservation of wetlands and mountainous regions.
- coping with ozone depletion.
- "smart transportation" systems and long-term elimination of petrochemical fuels.
- interdisciplinary urban planning.
- more effective use of telecommuting.
- creation of new "clean" jobs in industry and services.

Extensions of these projects could seek to utilize global information systems in new and innovative ways, create effective disaster-warning and recovery systems, provide effective search-and-rescue programs, interconnect electronic libraries and museums, as well as provide job retraining and professional recertification of a wide range of professionals.

The examples of what could be done to create a better world environment in the twenty-first century abound. In China, the National TV University is providing education in new and apparently highly successful ways. The Uttar Pradesh of India region has been economically and environmentally restored. The launch of the Triana environmental satellite into the L-5 Lagrangian point a million miles from Earth could answer basic questions about the energy exchange budget between the Earth and the Sun. It may also give rise to a new global space-environmental television channel to show us how to use our most advanced telecommunications, information, and space technologies to save not only our planet, but human life on our planet.

The key is as simple as seeking a "win–win" approach that advances knowledge, improves the environment, and creates an economic system that contributes to a "spiral of improvement" rather than to a spiral of blind growth and expansion within our fragile but rapidly evolving e-Sphere.

There are within the history of Western philosophy at least four important schools of thought: Idealism (Plato, St. Augustine, Ambrose, and others), Realpolitick (Machiavelli, Hobbes, Hegel, Nietzsche, Marx, and Schopenhauer), Democratic Liberalism (John Locke, Jean Jacques Rousseau, Montesquieu, John Stuart Mill, Jeremy Bentham, and Adam Smith), and Scientific and Technological Objectivism (Aristotle, Francis Bacon, Immanuel Kant, David Hume, René Descartes, Norbert Wiener, and Buckminster Fuller). Some believe that the key to the future in the twenty-first century and beyond involves simply turning the crank of technological progress ever faster. This is the view of "Extropists," those who believe that humanity is the intelligent force in the universe and that by turning the crank of technological innovation ever faster they will prove Isaac Newton and the Second Law of Thermodynamics wrong. They believe that with sufficient technology we can halt entropy and solve every problem that humanity faces. This is almost certainly wrong!

We must call on a balanced approach. This means drawing on both technology and humanist goals to survive even a millennium— let alone aspiring to last another eon. We are infants in the course of cosmic time. We are much too young and naïve as a species to aspire to change the course of history or Newtonian/Einstenian physics on a galactic scale. We must draw on the wisdom of all the historical schools of thought to survive. Balance, not speed, is the answer. Our new e-Sphere philosophy must be of survival over growth, of wisdom and knowledge over information, and of global systems and quality over technology. This is a philosophy based on fundamental changes that is key to building a successful e-Sphere culture in the twenty-first century.

These are not changes that can be made in a year or even a decade. As the third millennium begins there are some twenty-three active armed conflicts occurring around the world. These acts of savagery and aggression are occuring in parallel with the Internet's reshaping of our global economic network. We humans are a complex group of beings, at once magnificent and munificent, but also monstrous and malignant. Building a Global Village and ultimately a planetary electronic culture which I have called the e-Sphere seems to be our destiny. In short, if our descendants evolve continuously on this planet and go on to settle other planets and star systems over the next billion years, the future will hinge on the steps we take in this new century of a new millennium. The first step will be to develop a global consciousness—that is the World-Wide Mind.

## NEXT BILLION YEARS: A TIMELINE

### Formula for Calculating Supermonth Time

1 supersecond = 2 years

1 supermonth (equivalent to the history of humankind) = 5 million years

1 superyear = 60 million years

100 superyears = 6 billion years

### The View of the Universe in Supermonth Time

Some 250 years ago in supermonth time (15 billion years in the past) a "singularity" creates the universe with the Big Bang.

The universe holds many puzzles. These include such riddles as did this singularity begin expanding in as many as twenty-seven different dimensions? Are there more than the four known basic forces, represented by electromagnetic, gravitational, weak nuclear, and strong nuclear forces? Is there enough mass in the universe so that it will eventually contract back on itself? Is the universe smaller than we thought? Do distortions of space allow light to be reflected back on itself? Is our view of the universe thus equivalent to seeing a "wall of mirrors" (i.e., an illusion of distance)? Is there a process that can actually reverse entropy? Is Newton's Second Law of Thermodynamics correct? This law states that in any closed system, entropy (or the tendency toward "disorder" or the "arrow of time") will move systems or behavior toward chaotic behavior. Can there be instantaneous communications across the universe, for instance, by modulating gravitons? Could there be intergalactic communications of advanced civilizations using neutrinos, quasars, and so forth? What could the newly discovered "walls of galaxies" throughout the universe mean? What do black holes truly represent? Is there the possibility of intelligent life throughout the universe?

### Timeline

100 superyears ago (6 billion years) the second-generation or Type 2 star systems and galaxies were formed from the "stardust" of first-generation or Type 1 galaxies of which the Milky Way and our solar system were formed.

80 superyears ago (5 billion years in the past) the Earth and the planets of the solar system began to take shape.

16 superyears ago (1 billion years in the past) the Earth began to evolve the simplest types of lifeforms (algae, amoebas, paramesium).

2.5 years to 6 months ago in supermonth time (i.e., 150 million to 30 million years in the past) was the age of dinosaurs.

1 month ago (5 million years in the past) saw the earliest of early ape men.

1.5 hours ago (10,000 years in the past) was the start of the age of agriculture and towns and villages.

4 minutes ago was the Renaissance (500 years in the past, the age of Gutenberg and Newton).

2 minutes ago the Industrial Revolution begins with textiles and industrial mills (240 years in the past).

20 seconds ago (40 years in the past) is the age of computers, satellites, lasers, artificial intelligence, biotechnology, television, and spandex.

15 seconds ago (30 years in the past) the first humans walk on the Moon.

Now, at the start of the third millennium, we have the age of cloning, DNA engineering, terabit/second information systems, and virtual reality Donkey Kong.

7 superseconds from now (15 years from now) will come wearable, multipurpose antennas and computer systems for mobile communications, entertainment, navigation, and information processing.

15 superseconds from now (30 years in the future) will bring artificial islands, colonies under the oceans, mag-lev hypersonic tunnels between the continents, and molecular-level quantum communications and digital processing (a billion times faster than today's processors).

20 superseconds from now (40 years in the future) will come permanent colonies and hotels in space.

25 superseconds from now (50 years in the future) ecoeconomics may begin to evolve from capitalism (a new synergy of consumption, production, and recyclable products and services).

30 superseconds from now (60 years in the future) will come cybernetic organisms and smart robots, and bio-to-bio modems via alpha waves.

40 superseconds from now (80 years in the future) will bring the Von Neumann Machine (artificial machine evolution) and 200-year lifespans for *homo electronicus.*

50 superseconds from now (100 years in the future) Earth Guard will be in place (i.e., a space program to divert asteroids or comets from direct impact on Earth).

1 superminute from now (120 years in the future) will bring the space elevator in geosynchronous orbit and solar-power colonies in Lagrangian points (i.e., the stable gravitational point between the Sun and the Earth's gravity wells).

2 superminutes from now (250 years in the future) will bring creation of livable atmospheres on Mars and Venus and space-based mining and manufacturing on the Moon and asteroids.

5 superminutes from now (625 years in the future) will bring intergalactic communications, possibly via graviton waves or modulated neutrinos, and discovery of other intelligent life in the universe.

10 superminutes from now (1,250 years from now) will come the realization of GUTS (grand unified theory of the space–time continuum).

1 to 2 superhours from now (7,500 to 15,000 years in the future) will come "fundamental knowledge" as to whether we can reverse the arrow of time (i.e., discovery of a "reverse entropy" force that has been called, in concept, Extropism) or discovery of another dimension of the universe or a positron universe.

1 superyear from now (60 million years into the future) will we see colonization of the Milky Way?

16 superyears from now (1 billion years into the future) will the Sun, Earth, and solar system civilization be at risk from a solar nova?

# CHAPTER 14

## Coping with Life in the Age of the World-Wide Mind

As we begin a new millennium, a new awareness needs to begin. We need to learn to live a new type of life that springs forth from what might be most accurately called a nonlinear world. Change and adapting to change are the fundamental shifts that the twenty-first century brings to a world that is ill-prepared for this new environment. It is a launching pad into a critical period that may very well spell the difference between survival and a failed species. God has not provided an insurance policy for *homo sapiens* to live in peace and prosperity on our tiny planet in perpetuity. Our econiche is not insured. The initial challenge that faces all of us as we start a new age on this small planet is to recognize that a new age has actually begun to emerge. There is a paradigm shift actually occurring and the signs are everywhere, from the Internet to the Hubble Telescope, from the nonstop global stock markets to telecommuting, from genetic engineering and cloning to virtual reality entertainment. The world is now changing at superspeed and will never again be quite the same.

In the age of Isaac Newton, those who succeeded correctly claimed that their insights and achievements came from being able to stand on the shoulders of giants. Today the nature of change and innovation is remarkably different. We are building many new floors each week on the 10,000-story building of human knowledge (see Chapter 2). Teams of educators, research doctors, scientists, engineers, computer systems analysts, and entrepreneurs that number in the millions are reinventing our world even now. They are creating new educational software, developing and genetically engineering new drugs, inventing new seeds for agriculture, and creating new e-commerce business with truly global impact. They are doing all this in the blink of an eye.

These global innovators are not isolated inventors and tinkers like Alexander Graham Bell or Samuel Breese Morse, who gave us the telephone and the telegraph. They have gone well beyond the prototype industrial laboratory that Thomas Edison created in Menlo Park, New Jersey. No, these global innovators are redefining our world in timespans that are shrinking to microcosms. They are working within massive teams that are electronically linked together in sophisticated labs, universities, research centers, and board rooms that encircle the globe. It is difficult to know how or understand who created the Internet or e-mail or e-commerce or Beanie Babies or spandex. No one can keep track of the many thousands of products and services that are being spawned daily by the massive teams of faceless innovators who are changing our world, not step by step but at superspeed. In a time of innovation, which is now progressing at the rate of a fourth-order exponential, a systematic strategy for coping with change is needed.

The age of the World-Wide Mind will be increasingly complex and daunting, but not impossible. There are no simple solutions, but here are fifteen issues that must be addressed with new interest and intensity. There is no detailed agenda of fifteen steps that can be taken to save the world. The world of the World-Wide Mind is too complicated to be solved by a single plan of action. Nevertheless, there are some reasonable steps to be taken that may help us to adapt to the challenges of life in the twenty-first century. In each of these areas major changes, which might be called paradigm shifts (or nonlinear transforms), are altering our world forever. In each of these areas new plans of action are needed to address how to use technology to create positive evolution rather than simple economic growth.

### 1. Education

If there is a basic message contained in this book it is that education is the answer. Educational reform at virtually all levels is essential to living a successful life in the age of Telepower. Some of the most important tenets are the following:

- Implement life-long learning in order to keep pace, to keep your job, or to train for the next one.
- Develop self-paced and interactive learning systems.

- Return to greater reliance on "Renaissance education" as computers become our specialized information data sources.
- Use interdisciplinary learning concepts and employ interdisciplinary planning teams.
- Recertify professionals to keep up with exponentially increasing knowledge.
- Use experiential, hands-on learning processes on a continuous basis.
- Develop and apply the best of advanced tele-education systems.
- Expand efforts to provide truly global education to the 2 billion people without adequate education systems, but do so in a way that respects local societies, cultures, and languages.

We cannot try to speed up the same old "educational escalator" to simply run faster on the same old track. This will not work. We must reinvent our educational systems almost entirely and discard models of the past. Some of our most cherished educational institutions now block the way to needed change, but even now they are beginning to see a new way ahead. The wisdom of Socrates remains true even today as we enter the age of the World-Wide Mind: "There is only one evil, ignorance, and one good, knowledge."

## 2. Health Care

Almost one-quarter of the disposable income of Americans now goes toward education and health-care expenses: 13 percent to health care and 10 percent to education and training. Residents of OECD countries spend large portions of their income in a similar manner. Thus, Europeans and Japanese typically spend 15 to 20 percent of their income for health, education, and training as well. Telepower tools have already been effectively adapted to education and training via satellite, fiber, cable TV, and the Internet, but health care has lagged behind. The challenge of the next two decades will be to find better ways to apply telehealth techniques to disease prevention, health maintenance, and R&D to develop new medication at more reasonable cost.

The challenges in health and medical care are huge. We must adapt to a time in which there will be much longer lifespans. Ways must be found to extend adequate health care to all corners of the world. We must somehow control runaway costs. Technology can help, but totally new paradigms to allow individuals to take charge of their own health care are essential. In overall perspective, there must be care taken so that new biotechnological cures, cloning, and genetic engineering do not create an ultimate danger to the survival of the species.

### 3. Job Training

Careers in the twenty-first century are going to be dramatically different than those of the twentieth century. A new approach based on adaptability and acceptance of multiple careers must be developed for the age of the World-Wide Mind. One must ultimately come to the new perspective that having the opportunity to pursue several different careers and to be educated in more than one field or skill is actually desirable and fulfilling as opposed to being a sign of failure or loss. Likewise, the idea of working in teams will become both more necessary and more rewarding. Such cultural shifts are the most difficult of all. Telecommuting will be perhaps the biggest single change over the next ten years, as over 100 million people in service economies find a new way to travel to work—via electrons rather than by automobile.

### 4. Technological Unemployment and Deskilling

Closely tied to the idea of multiple careers, developing flexible telework skills, and working in electronic teams is the basic need to be flexible. This means we must avoid overspecialization. It also means developing jobs that are not just throwbacks to mindless repetitive activities that are better left to robots. By 2020 archaic assembly lines should become obsolete even in the most basic of the world's economies. It will be a challenge to Telepower management to create challenging jobs that make economic and intellectual sense for the next century. In the age of Telepower a worker's mind will be too great a resource to waste. Perhaps we will find creative ways to recombine patterns of production and consumption that Thorstein Veblen first warned us was of the fundamental concern in terms of creating a "sustainable economy."

### 5. Life, Leisure, and Entertainment

The most important growth sector for the near-term future may well be the sports, recreation, leisure, entertainment, hotel, and restaurant industries. This shift of growth toward nonessential enterprises contains a host of challenges. It raises the question of how to provide qualified and competent employees for essential industries. It suggests that such an economic shift could distort key social values. It even asks how a twenty-first-century world copes with what might become wholesale tendencies toward escapism. The key is to recognize that economic growth or economic incentives alone will not sustain any society on a long-term basis. Economic growth and intellectual and social growth cannot and must not be equated in the new nonlinear world of the World-Wide Mind.

Instilling the value of social worth and integrity, creating a work ethic, and providing intellectual stimulus to excellence are probably essential to the survival of the species. It is not clear in a nonlinear world that is moving at superspeed how we can successfully motivate future generations. In the new world of advanced entertainment and escapism it is important to have a strategy to retain a humane and progressive society. New forms of World-Wide Mind "collectives" that create core values of sacrifice, loyalty, dedication, diligence, and unrelenting effort for societal improvement seem essential to sustaining a viable human civilization. Exactly how to accomplish this in an age of "me first" and "escapism now" is far from clear. The dynamics of crime, drug abuse, and human savagery versus twenty-first-century escapism as a way of life is an area of special focus and concern.

### 6. Economic Reform

The key to almost every aspect of adapting to life in the new millennium will come from evolving and improving our economic systems from the capitalist concepts of John Locke and Adam Smith to new, more advanced, and survival-oriented economics. This new economics must increasingly take into account the survival of the species, the preservation of our biosphere, the importance of intellectual wealth over material wealth, and a wiser application of nonlinear math and evolutionary processes in the twenty-first century. This simply means applying survival values and environmental costs to pricing systems and attempting to reunite the production and the consumption exchange values in our complex global economy. When it is recognized that we pay ten times less for a gallon of gasoline ($1.50 to $4.00) that takes millions of years to produce than we pay for a ten-year-old bottle of wine ($15 to $40), the problems with our current economic pricing system becomes clear.

### 7. New Environmental Systems for the Age of the World-Wide Mind

There is ever-increasing evidence that manufacturers and service providers that pursue a green strategy in developing, producing, and delivering their products or services to market can achieve breakthrough success. They not only can be profitable, but also can be more profitable than their competitors. Those who wish to differentiate themselves and win in the new global market need to find ways to follow the e-Sphere algorithm. This is to bring products to market that are environmentally nurturing or sustaining and do so at a lower or neutral cost. The assumption that this is not possible is no longer true in the age of the World-Wide Mind. This is just one of the fundamental changes that is occurring. Success will actually be based on performing against this simple e-Sphere algorithm.

## 8. E-Commerce

One of the ways that the new economics and a new green economy can be achieved is through e-commerce. Increasingly, we will be able to move things and products rather than people. More and more of our economy will be in the form of services that are compatible with the sustainability of life on our planet. Much more rapid innovation in the design, improvement, and marketing of new environmental products and services will be achievable through a global information network that is available and responsive twenty-four hours a day, seven days or 168 hours a week. The problem is that just because these things are possible does not mean they will happen. Intelligent planning, wiser consuming, and longer-range perspective will all be needed. Closing the economic gap between developed and developing countries will be critical to making e-commerce truly global and green.

## 9. Living in the Age of Globalism

In the last five years the amount of global trading has increased over 5 percent and with the increasing spread of the Internet to perhaps a billion users by 2010 the spread of international trade and commerce will undoubtedly continue. It is possible to have global universities, research centers, corporations, and sporting teams. The basic question is what the role and responsibility will be of the nation state in this new electronic age of international collaboration and business. What will be the nature of conflict and wars in this new interconnected world. The book *McWorld vs. Jihad* clearly sets forth the clash in social values, cultures, and religions that besets our clearly schizophrenic world. It is not easy to make a smooth transition from a world of warring tribes to an interconnected global network of nonstop intellectual commerce. A lack of respect for differing values, languages, and cultures will only delay the evolution of a humane and effective world that represents the positive potential of Telepower and the World-Wide Mind. Bridging the gap between prosperity and poverty and finding common ground between ethnic groups and religious cultures will be one of the most difficult tasks of the twenty-first century.

## 10. Teleconvergence

The number-one force driving us toward the World-Wide Mind is the digital teleconvergence that is uniting the markets represented by the five Cs. These once separate markets of communications, computers, cable television, consumer electronics, and content will soon become one vast $5-trillion global market. Digital information and processing are creating a technical and market convergence that combines virtually anything that is electronic or optical together. It is one vast market for book publishers, newspapers, movie producers, television networks, telephone companies, computer and consumer electronic manufacturers, software developers, and on and on. This will give rise to new supercorporations with values greater than that of many nations of the world. Cisco and Microsoft are now valued at a half-trillion dollars. One-trillion-dollar corporations will ultimately follow. Teleconvergence will give us more sophisticated products and lower-cost services, but a world that individuals and even governments will find hard to control. The idea of a U.S. and European antitrust commission makes sense and a global antitrust commission probably makes even more sense. The need to channel teleconvergence in positive directions and to control abuses of monopoly is one of the great challenges we now face. The power of teleconvergence is ever increasing and reflected in the personas of Bill Gates, John Malone, Rupert Murdoch, Ted Turner, and an array of dot com billionaires.

## 11. Humanized Cities and Transportation Systems

Another paradigm shift that is coming is in the design and shape of our cities and the transporation systems that define their very existence. The powerful impact of telecommuting and the idea that your job or office is where you and your mobile telecommunications device happens to be is really hard to fully appreciate in the middle of this dramatic shift. This change will challenge the economic authority of nations, redefine the character of towns and cities, and force us to think in terms of the "global city" as well as the World-Wide Mind. The opportunity now exists to create major cities as centers of culture and education, but allow electronic communications to network areas of commerce together. This approach toward the creation of humanized telecities could allow our transportation systems to become smarter, more efficient, and better utilized. Communications and information systems would offload our highways and byways in new and innovative ways.

Under the new paradigm we could use our transportation systems on a twenty-four-hour-a-day basis rather than having highways always overloaded in rush hour and underutilized at other times of the day. This approach could allow more park land, and transfer real estate values to make land use more efficient with less sprawl. All of these changes stem from the paradigm shift that recognizes that the World-Wide Mind is more reliant on fiber-optic cables, satellites, and radio waves than on aircraft and highways.

### 12. Privacy

Too often the modern commercial world has been divided into the progrowth and probusiness sectors and the environmental and antigrowth factions. These divisions have also frequently been labeled conservative versus liberal or industrialist versus tree huggers. These types of divisions could be transcended in the age of the World-Wide Mind by redefining the objectives and the mechanisms for change. Why not attempt to create new algorithms that have universal support? This would involve defining new strategic aims that throw out the old zero-sum games that pit developer against environmentalist and liberal versus conservative.

The innovative application of new Telepower technology should allow us to redefine a world in which green products and services can also generate new jobs, create new prosperity, and allow important social goals to be pursued. These new technologies can give us improved transportation, reduced pollution, better health care, less crime, and improved education. Ironically, it seems that every new technology must give rise to new problems as well. One of the biggest problems to overcome will very likely be that of privacy. The need to create a more efficient economy, reduced pollution, and more efficient government and business will also give rise to the need for more data and information and more controls on individuals.

The key to survival may very well be more teamwork and more collective activities. How this can be done without being truly invasive to individual initiative and privacy is a major Telepower challenge. Indeed, we know that more data are being kept on computers. It is clear that more systematic tracking of individual and group behavior is occurring every year. At the start of a new age both big government and big business are to be feared, not only for abuse of privacy but for potential abuse of power. New legislation to protect health records, access to credit records, and so forth are positive steps currently underway, but further reforms and improvements are clearly needed. Aggressive antitrust steps and large fines and criminal penalties against the most significant abusers of privacy (both within industry and the government) are other recommended actions.

## 13. Information Overload

Another Teleshock concern is that of information overload. The amount of unwanted information and tension-creating stimulus that comes from living in a crowded urban environment is certainly on the rise. Information is growing at least 200,000 times faster than human population and this disparity in growth rates will soon be over a million times faster. The use of electronic filters, artificially intelligent knobots, and screening agents can be part of a technological fix, but the philosophical problem goes much deeper.

Will we actually be forced to take "smart pills" or have computer chips embedded in our brains to try to remember all that we should? Is there danger that when processes to "screen out" information begin we will potentially become subject to censorship or unwanted political or social controls? Some of these issues go to the heart of what it means to be a person and what we ultimately want our species to be and to achieve. Careful thought must be given to how controls are put on information that we receive or do not receive.

## 14. Combating Teleshock in Our Daily Lives

The assumption is often made that we have little choice about the character of the town or city in which we live. We note that tellers in banks are replaced by ATMs, gas-station attendants are replaced by "smart gasoline pumps," and now check-out clerks at grocery stores are being automated out of existence as well. The colleagues that we work with may be people on the other end of a WAN halfway around the world. There is legitimate concern that services are being automated and depersonalized. There is concern about value and quality decreasing as producers of goods and services are increasingly isolated from consumers and vice versa. Ralph Waldo Emerson, in the nineteenth century, said, "Technology is in the saddle and rides mankind." The question is if in the twenty-first century humans can recapture the control of advanced technological systems, humanize them, and make them compatible with the long-term survival of our biosphere.

If our world is depersonalized and dehumanized, what does that say about such things as pride in workmanship, diligence, or artistic appreciation? On the other side, what does it say about violence, theft and criminality, warfare and genocide, or the human ability to attack those who are out of sight or out of mind? Are these issues of social value, caring, and ethics always "fixable" by the use of yet more technology? At some stage do technology and complex automated systems actually become the problem themselves?

The solution seems to be in trying to find new balance between growth and environment, between efficiency and survival. There is also wisdom in trying to avoid the pitfall of overspecialization in planning and implementation of new systems. Large and complex systems should be designed not by specialized engineers, computer programmers, or scientists, but by a diversity of talents. Interdisciplinary teams can take broader values into account and create more humanized plans and designs. For instance, new urban environments, space stations, transportation systems, shopping malls, and museums, to name just a few examples, need a balanced and multidisciplinary group of planners to create a socially and culturally efficient design that considers more than economic efficiency.

The wisdom of the slogan, "Think globally and act locally," still remains. Individuals, corporations, governments, nongovernmental organizations, and international organizations all need to work together to create a more livable world. The simple concept of applying technology to solve social, economic, and environmental problems rather than using technology to create higher levels of economic throughput is an adjustment we need to make. We know how to consume more calories, build taller buildings, and build faster transportation systems. Now, in the twenty-first century, it is important to build a more humane society, preserve our biosphere, create improved educational and health-care systems, and explore human destiny in our expanding universe.

### 15. Releasing the Best of Telepower Potential: A Strategy for the Next Billion Years

Before the end of the twenty-first century it will become clear that humans can achieve material wealth sufficient for all to enjoy. The challenge is thus not economic wealth but rather the survival of the species and realization of the potential humans can achieve if we do not destroy our biosphere within the next few decades. It has been suggested that we could colonize and terraform Mars in a few hundred years, create a new star system within a million years, and spread human civilization throughout the entire Milky Way galaxy in less than 50 million years. The potential of what could be accomplished in the span of an eon is really hard to imagine.

Today only about 40 percent of the U.S. populace supports the continuation of the space program. Most of those who do would put their support in the context of new jobs, space applications, Earth observation, and other benefits to Earth and the current American and world economies. If *homo sapiens* as a successful species are to have a long-term destiny that will last a billion years we must go beyond the confines of Earth and the World-Wide Mind must ultimately become a "celestial brain" that reaches beyond the constraints of Earth's gravity.

The vision of a World-Wide Mind is one of how information technology and human society can work in tandem. What we know of technology and human intelligence is that progress has a strong sense of inevitability about it. If Darwin's concept of evolution and genetic progress is correct, the evolution of the species and of human civilization still has some way yet to go. Technology and intellectual progress always seem to be one-way gates. Once a discovery or invention has been achieved it is really not possible to "un-invent" knowledge unless we destroy all of civilization. The challenges ahead are thus great, but where we might ultimately go is even greater still. Teilhard de Chardin suggested that we humans have been sharing an ever-expanding intellectual "noosphere" ever since the start of the Renaissance. Marshall McLuhan saw that global satellite television was moving us toward a new reality—the Global Village. Now the Internet and cyberspace communications, driven by e-commerce and an emerging global interactive nervous system, is giving rise to the e-Sphere and the World-Wide Mind. Where we go next as a species is up to us, but the change imposed by future compression is neither slow nor subtle. For better or worse, we are being jerked into the new e-Sphere and leaving the Global Village quickly behind.

# Appendix A: Glossary of Terms

**AOL** One of the largest commercial ISP networks that serves over one-third of the U.S. Internet market by providing on-line services such as e-mail and data storage to private subscribers wishing to access the Internet.

**Archie** A program accessible through FTP that allows you to search various archives and databases stored on the Internet. Other programs are known as "Veronica" and "Jughead."

**ATM** Asynchronous Transfer Mode. This is an advanced "cell relay" type switch that is being increasingly used in the PSTN.

**BBS** Bulletin Board System. This is a convenient way to post information to be shared within a user group or community of interest.

**Bitnet** One of the largest computer networks that the Internet serves to interconnect.

**Browser** A general way of describing a program that allow Internet users to view, find, or navigate over the system to find desired information. See also Graphic Browser and Text Browser.

**Compuserve** Another major commercial vendor that allows individuals to access the Internet on an individual subscription basis.

**Common Signaling System Number 7** A global standard for allowing publicly switched telecommunications systems to become interconnected. It is based upon a seven-layer protocol that is designed to connect all forms of digital networks. TCP/IP can thus interconnect with public telecom networks by handshaking with a number-seven signaling protocol at a public point of presence or "switch."

**DSL** Digital Subscriber Loop. This allows high-speed data to be transmitted over short distances via copper telephone lines. It can be referred to as ADSL, HDSL, or XDSL depending on the speed of service.

**E-Mail** Electronic mail. Very brief to large documents can be sent to any addressee who has an e-mail address and is on the Net.

**Enterprise Network** A larger corporate private network that links individuals within a corporation. It can also be used to connect to suppliers and customers as well. Code words can be used to restrict access to various parts of an enterprise network.

**Eudora** One of several e-mail access and transfer systems commonly used on the Internet. Quick Mail is another commonly used system.

**Firewall** A computer encryption system that serves to separate confidential corporate or private data networks from the Internet or various other networks that the Internet interconnects.

**FTP** File Transfer Protocol. This is the standard protocol that is used to transfer files between computers or within a large network of computers. See also Telnet.

**Fuzzy Logic System** A logic system based on nonlinear math and the idea that choosing between many different options on a continuous basis allows greater flexibility and adaptability in control systems. This approach seeks to substitute systems that allow multiple choices on a continuous basis in lieu of having only two choices, such as between on and off or between "0" and "1" as in Boolean algebra as used in computer programs. In short, it is a logic system that seeks to model control or decision making after how humans think, as opposed to how digital computers operate.

**GII** Global Information Infrastructure.

**Geomatics** The combination of satellite imaging, space navigation, GIS, and communications into integrated services.

**Geoinformation** The integration of remote sensing, meteorological information, GPS navigation, data relay, and digital commmunications services to support the collection, processing, and distribution of information about the entire planet.

**Gopher** An entire system of Internet menus that was developed at the University of Minnesota (the Gopher name refers to the university's mascot). It works much like a menu on a personal computer.

**Graphics Browser** A browser system that allows access to hypertext graphics at Internet World Wide Web sites.

**High Data-Rate Services** This is not a precisely defined term. It is generally taken to mean services that are well above current conventional uses of telecommunications services. This is generally thought to range from the so-called T-3 (45 megabits/second level) for high definition television, interactive CAD/CAM, or big science, up to the OC-48 (2.488 gigabits/second) for supercomputer interconnect and so forth.

**Home Page** In effect, the entrance ramp or main doorway into a Web site. It is often equipped with pointers that allow direct interconnection with a variety of other Web sites that are interrelated.

**HTML** Hyper-Text Markup Language. The computer language used to prepare home pages and create Web sites. The key element of hypertext is the ability to combine text and images (including moving images) in an integrated home-page presentation.

**HTTP** Hyper-Text Transfer Protocol. A programming protocol that allows computers to interconnect to form the World Wide Web. Hypertext formatting allows the integrated transmission of text and images.

**Hypertext** The concept of allowing text, diagrams, graphics, video, and audio to be mixed together in an integrated presentation. See also Multimedia.

**Internet** A composite global network of networks that combines over 20,000 networks and nearly 40 million computer users together on a worldwide basis. Although initially focused on colleges, universities, and research centers, it is becoming increasingly a mass-communications network operating in most countries of the globe.

**Internet Explorer** An Internet browser developed and offered by the Microsoft Corporation in competition with Netscape, which is the major alternative in the U.S. market.

**IP** Internet Protocol.

**ISDN** Integrated Service Digital Network. A standardized system for digital communications within the publicly switched network devised and agreed to by the International Telecommunication Union (ITU) and the International Standards Organization (ISO). It allows all types of services to be offered within a common bearer channel with a separate signaling channel being used to add intelligence to a network. For multimedia, video, and other digital services there are broadband ISDN standards as well.

**ISP** Internet Service Provider. Serves to re-sell access to the global network. Some of the key ISPs are America On-Line, AT&T, Compuserve, Prodigy, MCI, and Sprint.

**LAN** Local Area Network. A private computer network that serves to connect computers, computer printers, fax machines, and other office equipment together via a modem-based system. LANs can be provided via wire (i.e., Appletalk, ethernet, FDDI, etc.) or via wireless or radio-based networks. Most users access the Internet via an office-based LAN.

**LISTSERV** How messages are distributed to a discussion or news group. All subscribers to such a group are routinely sent messages that are posted for distribution via the mailing list server or LISTSERV.

**LYNX** One of a number of text-based Web browsers.

**Mailing Lists** Mailing lists are used within discussion groups or newsgroups to which users sign up or subscribe. Once a message is posted on a list server it is automatically routed via e-mail to all current subscribers.

**MAN** Metropolitan Area Network. A large-scale LAN that is extended to interconnect a number of office campuses or corporate facilities together within a private network that covers a city or region.

**MCI Mail** A commercial access service to the Internet provided by MCI.

**Multimedia** A computer-based presentation that allows text, graphics, video, and audio to be integrated together. See also Hypertext.

**Netscape** A commercially successful Internet browser. When Netscape went public in late 1995 as a new NASDAQ stock under an initial public offering it became one of the most successful new stocks of all time. Microsoft Explorer is currently challenging Netscape in this software market. AOL has acquired Netscape and thus positioned itself as a major competitor to Microsoft in the Internet market.

**NSFNET** This is the backbone TCP/IP computer network operating in the United States under NSF funding. It constitutes the largest single network that is interconnected by the Internet. There are currently over 30,000 computer networks interconnected on the global Internet.

**Open Networks** Networks designed to operate with standardized protocols so that anyone operating with these protocols can interconnect. Private networks are designed to operate as proprietary and secure networks that are not "open."

**OSI** Open Standard Interface. The predominate open network standard. It is based upon the seven-layer protocol used within the Number 7 Signaling System. The concept of ISDN and broadband ISDN is built around the use of the OSI standards.

**PPP** Point-to-Point Protocol. Allows high-speed computer links. Also see SLIP.

**Private Network** A closed computer network that is used to communicate via LANs, MANs, or WANs within a corporate environment. These private networks can at selected points be designed to link to the open network that represents publicly switched networks.

**Prodigy** An on-line service that allows individual subscribers to access the Internet. It was created as a partnership between Sears and IBM.

**Protocol** The "handshakes" or standardized recognition codes that must be used to interconnect computer networks.

**PSTN** Public Switched Telephone Network.

**Quick Mail** One of several e-mail systems commonly used on the Internet. Eudora is another commonly used system.

**Search Engines** On-line software that is available to help Internet users find specific information or Web sites they are seeking. Some of the more popular search engines, which are based upon shareware and search the entire Net, are known as "Veronica", "Archie," and "Jughead" of comic-book fame. These shareware search engines, however, can be slow because of the breadth of search. Popular commercial search engines with a more targeted and faster approach include Yahoo!, Lycos, and InfoSeek.

**SLIP** A point-to-point protocol for interconnecting computers at high speeds of 1.5 to 2 megabits/second.

**Spam** A derogatory term that refers to a commercial message posted on one or more newsgroups, especially if it is not directly related to the specific interests of the users. Also used to describe junk and unsolicited e-mail.

**TCP/IP** Transmission Control Protocol/Internet Protocol. This is the main computer protocol that is used to link the Internet system together.

**T-1** A transmission speed of 1.544 megabits/second that is going to be used increasingly for broadband multimedia and Internet access. In Europe the transmission speed known as E-1 is the standard for broadband transmission system. This is a speed of 2.048 megabits/second.

**Telnet** A special program that allows access to specific Web sites and the ability to download files from these sites. This is particularly useful for Web sites that are libraries or scientific archives.

**Text Browser** A software package that gives you efficient access to Web sites.

**UAV** Unattended Autonomous Vehicle. Also called stratospheric platform.

**URL** Uniform Research Locator. The address of a Web site. Using a Web browser, you can go directly to a Web site if you know the URL.

**United Connection** One of several software packages that allow one to book airline and travel arrangements on a worldwide basis.

**Usenet** The collection of discussion or newsgroups on the Internet.

**USAT** Ultra Small Aperture Terminal.

**User Group** A specific list of users who have set up a bulletin board to share messages and to allow efficient communications within the group.

**VR** Virtual Reality.

**VSAT** Very Small Aperture Terminal. Used for interactive satellite communications.

**WAN** Wide Area Network. A private computer network that covers a very large geographic area. The Internet is in a sense the world's largest WAN.

**Windows NT** Microsoft software released in mid-1996 to provide a wide range of personal-computer functionality (similar to Windows 98) plus effective access to the Internet. This offering together with Microsoft Explorer is a direct challenge to Netscape.

**World Wide Web** A specific address on the Internet that is unified within a common addressing system. The use of HTML programming language allows text, graphics, video, and sound to be stored on an integrated basis. The result is a very appealing and user-friendly graphic or hypertext presentation of information. The entry point into each Web site is called a home page. This has now become the largest and most commercial part of the Internet.

# Appendix B: A Brief Guide to Cyberspace and Telecommunications Technologies and Services

The rapid spread of new information, communications, and entertainment technologies is difficult to follow. We have seen the convergence of many once separate industries into overlapping markets. The merging of markets now includes the 5 Cs: communications, cable television, consumer electronics, the computer, and the content/software companies. Finally, smart energy companies are joining the fray. Figure 1.7 suggests the complexity of the current digital market. In this massive new market, which will soon represent $5 trillion in annual turnover, everyone is getting into the act and potentially colliding with virtually everyone else.

The following guide, presented in alphabetical order, summarizes the key elements of the leading new technologies in terms of how they function, what services are delivered, and some of the key companies providing the services.

## Cable Television (CATV)

*Technology*

The initial CATV systems of the 1950s were very simple. A high-gain antenna was built to receive a remote television signal and then coaxial cable was used to hook up a rural town or village. The invention of the satellite allowed the idea of a superstation that could take programming off of a satellite and create a twenty-four-hour-a-day service on many different CATV systems. The satellite also allowed premium channels like HBO or CNN to be distributed to CATV networks. These changes allowed the growth of MSOs (Multi-Service Operators) like ATT/TCI, United Video, Cox, Jones Intercable, Continental, Time-Warner, and so on.

### Service

Today CATV systems offer 30 to over 120 video channels and soon will grow to a remarkable 500 channels. This increase in channel capacity is largely due to the new digital standard known as MPEG 2 that can allow a high-quality television channel to be transmitted via direct-broadcast satellite or CATV cable at a speed of only 6 megabits/second. These coax or fiber-optic cable TV channels can also be used to transmit (usually for an additional fee) high-quality audio, and even interactive services like pay-per-view movies and home security. In the future cable television systems would like to offer telephone service (interactive), T-1 broadband and multimedia services to business and home consumers, as well as node interconnections for personal communications services. In order to provide interactive services the cable network must be replaced by two-way repeaters that allow signals to travel both ways on the network.

### Key Service Providers

Key service providers are ATT/TCI, Cox, United Video, Time-Warner, Westinghouse, and so forth. Increasingly, we will see a merger of telephone and cable television systems to allow high-speed pipelines into the home to support interactive services, especially broadband Internet.

### Comments

CATV is very good at providing broadband capacity but has limited switching capability. CATV companies are frequently heavily in debt, often with something like a 90/10 debt to equity ratio, as indicated in the latest Dun and Bradstreet survey report.

### Cellular Telephone Service Including Cellular Digital Packet Data (CDPD) Services

### Technology

Cellular telephones began in the mid-1980s as a way to provide a much-higher-capacity system for voice service through the reuse of the limited frequency bands available for this service. Each of these cells is separated from other cells by the use a different set of frequencies in the adjacent cells. Thus, in the early systems every seventh cell could use the same frequency band over and over again. (Since that time even more efficient schemes for data reuse have been developed within analog as well as new digital systems). The original cellular service in the United States was developed by AT&T and was an analog service known as Advanced Mobile Phone Service (AMPS). It could, to a limited degree, also support data service. This data service was a limited-capacity Frequency Division Multiplexing (FDM) based service. A new type of analog carrier developed to send data entered service in 1995. It is called Cellular Digital Packet Data service and has largely been replaced by digital systems that offer so called Personal Communications Service (PCS).

### Service

Voice and data service is provided to and from the car or mobile site by radio wave from a radio tower. A Mobile Telephone Switching Office (MTSO) interconnects the mobile subscriber with the PSTN.

### Key Service Providers

In the United States one cellular service is provided by the Regional Bell Operating Company in each major metropolitan area and another competitive service is provided by an organization selected by the FCC in a lottery drawing. Cellular One and AT&T Wireless (formerly McCaw Communications) are the biggest "other" cellular providers. Sprint and Bell Atlantic/Vodafone/Air Touch are the other big digital PCS providers.

### Comments

Strong competition will occur as digital cellular (especially Nextel) and PCS become widely available.

## Digital Cellular and Enhanced Mobile Radio Telephone Service (EMRS)

### Technology

There are new standards that allow mobile communications in the United States based upon digital technology but using the 800 to 900 MHz frequencies allocated for the initial wireless cellular service. There is currently a marketing struggle between digital cellular and EMRS operating in the 800 to 900 MHz band and the new Personal Communications Service that operates in the 1,900 to 2,100 MHz band. Many believe that PCS will become the predominant service in the longer term. In Europe there is a French-based standard known as Global Standard for Mobile (GSM). This is based on a digital multiplexing concept known as TDMA (see Glossary) and is a key standard for most PCS services. Many service providers in the United States, however, want the next generation of digital PCS mobile service to be based upon another multiplexing concept known as spread spectrum or CDMA. In short, there is confusion as to which of several possible standards will be used as the predominant one in the United States and around the world over the longer term. Only time will resolve this issue with respect to digital cellular, GSM/PCS, and other PCS services. Worldwide, the dispute over whether to use TDMA or CDMA standards also continue.

### Service

Cellular, digital cellular, and EMRS are restricted to the 800 to 900 MHz band today. Digital cellular service is still limited to just voice and data. The idea is to eventually provide much more capacity through the advantages of digital compression techniques and improved frequency techniques. In time it could be able to provide higher quality, but at this time many believe that analog service is still better.

### Key Service Providers

Many of the same organizations providing cellular services are also providing PCS. Conventional cellular can be used as a backup to PCS in cases where there is a "dual mode" telephone capable of operating with both standards.

### Comments

Eventually digital cellular and PCS will become more or less the same, except that PCS frequencies are about twice as high (i.e., digital cellular is offered at 800 to 900 MHz while PCS is offered at 1.9 to 2 GHz).

### Direct Broadcast Satellite Service (also Direct-to-the-Home [DTH] Service)

### Technology

The basic concept is similar to that used with conventional fixed satellite services that have been provided on geosynchronous satellites for some thirty years. What is different is the idea of creating very high-power beams so that video signals can be sent directly to the home and received by very small and low-cost terminals. These are fourteen to eighteen inches in size for U.S. systems and as small as forty-five centimeters in the latest Japanese DBS systems. There are nearly 30 million direct-broadcast or direct-to-the-home television receivers in operation worldwide, and this number is projected to grow to 80 to 100 million by year-end 2005.

### Service

Most systems offer 30 to 100 channels. This includes premium entertainment services, educational and health channels, information services, home shopping, and high-fidelity audio. The key lack is local programming. Typical frequencies are 18 and 12 GHz. The Echostar or dish system is scheduled to be first to provide local programming in most large urban markets in the United States starting during late 2000 or early 2001.

### Key Service Providers

In the United States these include Hughes DirecTV, Primestar, USSB of the Hubbard Broadcasting Service, and the Echostar (or dish) DBS system. In Japan the DBS systems include SCC, JBS, and the NHK systems. For the rest of Asia there is Asiasat, Apstar, Indostar, Insat, Optus, Thaisat, and Koreasat 3. In time Koreasat 4 could cover most of Asia as well. In Europe the DBS systems include TV-Sat (Germany), TDF (France), Astra and Eutelsat's Hot Birds. Sweden plans to redeploy BSB's Marco Polo satellite to provide coverage to the Nordic countries. Several DBS systems for South America are planned as well. These include the use of Brazilsat, Cyberstar's SatMex system, the News Corporation's network on Intelsat 8 satellites, and an Argentine system called Nahuelsat that redeployed a Canadian satellite system for this purpose. Worldspace will provide radio broadcasting to Africa, Latin America and the Caribbean, and Asia. Sirius, XM Radio, AMSC, and TMI will provide direct radio satellite broadcasting in North America.

### Comments

DBS is proving capable of competing with cable TV systems. DBS is well positioned to provide new digital television and HDTV. In fact, the Japanese DBS systems are already providing HDTV service to over 200,000 commercial users, plus nearly ten million conventional DBS subscribers.

### Fiber-Optic Cable

*Technology*

The first fiber-optic technology was multimode fiber of relatively low capacity. The next step was the much higher capacity and very low-loss monomode fiber. The latest technology has made tremendous gains with a doubling of capacity every year. There is the so-called soliton-pulse fiber system that makes possible "repeaterless" fiber-optic cables. Even more important is the use of wave division multiplexing that will support monofiber systems transmitting at rates of 160 gigabits/second in submarine cables. Level 3 Corporation is deploying a terrestrial trunk fiber that sends 80 megabits/second transmissions over a single fiber. With forty fibers in the L-3 cable, a total speed of 3.2 terabits can be achieved over their network. Such land-based fiber systems are now being deployed that can operate at 1 to 10 terabits/second in the United States, Japan, and Europe.

*Service*

High-capacity fiber systems can now operate in the terabit/second range and can carry all forms of communications. It is best for high-volume trunk traffic and for video and multimedia distribution between urban areas. By 2010 fiber to businesses and curbside pedestals in housing developments will also become very prevalent. The key switching technology for fiber systems will be called Asynchronous Transfer Mode (ATM) although IP-based systems will also increasingly be used.

*Key Service Providers*

The key service providers are Corning, Scientific Atlanta, Alcatel, NEC, Lucent Technologies, Ciena, and Sycamore.

*Comments*

The key technology for the Information Highway is clearly fiber-optic cable. In the future the strength of fiber-optic transmission systems will be further leveraged by opto-electronic switching. Nevertheless, wireless and satellite technology will be a key part of the mix. This future of hybrid or mixed fiber and wireless systems has been described as a model for coming interactive broadband telecommunications systems. The key to this happening are so-called open network standards that allow these systems to seamlessly interconnect. IP and ATM standards are the primary means to achieve the so-called "Pelton Merge" (see Figure B.1). This model of the future appears to have become a better predictor of market behavior than the initial model offered by Nicholas Negroponte, called the Negroponte Flip (see Figure B.2).

### Fixed Satellite Service

*Technology*

There are some 300 operational geosynchronous satellites. Most of these use assigned frequency bands (i.e., the Cband, 6 and 4 Ghz; the Ku-Band, 14 and 12 Ghz. In the near future there will be Ka Band, 30 and 20 GHz and by 2010 millimeter wave-band frequencies of 38 and 48 GHz). The UHF, S, and X bands are used by military and government research satellites as well. High-gain Earth-station antennas send and receive signals to geosynchronous satellites. Transponders on the satellites receive, filter, and translate signals into the frequencies for the downlinks at an amplified level.

**Figure B.1**
**The Pelton Merge**

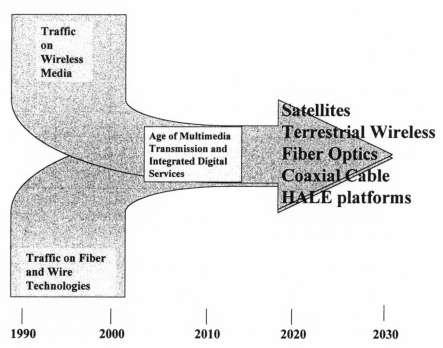

**Figure B.2**
**The Negroponte Flip**

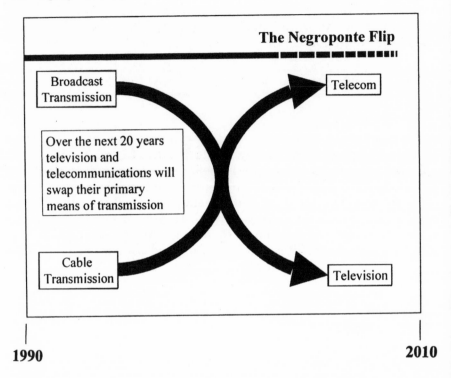

## Service

Satellites are broadband and can carry all types of services, including data, telephone, fax, video, high-quality radio, and multimedia.

## Key Service Providers

In the United States these include Hughes PanAmSat, Loral Skynet, Orion, and SatMex (now known as Cyberstar), GE Americom, Alascom, and others. Internationally they include Intelsat, New Skies, GE Americom plus the Columbia system, PanAmSat, Cyberstar, and the Lockheed Martin (LM), and others. Comsat is the U.S. carrier for both Intelsat, the global fixed satellite system, and Inmarsat, the global mobile satellite system, which is being acquired by Lockheed Martin Global Telecommunications. Up to twenty broadband, multimedia satellites for regional and global satellite systems to be deployed early in the twenty-first century have now been proposed by U.S. and European aerospace companies. These include Teledesic (Bill Gates, Craig McCaw, and Motorola), Skybridge (Alcaltel and Loral), Hughes (Spaceway), Loral (Cyberstar), and Lockheed Martin (Astrolink).

## Comments

Satellites are well suited for rural and remote services, overseas services, television distribution, multicasting, and large-scale business networks connected together by very small aperture terminals. These VSATs are typically under two meters in diameter, and the new Digital Video Broadcasting terminals are usually one meter in size. In the future antennas will be even smaller and will be known as ultra small aperture terminals (USATs). These will typically be 50 to 65 cm diameter. In general, satellites are getting larger, more powerful, and equipped with larger antennas in space so that ground antennas can be smaller and cheaper. Among the coming technologies for space and ground antennas are phased array antennas that allow flat or conformal antenna shapes.

## Intermediate (or Sometimes Instructional) Frequency Television Service (IFTS)

### Technology

This is a band of microwave frequencies that is reserved for television broadcasting for educational purposes. This band has been reduced due to underutilization. Some of the IFTS frequencies have been reassigned to the Multichannel Multipoint Distribution Service (MMDS) or wireless cable bands and others for low-power television. The simple system of broadcast radio involved with IFTS allows start-up and operation with little capital investment and modest operating costs.

### Service

Broadcast video and audio programming can be analog or digital in format. The imported signal received by satellite can be rebroadcast over an IFTS system.

### Key Service Providers

These are local operations, typically involving city governments, universities, or school systems. These are now often released to commercial organizations for mobile telecommunications or wireless cable television services.

## The Internet and Internet Service Providers

### Technology

This computer-network communications system was first created by the department of defense as the Advanced Research Projects Agency Network. Initially it was only an e-mail system. Today this system, which was "civilianized" and taken over in the United States by the National Science Foundation (i.e., NSFNET), has grown into a global network of networks. An estimated 100,000 computer networks link together 200 million users (as of year-end 2000 almost equally divided between the United States and the rest of the world). They are linked worldwide via a common protocol known as TCP/IP. Today, with high-speed fiber and satellite "pipes" operating at 155.5 to 622 megabits per second, the "super WAN" can handle everything from e-mail to video and high-resolution imaging services. Most links on the Internet are fiber, cable, or wire, but many satellite and wireless links also exist.

### Services

Initially e-mail was the predominant use. Today, with the higher-speed T-1 interface to support video and multimedia services, the newer broadband services such as the World Wide Web and Gopher represent the majority of uses. Many commercial users have established World Wide Web and Gopher sites to sell products and services. ISPs like America On-Line, MSN net, PSI net, Compuserve, MCI-Mail, and Prodigy, dominate the U.S. market. According to the Internet Society, of over 200 countries in the world, some 180-plus are now connected and growth rates in South America and Asia are on a percentage basis growing the most rapidly in the world. Currently a new broadband network known as Internet 2 is being implemented to interconnect research agencies and major research universities in the United States.

### Key Players

Key players are most science and technology agencies around the world, most colleges and universities, and most on-line ISPs. New ISPs like Zero and Net Zero that provide free Internet access are beginning to make an impact on the market.

*Comments*

The overly rapid growth of the Internet, the lack of privacy and security, and the lack of content and quality control on what is placed on the system are issues of great concern.

## LANs, MANs, WANs, and Enterprise Networks

*Technology*

Local Area Networks, Metropolitan Area Networks, and Wide Area Networks are private networks separate from the PSTN that support private business communications networks. LANs, which connect computers, printers, fax machines, and telephones, operate on such systems as Appletalk, Phonenet, Fiber Distributed Digital Interface (FDDI), and Ethernet at speeds of 10 to 100 megabits/second, and recently at even higher speeds over Gigabit Ethernet. MANs and WANs tend to operate on systems called X.25, Frame Relay, Switched Megabit Digital Service (SMDS), and the new Asynchronous Transfer Mode. Over time it is expected that these systems will migrate toward IP-based systems and in ten years IP and IP over ATM systems will largely predominate. The largest and most sophisticated of these networks are sometimes call enterprise networks. These enterprise networks (and their externally accessible networks for customers and suppliers, called Extranets) are crucial to business success in the age of the Information Highway and the emerging World-Wide Mind.

*Service*

Some networks can only handle data communications, but others are designed for data, voice, video, imaging, and multimedia. The new broadband switching technology called ATM is perhaps the long-term approach to providing all forms of services on a flexible basis for enterprise networks.

*Key Service Providers*

Key service providers are IBM, GTE, Cisco, Fore systems, DEC, Novell, and others.

*Comments*

Some large companies have outsourced their private networks to organizations like Anderson Consulting, EDS, AT&T, and IBM.

### Local Multipoint Distribution Service (LMDS)

*Technology*

This service is a broadband terrestrial radio service in the 28.5 to 30 GHz band that allows very intensive reuse of frequency bands so as to achieve very-high-capacity video-distribution systems. Wireless cable television systems of 50 analog video channels to 200 digital video channels can be achieved in this manner. The LMDS frequency bands have recently been auctioned by the FCC in a fashion similar to that used for the PCS frequency auctions.

*Service*

The primary application of this service band is for video and high-quality audio channels. It would be possible to use these bands for mobile services as well. Interference and ghosting by buildings and blockage by trees and other vegetation is a problem for this frequency band, which requires direct line of sight to maintain service.

*Key Service Providers*

The most likely users of these bands are local exchange carriers based upon field trials to date. New market entrants, such as Competitive Access Providers (CAPs), teleport operators, existing wireless cable (MMDS) operators, and others may enter this field.

*Comments*

Initial field trials indicate that operational use of these frequencies will be difficult. The success or failure of the FCC auction for these bands will be a key indicator of how important this service will become.

### Multichannel Multipoint Distribution Service

*Technology*

This is a service that is sometimes called wireless cable television. The microwave bands assigned by the FCC to this technology are reassigned channels that were initially reserved for instructional broadcast as the IFTS bands. Broadcasters such as CNN, HBO, Showtime, and other premium channels send out coded signals and subscribers can thus buy the service they want and the subscriber only needs a very simple microwave receiver. Only small, low-cost ($3,000) microwave antennas are needed to cover an entire community and no cable or fiber is required.

### Service

The service is today very limited as a niche market to in-fill around cable TV systems. The IFTS service for broadcast education is still very important.

### Key Service Providers

These are largely local operations on a city-by-city basis. There are few major players involved in MMDS or IFTS service, although several of the Bell operating companies are now beginning to invest in these areas. It is anticipated that the wider-band LMDS service may attract some of the key telecommunications organizations.

### Comments

The MMDS service can provide subcarrier transmissions for educational or emergency communications service.

### Mobile Satellite Service

### Technology

There are already several geosynchronous satellite systems that can provide international mobile telecommunications for maritime and aeronautical services. There is the global network known as INMARSAT and there are two land-mobile systems for North America. These are the American Mobile Satellite Corporation (a consortium of seven companies headed by Hughes Aircraft) and Telesat Mobile Inc. (a Canadian system). In the next few years we will see a host of new geosynchronous and Low Earth Orbit systems optimized to provide land-mobile service to hand-held transceivers. Despite the market failure of the Iridium Low Earth Orbit system and the problems with the ICO systems, there are still the Globalstar, Thuraya, and ACeS systems. The Inmarsat aeronautical and maritime mobile satellite system has been in successful operation since the early 1980s. Most of these systems seek to provide anytime and anyplace communications to users with small compact and low-cost transceivers that are handheld, although Inmarsat operates to larger antennas. Most of these systems are often designed for "dual mode" operation so that one handset can talk or send data to both satellites and terrestrial cellular systems.

### Service

The initial service will be largely voice and data and in some cases GPS positioning. These services cost $1 to $3 per minute. Simpler satellite systems called store-and-forward systems (e.g., Orbcomm) provides just messaging at about $0.01 per byte of data.

### Key Service Providers

These are broken down by satellite system type:

1. LEO satellite systems: Iridium (now filed for bankruptcy), Globalstar (Loral and Qualcomm), and Aries Constellation (yet to be financed).
2. MEO satellite systems: International Circular Orbit (ICO) network (filed Chapter 11 but with new financing provided by Craig McCaw) and Ellipso (Boeing, Westinghouse, etc.) (yet to be financed).
3. GEO satellite systems: These regional GEO systems are called Agrani (for Asia and Africa service), Thuraya (for Arab world service), and ACeS (for Asia). The initial GEO mobile satellite systems now over seven years old are known as the American Mobile Satellite Corporation (AMSC) and the Telesat Mobile Inc. (TMI) systems and have had trouble achieving a large customer base.

### Comments

It is estimated that these systems may capture only a small portion of the global mobile traffic, but total revenues will be proportionately higher because of the higher value added. This may be enough revenue to add many billions in total telecommunications revenues over the next twenty years. The disappointing uptake of traffic on the Iridium Low Earth Orbit Satellite System, its filing on August 13, 1999, for Chapter 11 bankruptcy, and its shutdown in March 2000 has cast a pall over the entire mobile satellite industry.

## Personal Communications Service

### Technology

This is a new form of wireless telecommunications that uses all digital technology and utilizes much smaller cells operating at much lower power. The increase in the number of cells, since they are typically about 800 to 1,500 meters in radius, allows much more frequency reuse and thus more system capacity. This service operates in the 1.9 to 2 GHz band as opposed to the 900 MHz band used for regular cell-phone operation.

### Service

The auction of frequencies for narrow band (paging and messaging) and for cell-phone service was held in late 1994 and well over $10 billion was spent to obtain access to these bands (although some of these bidders have defaulted). Existing users of these bands have to migrate to other bands before PCS service can start. PCS in the United States began service in 1996–1997 and has grown swiftly. The PCS is very good for portable and pedestrian service, but its suitability for automobiles is still in question. Low-tier PCS, in particular, cannot support service to automobiles.

### Key Service Providers

Key service providers are AT&T, MCI, Sprint, Air Touch, the regional Bell operating companies, and others.

## Public Switched Telecommunications Network

### Technology

The public switched telecommunications network in the United States was broken up by the AT&T divestiture in 1984. There are now two types of PSTN carriers. These are the interexchange carriers (IXCs) and the local exchange carriers (LECs). These systems have switching systems, twisted copper pair, coax, and fiber-optic cable transmission systems. A huge investment will need to be made in new electronic switching, fiber-optic cable, and other technology to bring these systems up to the needs of the Information Highway. In general most of the Bell company PSTN systems are not broadband enough to meet the telecommunications needs of the twenty-first century.

### Services

The primary demand for PSTN is today still voice service. There is, however, increasing demand for video, multimedia, e-mail, and fax services. Under the 1996 U.S. Telecommunications Act there will be increased competition for the provision of these various services.

### Key Service Providers

The interexchange or long-distance carriers include AT&T, MCI, Sprint, WilTel, and over one hundred smaller organizations. The local exchange carriers in the United States include the regional Bell organizations (Ameritech, Bell Atlantic, Bell South, SBC, and Global Crossings/US West, plus GTE and over a thousand smaller independent carriers).

### Comments

Today there are about $180 billion in revenues per year for PSTN services in the United States divided primarily among the big-four IXCs and the LECs. New competition is expected to increase the range of services and the volume of total business sharply over the next decade.

### Teleports and Alternative Network Providers

### Technology

The concept behind a "typical" alternative network provider (ANP), also known as a Competitive Access Provider (CAP) or Alternative Local Transport (ALT) or Competitive Local Exchange Carrier (CLEC), is to connect large business users together with long-distance interexchange carriers and/or with various satellite system operators. This requires a number of satellite earth stations to connect to the satellites (usually in C band and Ku band) and a fiber-optic loop that runs from the satellite teleport to all of the major office buildings in an urban area. The key is low-cost, high-quality digital transmission using the latest in fiber and satellite technology. Increasingly the long-distance telephone providers are acquiring these companies to obtain access to major businesses in key cities around the United States.

### Service

The service is digital and very high quality (i.e., bit error rates of less than ten to the minus seventh). The key is the local exchange carrier is bypassed and thus no access charges are charged. Since this is about 45 percent of total long-distance charges, this is a big savings. High-quality satellite video can also be obtained on demand without elaborate set-up or difficult preparations.

### Key Service Providers

There are on the order of 100 ANPs and teleports in the United States. You can be an Alternate Network Provider and not have a teleport, but usually large corporations offering such services in a number of cities will have both a fiber loop and a satellite teleport. For instance, the publicly-traded ICG Corporation operates fiber loops in some thirty cities and also has teleports in virtually all locations. A number of the companies are publicly traded on the stock exchange and operate in multiple cities. IBD is currently the most extensive teleport operator in the United States, while Globecast (owned by France Telecom) operates the largest video-broadcast teleport network in the United States. The concept of ANPs or CLECs is essentially a U.S. mode of operation and is not found in most other countries.

### Comments

A number of cable television companies are investing in these companies as a head start into competing with the regional Bell operating companies. ATT/TCI has invested in the New York City teleport, for instance.

## Unlicensed Wireless Communications

### Technology

The radio frequency and infrared bands available for this wireless service are known as the industrial, scientific, and medical services bands. Thus, everything from pacemakers to microwave ovens are in this category. There are several bands designed for interoffice communications, communications between computers and printers, and even wireless Local Area Networks.

### Service

This is for short-distance communications (i.e., 100 meters or less). It is usually for voice and data, even though at higher frequencies (20 to 30 GHz or infrared) it can be for video or multimedia. The key is that any manufacturer can produce equipment in these bands according to standards and any user can use it according to guidelines. No license is required.

### Key Service Providers

Major suppliers in this area include Motorola (product name Altair), Spectrallink, and others.

### Comments

This can be added as an adjunct to a corporate telephone. This is not a large market (i.e., less than 1 percent of the overall telecommunications market).

# Bibliography

## BOOKS AND KEY REPORTS

Arthur C. Clarke Institute for Modern Technologies (ACCIMT). *Confer-ence Proceedings: Science and Technology Application for National Development*. Columbo, Sri Lanka: ACCIMT, 1999.

Ayres, Richard. *Technological Forecasting*. New York: McGraw-Hill, 1970.

Bamford, James. *The Puzzle Palace*. Boston, Mass.: Houghton Mifflin, 1982.

Barnett, Richard, and Ronald Muller. *Global Reach*. New York: Simon and Schuster, 1979.

Bronscomb, Anne Wells. *Who Owns Information?* New York: Basic Books, 1994.

Centre National Espace Studies (CNES). *Strategic Plan: Innovations for the Development of Space Applications*. Paris: CNES, 1999.

Clarke, Arthur C. *1984: Spring-a-Choice of Futures*. New York: Ballantine Books, 1984.

Cherry, Colin. *On Human Communications*. Cambridge: MIT Press, 1971.

Commission of the European Communities. *Eurofutures*. Luxembourg: CEC, 1984.

Crichton, Michael. *Congo*. New York: Alfred A. Knopf, 1985.

Didsbury, Howard, Jr., ed. *The Future: Opportunity Not Destiny*. Bethesda, Md.: World Future Society, 1999.

Dizard, Wilson. *Old Media, New Media*. New York: Longman Press, 1999.

Dunlop, J. T., ed. *Automation and Technological Change*. Englewood Cliffs, N.J.: Prentice Hall, 1963.

European Space Agency. *Strategic Plan for Telecommunications*. Noordwyck, The Netherlands: ESTEC, 1999.

Haigh, Robert, George Gerbner, and Richard Byrne. *Communications in the 21st Century*. New York: Longman Press, 1987.

Hofstadter, Douglas. *Godel, Escher, Bach*. New York: Vintage Books, 1980.

International Engineering Consortium (IEC). *Competition for Access Services in the Local Loop*. Chicago: IEC, 1996.

Irwin, Susan. *The Compression Revolution*. Washington, D.C.: Irwin Communications, 1995.

Irwin, Susan, and Adam Toll. *Internet Delivery via Satellite*. Potomac, Md.: Phillips Business Information, 1999.

Johnston, William B. *Workforce 2000*. Indianapolis: Hudson Institute, 1987.

Jones, Glenn R. *Make All America a School: Mind Extension University*. Englewood, Colo.: Jones 21st Century, 1991.

Logsdon, John, and Russell J. Acker. *Merchants and Guardians: Balancing U.S. Interests in Global Space Commerce*. Washington, D.C.: George Washington University Press, 1999.

Lundstedt, Sven. *Telecommunications Values and the Public Interest*. Norwood, N.J.: Ablex, 1990.

McLuhan, Marshall. *Understanding Media: The Extension of Man*. New York: Signet Books, 1966.

McPhail, Thomas. *Electronic Colonialism*. Beverly Hills, Calif.: Sage, 1981.

Merrill Lynch. *Global Satellite Marketplace 99*. New York: Merrill-Lynch, 1999.

Naisbitt, John. *Megatrends 2000*. New York: Morrow, 1990.

National Science and Technology Center. *Networked Computing for the 21st Century*. Washington, D.C.: NSF, 1999.

Passes, Greg, William Casola, Larry Harbour, and Robert Ackerman. *Orbiting Internet: A Price Performance Model for Broadband Satellite*. Washington, D.C.: George Washington University Press, 1998.

Pelton, Joseph N. *Future View: Communications Technology and Society in the 21st Century*. Boulder, Colo.: Baylin, 1994.

Pelton, Joseph N. *The Wireless Industry and the Coming Personal Communications Revolution*. Chicago: International Engineering Consortium, 1997.

Pelton, Joseph N. *Developing Innovative New Global Approaches to Frequency Allocations for Communications Satellites in the 21st Century*. Washington, D.C.: Institute for Applied Space Research, George Washington University, 1999.

Pelton, Joseph N., and Al MacRae. *Global Satellite Communications Technology and Systems*. Baltimore, Md.: ITRI, 1998.

Price-Waterhouse. *Technology Forecast 1999*. Menlo Park, Calif.: Price-Waterhouse, 1999.

Reich, Richard. *The Work of Nations*. New York: Alfred A. Knopf, 1991.

Rossman, Parker. *The Emerging Worldwide Electronic University*. Westport, Conn.: Greenwood Press, 1992.

Roszak, Theodore. *The Cult of Information*. New York: Pantheon Books, 1986.

Sagan, Carl. *The Dragons of Eden*. New York: Ballantine Books, 1977.

Sagan, Carl. *Broca's Brain*. New York: Knopf, 1978.

Schlain, Leonard. *Art and Physics: Parallel Visions in Space, Time and Light*. New York, William Morrow, 1991.

Shapiro, Carl, and Hal R. Varian. *Information Rules: A Strategic Guide to the Network Economy*. Boston: Harvard Business School Press, 1999.

Smith, Anthony. *The Geopolitics of Information.* New York: Oxford University Press, 1980.

Telegeography, Inc. *Telogeography Report 2000.* Washington, D.C.: Telegeography, Inc., 2000.

Toffler, Alvin. *The Third Wave.* New York: William Morrow, 1987.

U.S. Space Command. *Long Range Plan: Implementing USSpacecom Vision for 2020.* (Colorado Springs, Colo.: U.S. Air Force, 1998.

Vonnegut, Kurt, Jr. *Player Piano.* New York: Delacorte Press, 1952.

Waldorf, Michael. *Commplexity: The Emerging Science at the Edge of Order and Chaos.* New York: Ballantine, 1995.

*The World Fact Book 1999.* Washington, D.C.: C.I.A., 1999.

## ARTICLES

Allery, M. N., H. E. Price, J. W. Ward, and R. A. da Silva Curiel. "Low Earth Orbit Microsatellites for Data Communications Using Small Terminals." Presented at the International Conference on Digital Satellite Communications, Brighton, U.K., 1995.

Ananasso, Fulvio, and Francesco Delli Priscoli. "The Role of Satellites in Personal Communications Services." *IEEE Journal of Selected Areas in Communications* 13, no. 2 (1995): 107–115.

Deutsch, Sarah B. "New Copyright Rights for the Digital Age." *Intermedia* 26, no. 1 (1998): 6–7.

Dodge, James C. "The Earth Observing System: Direct Broadcast and Receiving Stations." *EOM Magazine* 8, no. 2 (1997): 22–25.

Evans, John. "New Satellites for Personal Satellite Communications." *Scientific American* 278, no. 4 (1998): 61–67.

"Global Survey on Telecommunications Development." *ITU Report,* December 1999.

Gubbels, Timothy, and Martha Malden. "Access to ESE and EOS Data and Information." *EOM Magazine* 8, no. 2 (1999): 18–21.

Guntsch, Alexander, Mohammed Ibnkahia, Giacinto Losquadro, Michel Mazzella, Daniel Roviras, and Andreas Timm. "EU's R&D Activities on Third Generation Mobile Satellite Systems (S-UMTS)." *IEEE Communications Magazine,* February 1998, 104–110.

"ICO to Provide Rural Telephone Service in Mexico." *Space News,* 12 July 1999, 5.

"ICO Wins Regulatory Nod at FCC, Eyes Way to Wrap Up Financing." *Space News,* 12 July 1999, 6.

International Bank for Reconstruction and Development (IBRD). "IT and the New Economy." Washington, D.C.: IBRD, September 1999.

Irwin, Susan. "Internet Delivery Via Satellite." *The Orbiter,* August–September 1999, 1–2.

Lohr, Steve. "Welcome to the Internet, the First Global Colony." *New York Times,* 9 January 2000, 4: 1–4.

Lucantoni, David M., and Patrick L. Reilly. "Supporting ATM on a Low Earth Orbit Satellite System." Available at http://www.isoquantic.com/pr/ATMsatellites-1.html.

Mansell, Robin. "Citizen Expectations: The Internet and the Universal Service Challenge." *Intermedia* 26, no. 1 (1998): 4–5.

Morris, Bob. "ESE DAT and Information in the Marketplace." *EOM Magazine* 8, no. 2 (1997): 26–29.

"Officials Worried Over a Sharp Rise in Identity Theft: Internet's Role Is Cited." *New York Times*, 3 April 2000, A1, A19.

Pelton, Joseph N. "Cyberlearning vs. the University." *The Futurist* 30, no. 6 (1996): 17–20.

Pelton, Joseph N. "The Information Superhighway: CEO Perspectives on NII Development." *Telecommunications*, September 1997, 27–34.

Pelton, Joseph N. "Low Earth Orbit Satellites." *Journal of Space Communications* 12, no. 4 (1997): 233–247.

Pelton, Joseph N. "Telecommunications for the 21st Century." *Scientific American* 278, no. 4 (1998): 68–73.

Pollack, Andrew. "Even the Sky Can Have Limits." *New York Times*, 4 August 1999, 1, 9.

Pollack, Andrew. "Chase Seeks Loan Default in Iridium Financing." *New York Times*, 10 July 1999, 9.

Ro, Enrico. "A Coordinated European Effort for the Definition of a Satellite Integrated Environment for Future Mobile Communications." *IEEE Communications Magazine*, February 1996, 98–104.

"Satellite Operators Gain Nod to Expand into Brazil and Mexico." *Space News*, 12 July 1999, 5.

Seidman, Lawrence. "Satellites for Wideband Access." *IEEE Communications Magazine*, October 1996, 36–43.

UNESCO. "Unmet Educational Needs of the 21st Century." Paris: UNESCO, 1998.

## WEB SITES

http://www.erols.com/astrolink/pages/english/index_eng.html
http://www.comlinks.com/sys/astrol.html
http://news.wirelessdesignonline.com/industry-news/19990507-932.html
http://www.trw.com
http://biz.yahoo.com/bw/990722/ca_trw_1.html
http://www.aviationweek.com/spacebiz/sb_gov.html
http://dailynews.yahoo.com/headlines/tc/story.html?s=v/nm/19990712/tc/
  telecoms_teledesic_4.html
http://www.teledesic.com/index.html
http://www.forbes-global.com/forbes/98/1130/0118044a.html
http://www.gcndir.com/gcn/1999/February22/46a.html
http://www5.zdnet.com/anchordesk/story/story_878.html
http://www.comlinks.com/sys/teled.html
http://www.commlaw.com/pepper/Memos/International/diracc.html
http://dowjones.wsj.com/archive/gx.cgi/AppLogic+retrieve?id=PR-CO-
  19990618-001014.djml&d2hconverter=display-d2h
http://dowjones.wsj.com/archive/gx.cgi/AppLogic+retrieve?id=ON-CO-
  19990719-001314.djml&d2hconverter=display

http://dowjones.wsj.com/archive/gx.cgi/AppLogic+retrieve?id=PR-CO-
    19990602-001805.djml&d2hconverter=display-d2h
http://www.lmgt.com/lmgt/products/satellite_LMI.html
http://www.astrolink.com/pages/english/framesets/global/global_set.html
http://www.trw.com/astrolink/dpsp.htm
http://www.marketguide.com/cgibin/chart.cgi?companyname=APT+Satellite+
http://www.hughes.com/earnings/invest_pr/hts_pr_invest/04_09_96_proton.
    html
http://www.hughespace.com/hsc_pressreleases/99_06_11_ses.html
http://www.isoquantic.com/pr/ATMsatellites-1.html
http://www.comp.lanes.ac.uk/medstud/yorkdoom/
http://www.fright.com/spam/spamcan.html

# Index

## ABOUT THE AUTHOR

**Joseph N. Pelton** is Professor at the Institute for Applied Space Research at George Washington University and Director, Accelerated N.S. Program in Telecommunications and Computers. He is the author of fifteen books and has received several major awards, including a Pulitzer Prize nomination. Former Chairman of the Board and Dean of the International Space University of Strasbourg, France, he is founding president of the Society of Satellite Professional International, senior member of the International Academy of Astronautics, and Director of the newly formed Arthur C. Clarke Institute of Telecommunications and Information.